To those who have enriched our love and understanding of nature, we extend our thanks.

To those who are motivated by these Northern California nature excursions, we hope your journeys answer the call for adventure and deepen your appreciation of California's natural wonders.

Help Us Keep This Guide Up to Date

Every effort has been made by the authors and editors to make this guide as accurate and useful as possible. However, many things can change after a guide is published—trails are rerouted, regulations change, techniques evolve, facilities come under new management, etc.

We would love to hear from you concerning your experiences with this guide and how you feel it could be improved and kept up to date. While we may not be able to respond to all comments and suggestions, we'll take them to heart and we'll also make certain to share them with the authors. Please send your comments and suggestions to the following address:

The Globe Pequot Press
Reader Response/Editorial Department
P.O. Box 480
Guilford, CT 06437

Or you may e-mail us at:
editorial@GlobePequot.com

Thanks for your input, and happy trails!

Contents

Overview

Pacific
Ocean

N

Kilometers
0 ——————— 100

Miles
0 ——————— 100

OREGON

NEVADA

CALIFORNIA

REDWOOD
NAT'L PARK

LASSEN VOLCANIC
NAT'L PARK

YOSEMITE
NAT'L PARK

KINGS CANYON
NAT'L PARK

Medford
Crescent City
Yreka
Eureka
Redding
Susanville
Reno
Carson City
Fort Bragg
Santa Rosa
Yuba City
Sacramento
Lake Tahoe
San Francisco
Oakland
Modesto
San Jose
Monterey
Salinas
Fresno
Tulare
Bakersfield
San Luis Obispo

Acknowledgments

Northern California Nature Weekends has become a reality with the help of family, professional associates, and many supportive people at public agencies and private organizations. We give special thanks to Jeanne's husband, Bill, and Bob's wife, Lisa, and son, Sean, for their enthusiasm for this project and patience with long hours on the road or at the computer.

We are grateful to the many photographers whose images complement our descriptions. And we especially appreciate the people at each of the fifty-two sites who made time for interviews, to answer questions, and to review the draft manuscript. All gave generously of their time, including:

Steve Arrison, Mary August, Nancy Bailey, Stan Bales, Chuck Bancroft, Richard Banuelos, Deborah Bartens, Michael Behney, Misty Bell, Liz Bellas, Jim Belsher, Anthony Botello, Virginia Boucher, Chris Bramham, Carl Brenner, Liz Burko, Tim Caldwell, Darren Cooke, Denise Dachner, Steve Dirken, Alison Dunbar, Loretta Farley, Bruce Forman, John Fulton, Scott Gediman, Bill Grenfell, Bill Griffith, Scott Hamelberg, Christina Han, Myrna Hayes, Ken Huie, Nancy Hutchins, Sandra Jerabek, Conrad Jones, Jerry D. Jordan, Bern Kreissman, Ken Labini, Kari Lewis, Dennis Lewon, Dave Lydick, Dave Marquart, Kirk Marshall, Dave Menke, Greg Mensik, Cameron Morrison, Martha Nitzberg, Rex Norman, Holly Palmer, Kenton Parker, Mark Pupich, Dan Reasor, Vince Sereno, Nicky Sexton, Bob Smith, Dave Stockton, Denize Springer, Steve Waddell, John Werminski, Jim Wheeler, Kevin Williams, and Michael Wisehart.

Finally, many thanks to Rich Krivcher, Jean Yun, and Jeremy Garrett for their untiring assistance with research.

Introduction

California's scenery, natural wonders, and diversity are nothing short of legendary. The state that leads the nation's economy is also known for its rugged Sierra Nevada vistas, pristine wild rivers, picture-postcard coastline, and sprawling wetlands. Visitors come from around the world to see and photograph huge gatherings of ducks and geese on marshes, herds of tule elk on native grasslands, battling elephant seals on sandy beaches, and clusters of monarch butterflies on weathered eucalyptus trees. Whether you hike, birdwatch, kayak, bicycle, or snowshoe, a wealth of nature destinations are often less than a few hours' drive from home or your lodging. If you're like most other travelers in the state, you're looking for a weekend experience that's ready-made, usually just two to three hours away—one that provides a diversity of activities to enjoy. *Northern California Nature Weekends* makes it easy to explore nature by providing one getaway for every weekend of the year, timed to allow you to experience peak viewing or a seasonal wonder. Every getaway is located in an area where you can also enjoy a range of other recreational activities.

How to Use This Book

As you glance through the pages of this book, you'll notice that each description follows the same format, making it easy to compare trips and find important information. Some weekend adventures are highlighted with a photo or include a sidebar that provides more in-depth information about a topic of interest.

The **site** name includes a reference to the closest town and usually an estimate of distance or the amount of time it takes to reach the site from that town. You will need to factor in travel time to the closest town from your point of departure.

Each description includes a **recommended time** to visit the site. The trip may be timed to capture peak wildlife populations or the best of fall colors, or to allow you to enjoy a normally popular area at a less crowded time of year. You may find that a trip has been placed in a particular month to highlight a nature festival, but the featured species or experience may be something you can enjoy during other times of the year. If you're excited about the prospect of enjoying one of the nature festivals described in the book, be sure to double-check the actual date with the site. Nature festivals are generally timed for the return of a migratory species or other seasonal event, but the actual date of the festival can vary from year to year.

The **minimum time commitment** is our highly subjective guess regarding the *least* amount of time needed to experience the site. Some of you may be content to visit only the nature center or walk on one short trail. Others may expect to explore a few trails, take a guided tour, or, if attending a nature festival, spend the entire day. It is important to remember that this estimate does *not* include the time it will take you to drive to the site. Since some sites may require several hours' driving to reach, you will probably want to spend the better part of a day, or the weekend, at the site or enjoying other attractions in the area.

When possible, information about entry or parking **fees** has been provided. Fee information can become dated in a matter of months, so be sure to check if it is important to know these costs before you arrive. Phone numbers and Web addresses are provided at the end of each description to help you make these contacts.

Whether you're going to leave home for part of a day or stay in local lodging over the weekend, it is helpful to know what to bring. **What to bring** focuses on what you may need to enjoy the site during a day visit. Consider it a starting point, and develop your own travel list. For example, binoculars are normally listed because you will need them if you want to enjoy close-up views of scenery and wildlife almost anywhere you go. Cameras are sometimes mentioned, but if you're a shutterbug, you'll probably want to add a camera to your regular travel list. If you plan to camp or stay in lodging as you travel, you will need to bring the necessary supplies based on your destination, the number of travelers, and other recreational plans.

The book also provides information about the **entry hours** at each site. As with fees, hours may vary with the seasons and may change from year to year. If you are trying to pack a lot into your trip and want to be at the destination first thing in the morning, at the end of the day, or on a weekday, call ahead to confirm the hours—especially if you are visiting during a time of year other than the featured time.

Most **directions** are provided in the text, although occasionally maps will illustrate driving tours or complicated routes. Take advantage of road maps and online services to verify the routes that are provided, which are normally the most direct routes. If you plan to make other stops en route, you may need to modify the given driving directions.

The **background** and the **fun** are the heart of each description, providing interesting or essential information about the experience. In some cases, entire books have been written about the site. We have selected trips that focus on a unique type of activity, location, or seasonal event, and these sections provide enough information to plan your trip. All the destinations have Web sites that will allow you to learn more about the area before your visit.

Every weekend destination has challenging features, whether poison oak or a road that floods during winter. In **special tips** we've provided information that will alert you to hazards, reinforce site requirements, or otherwise better prepare you for the visit.

Food and lodging offers information about the closest available restaurants, camping, and lodging to the site. We've made an effort to provide some specific camping information, with the caveat that overnight rates and reservation policies may change. If you're interested in learning more about the food and lodging choices near a site, the name, phone number, and Web address of a local Visitors Bureau or Chamber of Commerce has been included.

According to tourism trend information, most travelers like to pack diversity into their trips. The **next best** section may include other sites in Northern California that provide the same type of experience, whether it's wildflower viewing or a fall migratory bird gathering. We've also included natural areas near the site, interesting local attractions, and other activities that may have little to do with nature but are unique to the area you are visiting.

Finally, in the Best Bets appendix we have tried to sort the trips by several categories. Please remember that many of these categories, such as Good Scenery, Best for Families, and Easiest to Enjoy, involve subjective judgments on our part. We hope you'll find them to be helpful.

Making the Most of Your Trip

Northern California Nature Weekends helps take some of the guesswork out of planning your weekend getaway. It can help you choose the right time of year to visit a site, provide good driving directions, give you a taste of what is interesting to see and do at that time of year, and offer resources to check to enrich your trip.

Before you leave, contact the site. If you only have time for a short visit, check with the staff. Describe the type of experience you want based on the abilities and stamina of the people in your group. You won't want to take a toddler on a 2-mile hike. If you are bringing someone using a walking aid or wheelchair, you'll want to find out what surfaces and routes are friendly to people with disabilities.

Wildlife and natural events do not perform on cue! If you want to arrive in time for the peak migration of snow geese or at low tide to maximize tidepooling opportunities, ask the locals to confirm the best time to visit. Such planning will help you get the most out of your trip and avoid disappointment.

Most of the experiences described in this book will be enhanced by binoculars or a spotting scope. Binoculars are strongly recommended for anyone interested in viewing wildlife. Generally, binoculars between seven and ten power (the first number identified on the binoculars, such as 7x35) will be suitable, but the quality of the optics, size, and price vary greatly. Lightweight, compact binoculars are easier to carry while hiking but do not always provide the same quality views as the full-size variety. Try out a number of styles before you buy. Spotting scopes are great for viewing wildlife at great distances but are not as portable as binoculars.

The weekend trips will take you to places where there are beautiful wildflower displays, groves of trees, gatherings of wildlife, legions of insects, and many types of habitat to enjoy. You can learn from experts on guided tours or sometimes by just listening to other hikers (chances are someone with a spotting scope on a tripod knows something about birds). But the best way to become proficient at identifying and understanding what you are seeing is by using a nature identification guide. See the Selecting a Field Guide sidebar on pages 56–57, which provides tips on how to select the right type of guide for your needs and experience level.

It is impossible to include all the many activities these areas offer. There are excellent guides and resources available for those who enjoy hunting and fishing. Specialized books cover bicycling tours and rafting adventures. This book aims to give you a small sample of just fifty-two nature destinations to visit, including everything from traditional hikes and bicycle rides to kayaking, houseboat trips, rafting, cross-country skiing adventures, and wildlife viewing at a winery wetland. Consider these a starting point: California's diversity makes the opportunities for nature adventures limitless.

Wildlife Viewing Tips and Ethics

When watching wildlife, always ask yourself if your presence or actions will disturb or displace the animals. To help minimize your impact and improve your viewing experience, follow these simple steps:

—Use binoculars for a close-up view.

—Watch at dawn and dusk, when wildlife are the most active and visible.

—Keep your distance; back away if the animal appears to be disturbed by your presence.

—Move slowly and quietly.

—Do not feed wildlife.

Some wildlife can pose a threat to humans. Mountain lions, black bears, elephant seals, and even deer have been known to attack people. Hike with a partner, and stay well away from visible wildlife. Though the likelihood of seeing a mountain lion or bear is low at most of these destinations, if you're visiting mountain lion or bear country, ask for tips from the staff regarding how to respond if you should encounter one of these animals. The California Department of Fish and Game (www.dfg.ca.gov) also has information on how to avoid or handle mountain lion and bear encounters. Animals habituated to people by illegal feeding pose the greatest threat. Report these types of interactions to local park authorities.

Come Prepared

Much of your pleasure during your trip will derive from being prepared. This will involve planning and following simple courtesies.

Check road and weather conditions: Winter trips can be spoiled, even turn hazardous, during bad weather. Check the newspaper or an online Web site, such as www.accuweather.com, for the weather forecast during your intended visit. Check with Caltrans (800–427–7623 or www.dot.ca.gov/hq/roadinfo) for road detours or closures.

Prepare your vehicle: Some adventures will take you off the beaten track. Be sure you have plenty of fuel before you leave towns with major services. Carry a flashlight, flares, a spare tire, and chains if you're traveling in areas where it can snow. It's always a good idea to have spare drinking water, food, and a blanket if you are traveling in winter. Bring your cellular phone, but remember that you cannot always count on a signal in remote areas. More important, check with your provider regarding how to call 911 when you are traveling outside your regular service range.

Bring maps: The directions included with each description normally start from the closest major city or town. Get up-to-date maps or use the Internet to plan your complete travel route. Bring them with you in case there are detours or you wish to make last-minute changes in your itinerary. And by all means, plan enough time to take the back roads to get a real feel for the local scenery.

Bring suitable clothing: California's weather can be variable. From fall through spring, the difference between daytime and evening temperatures can vary 40 degrees or more in the foothills and mountains or in portions of northeastern California. It's always a good idea to dress in layers so that you can add or subtract clothes as the conditions change. Carry a light-weight windbreaker or rainproof jacket in your day pack as "insurance" to allow you to extend your visit when the weather turns bad, or at least get back to your vehicle without becoming chilled or soaked. Don't forget a hat, which can help prevent overheating or protect you from cold, wet conditions. If you're planning on doing some serious hiking, leave the sneakers back at the vehicle and invest in hiking boots that will provide you with ankle support and good traction on a variety of surfaces.

Carry plenty of fluids: Whether you're a recreation veteran or an admitted couch potato, you need to replace the fluids you lose through perspiration while hiking, bicycling, or other activities. Fluid replacement may seem obvious if you're outdoors when it's 90 degrees, but you also lose fluids when it's windy or doing winter sports. Don't wait until you're thirsty to drink; sip frequently while you're active to *avoid* becoming dehydrated.

Be a courteous visitor: Try to travel gently on the land. Avoid littering. Be respectful of other visitors. Whether you're on a well-traveled path or a wilderness trail, follow the tenets of zero-impact travel: Take only memories, and leave only footprints.

A Final Word

Both of us have spent much of our professional lives writing and teaching about nature to help others better connect to, understand, and appreciate the outdoor world. This calling is much more than a livelihood; it is also an expression of a deep and lasting bond with nature that we each share with our families and friends—and with you. As schedules fill and life becomes more complex, it is more important than ever to immerse yourself in the beauty and wonder of the natural world, enjoy the tonic of nature, and feel the sense of spiritual renewal that nature can provide. For all of California's complexities, opportunities abound to enjoy the greatest natural diversity in the nation—often just a few hours drive from home.

Chances are there are natural areas very close to where you live. Make time to volunteer at one of them. Join a conservation organization dedicated to preserving the state's legacy. There are hundreds of them, from groups dedicated to saving sea otters to those working to restore botanical diversity. Get your children involved. When a child helps to clean up a beach or plant a tree, video games and missed television programs are easily forgotten.

The flower-shaped sea anemone—found at Fitzgerald Marine Reserve —captures prey with miniature stinging barbs on its "petals." ROBERT W. GARRISON

Map Legend

Symbols

✈ Airport

⛰ Campground

🐟 Fish Hatchery

🏇 Horse Trail

⚓ Marina

⛪ Mission

🅿 Parking

🛆 Picnic Area

■ Point of Interest

⚑ Ranger Station

🚻 Restroom

○ Town

■ Visitor Info

🦌 Wildlife Refuge

Transportation

 Interstate Highway

━[101]━ U.S. Highway

━(16)━ State Highway

─────── County, Local, or Forest Road

- - - - - - - - - - Trail

Administrative Boundaries

CALIFORNIA ─── State Boundary

Recreation Area Boundary

A Bonanza of Waterfowl

Watch hundreds of ducks bank, wing to wing, as they land on a quiet pond. Listen to their vibrant calling and chuckling as they feed and preen. Hear their wings churn the wind—and then the sudden silence after they depart. Breathe the crisp winter air and let the serenity of the marsh fill you with calm.

Site: Sacramento National Wildlife Refuge Complex, Sacramento NWR (headquarters) 6 miles south of Willows (ninety minutes from Sacramento).
Recommended time: November through February for ducks and geese.
Minimum time commitment: Half day; more if you visit several refuges.
What to bring: Binoculars, bird and mammal field guides, warm/waterproof clothing, water, and food.
Hours: Auto tours and walking trails open sunrise to sunset, year-round. Visitor center at Sacramento NWR open daily 7:30 A.M. to 4:00 P.M. October through March; weekdays only the rest of the year.
Admission fee: Sacramento NWR only: $3.00 day pass per vehicle, $12.00 Annual Refuge Pass, or $20.00 commercial pass (an automated machine accepts credit cards; the fee helps with refuge visitor facilities and wildlife habitat projects). Holders of a Federal Duck Stamp, or Golden Eagle, Age, or Access Passport are admitted free.

Directions: Sacramento NWR is south of Willows on Interstate 5; take the State Road 68 exit (exit 595) and travel east on SR 68. Turn left (north) at the intersection of SR 68 and California Highway 99W. Sacramento NWR headquarters is 1 mile north on CA 99W. From the Bay Area, travel on Interstate 80 east to Interstate 505. Follow I–505 north to I–5 and follow directions above.

The background: Did you put "connect with nature," "reduce stress," or "lose a few pounds" on your list of New Year's resolutions? If you did, the Sacramento National Wildlife Refuge Complex may be just the place to do them all! From lush wetlands and vernal pools filled with winter rain to the shady curves of the Sacramento River, the Sacramento, Colusa, and Sacramento River NWRs offer nature, tranquility, and ample opportunities to hike.

Tens of thousands of northern pintails winter at Sacramento National Wildlife Refuge.

If you're a bird navigating the Pacific Flyway, the 35,000 acres at six Sacramento Valley refuges are *the* four-star stopover or winter destination! Great weather, with temperatures normally above freezing. Lots to eat, with aquatic plants and other food in the wetlands and rice stubble to forage in the surrounding farmlands. And excellent accommodations, with wetlands managed and timed to have just the right amount of water and aquatic vegetation for a waterbird's needs.

One of the most important wintering areas in the entire Pacific Flyway, this complex of six refuges attracts ducks and geese by the millions. Birds from the prairie potholes and as far away as Siberia leave subzero winter temperatures behind and fly thousands of miles to this "balmy" winter respite. The mix includes tens of thousands of mallards, wigeon, shovelers, green-winged teal, and others; half of the pintails in the Pacific Flyway; and three-quarters of a million geese, from the Aleutian Canada goose to Ross', snow, and white-fronted geese. Shorebirds by the thousands, from plucky killdeer to yellowlegs. Refuge residents also abound, such as statuesque herons and egrets, playful river otters, and wary black-tailed deer—more than 300 wildlife species in all!

All of this in a setting that has been photographed by such highly recognized photographers as George Lepp, Moose Peterson, Tupper Ansel Blake, and Jim Clark—each able to see Escher-like scenes of multitudes of birds, a solo American peregrine falcon, or a stunning crimson sunrise or sunset. To accommodate photographers, the Sacramento Refuge has two photo blinds; they are popular, so be sure to reserve in advance.

The fun: Begin your experience at the Sacramento NWR. As you drive through the gate, you'll notice some attractive interpretive panels and a fee-collection station on your right. Stop here and enjoy the view of the wetland before you begin your tour.

Take the 6-mile auto tour to get a sampling of the area without disturbing the birds. Enjoy the upbeat, cartoonlike graphics telling you where to stop, stretch, and view. While you're driving, tune into FM 93.1 and listen to a continuous loop recording about wildlife on the refuge.

There are two areas where you can get out of your vehicle and enjoy views of the wetlands. Don't rush; relax and let yourself be captivated by the sights and sounds of California wetlands, much as they were a century ago. Today only 5 percent of the Central Valley's wetlands remain, and this is an important one.

The driving loop brings you back to the visitor center. Stop in to find out where you can hike, to see the interpretive displays, and to visit their bookstore.

You can enjoy a similar, 3-mile auto tour and 1-mile hiking trail at nearby Colusa NWR, which has much the same feel and ambience as the Sacramento NWR, though it is smaller. Or you can visit the complex's newest refuge, the Sacramento River NWR. The Llano Seco Unit includes a 0.6-mile trail with two elevated viewing platforms in a freshwater wetland. Get directions to both refuges at the complex headquarters.

Special tips: The auto tour routes have been designed to create excellent viewing. Multilevel viewing platforms, park and stretch areas, loafing islands, and mowed viewing lanes allow you to view right from the car, without disturbing the wildlife. Very secretive species like the Virginia rail and American bittern have been spotted from just 20 feet away. The tour and viewing facilities are accessible to people with disabilities.

Food and lodging: Bring a picnic or pick up supplies at Williams, Willows, or Chico. There are campgrounds at Sacramento River State Recreation Area. Contact the Willows Chamber of Commerce at (530) 934–8150 or www.willowschamber.org or the Chico Chamber of Commerce at (530) 891–5556 or www.chicochamber.com.

Next best: Also considered one of the premier birding areas in the state, Gray Lodge Wildlife Area is located near Gridley and Live Oak off California Highway 99E. Black Butte Lake is just north on I–5, set amid oak woodlands, rugged lava flows, and lofty buttes. Chico's Bidwell Park, the third largest city park in the nation, lies to the east. You can combine this refuge excursion with a trip to Battle Creek (see Weekend 46) or Clear Lake (see Weekend 51). If you pass through Williams and love garlic, stop for a meal at Louie Cairo's on Main Street.

For more information:
Sacramento National Wildlife Refuge Complex
752 County Road 99W
Willows, CA 95988
(530) 934–2801
http://sacramentovalleyrefuges.fws.gov

Winter Sports with an Environmental Twist

The Sierra Club's historic Clair Tappaan Lodge offers a cozy, communal, and cost-effective winter getaway for the beginning or intermediate cross-country skier and snowshoer.

Site: Clair Tappaan Lodge, at Donner Summit on Interstate 80.
Recommended time: During the snow season, November through February, or later.
Minimum time commitment: Two days.
What to bring: Multiple changes of winter clothes, skis or snowshoes (or rent on-site), hiking boots, day pack, water bottle, sunscreen, sunglasses, sleeping bag, pillow, flashlight, swim suit, and a favorite book.
Hours: Always open.
Admission fee: $50 per night; includes meals and lodging.

Directions: From Sacramento, travel east on I–80 toward Donner Summit. Take the exit for Soda Springs/Norden and go 2.4 miles east on Donner Pass Road. Look for the lodge sign slightly up the hill on the left side of the road. Park on either side of the road.

The background: Donner Summit has attracted winter sport enthusiasts for more than a century. The trans–Sierra railroad and, later, I–80 were the first winter routes opened across the Sierra, offering access to winter sports and exploration. At an elevation of 7,000 feet, the summit receives the highest average snowfall of the entire Sierra Nevada range, over 30 feet. The combination of winter access and great snow makes Donner Summit one of the Sierra's most popular winter sports areas.

The Sierra Club, founded in 1892 by John Muir and other conservationists, offered some of the first organized winter trips to the Sierra. The Clair Tappaan Lodge was built in 1934 by a group of Sierra Club volunteers to provide low-cost, communal accommodations for its members. The lodge is open to everyone today, but the spirit and camaraderie that built the lodge are very much a part of the experience.

COPING WITH WINTER

True to California's reputation for great weather, the state's western and central regions enjoy mild winter conditions, but not the northeast, where subzero weather and howling snow storms are common. Wildlife cope with winter weather in many ways. Beginning in fall, birds migrate to more temperate climates, sometimes traveling thousands of miles to escape harsh winter weather. Waterfowl aren't daunted by winter storms; they are warmed by soft down and moisture-repelling feathers, even as they bob on the frigid water. Songbirds and hawks find shelter in trees, where their fluffed up feathers trap insulating pockets of air.

Deer, pronghorn, and elk migrate to find food and stay warm. Those exposed to cold weather grow thick winter coats. Pronghorn have hollow hair, which provides insulation against both cold and heat. Plush fur protects muskrats, rabbits, foxes, beavers, and river otters—a reason that some were hunted to near extinction. The dark-brown ermine grows a dense, white coat that provides both warmth and camouflage in the snowy environment.

Foxes, coyotes, and other canids can navigate through snowbound country, relying on webbing between their toes that allows them to spread out their feet and balance on top of the snow. Some California black bears hibernate, relying upon heavy fur, layers of fat, slowed metabolism—and a cozy den—to sleep through the harsh weather. The females even give birth in their winter dens before emerging. Other mammals that don't migrate or hibernate, such as squirrels and foxes, cope with cold or storms by sleeping or simply curling into a tight ball to conserve heat.

If you visit a natural area during winter, remember that many of its wildlife visitors arrive and depart with the changing seasons. Find out in advance what species you can expect to see and how you can improve your chances of seeing them. Also remember that road conditions can be vastly different during winter. Check with the area before you visit to see if snow or winter flooding will affect your visit.

The lodge maintains more than 8 miles of groomed beginning and intermediate cross-country skiing trails right outside the back door. They offer lessons ($14) and rental equipment ($13 per day for skis, boots, and poles; $11 for snowshoes). A free shuttle runs from the lodge to nearby downhill skiing resorts if a member of your party prefers downhill skiing.

Clair Tappaan Lodge provides accommodations for up to 140 people in dormitory-style rooms and a limited number of closet-size private rooms. All guests share communal bathrooms. Dinner and breakfast are served family style in the rustic dining room, and guests are welcome to prepare their own bag lunch. A huge granite fireplace and comfortable seating in the living room encourage friendly talk or a game of checkers. There is even a hot tub available to soak sore muscles. To keep costs low, guests are asked to sign up to help with daily chores. This is a popular lodge on winter weekends, so make reservations early.

The fun: The high Sierra can be a magical but somewhat intimidating destination in winter. Unless you already ski or snowshoe, it's hard to find a location that offers safe beginning trails, a place to warm up when you get cold, and a sense of wildness. With 8 miles of groomed trails behind the lodge, there is plenty of room to experience the solitude and silence of the Sierra in winter. At the same time, you will be close enough to the lodge, or to other recreationists, to seek guidance or assistance if you need it.

Cross-country skiing requires some skills and practice. If you are a beginner, take advantage of the one- to two-hour lessons on your first day, and stick to the groomed tracks. However, if you can hike, you can snowshoe. Snowshoeing is a great way to explore the backcountry, and you aren't limited to the groomed tracks used by skiers.

The Sierra Club offers occasional guided tours and programs, so check with the staff when you arrive. Even if there are no guided trips being offered, chances are good that you can team up with some guests that have been visiting the lodge for years and have some favorite treks.

If you have energy to burn and the weather and moon cooperate, try a night hike across the moonlit slopes. There is nothing more peaceful and beautiful than viewing the snowcapped peaks and canyon at night under a full moon.

Special tips: Carry chains in your vehicle—and know how to use them. Drink plenty of water and use sunscreen, even on overcast days. Check winter road conditions at (800) 427–ROAD or www.dot.ca.gov/hq/roadinfo.

Food and lodging: Clair Tappaan Lodge has everything you need. Bring your own bottle of wine if you would like to have a glass with your dinner.

Next best: Try snowshoeing or skiing at nearby Donner Memorial State Park. The park has an excellent museum about the plight of the Donner Party, and visiting the site of the tragedy in winter makes the story even more compelling. Also consider visiting Royal Gorge, a private cross-country skiing resort in Soda Springs.

For more information:
Clair Tappaan Lodge
P.O. Box 36
Norden, CA 95724
(530) 426–3632
www.sierraclub.org/outings/lodges/ctl

Wintering Eagles and Summer Canoe Trails

Rising from his shoreline perch, the bald eagle glides on powerful wings toward movement on the lake's ruffled surface. As he approaches, a thousand mallards and pintails rise and fill the air with beating wings and strident calls, hoping to escape the lethal talons and crushing beak.

Site: Klamath National Wildlife Refuge Complex, 145 miles (three hours) from Redding.

Recommended time: For bald eagles, late November to March, with peak viewing January and February. Migrating ducks, geese, and other water birds begin arriving in September, with more than a million present by late November. Spring waterfowl migration occurs during late March and April. Canoeing is best late spring through fall.

Minimum time commitment: At least one full day.

What to bring: Binoculars, bird guide, suitable winter clothing, ice chest and food, and camera.

Hours: Open daily, during daylight hours. Visitor center hours are 8:00 A.M. to 4:30 P.M. weekdays and 10:00 A.M. to 4:00 P.M. weekends and holidays.

Admission fee: $3.00 per vehicle auto tour route fee.

Directions: To reach the complex visitor center, head north on Interstate 5 to Weed. Take California Highway 97 northeast for 45 miles to the Oregon border. Take Stateline Road (California Highway 161) east toward Tulelake to Hill Road. Turn south onto Hill Road and drive 4 miles.

The background: Everything about this place is big! Big country, big waterfowl numbers, and the largest wintering population of bald eagles south of Alaska. This complex of six separate refuges is over 175,000 acres, making up almost half of the Klamath Basin's 385,000 acres. Close to 350 bird species have been tallied, and 170 of them breed here, from white pelicans to greater sandhill cranes. Several million birds migrate through the basin, 70 to 80 percent of the birds in the entire Pacific Flyway! You can see 150,000 snow geese and many of the more than 60,000 goslings and ducklings that hatch here annually.

Wintering bald eagles perch on shoreline trees to watch for fish or an unsuspecting duck. D. MENKE/USFWS

And then there are the bald eagles. Once endangered, 500 to 1,000 bald eagles winter in the Klamath Basin. You won't just see them in ones and twos. From some viewing areas along the auto tour, you can watch up to fifty or more of these monarchs of the skies flying and hunting or perched on a snag while eating.

The best eagle viewing occurs from December to early March. During the same time you'll also be treated to views of an incredible array of water-associated birds that winter in the basin.

This vast area was once naturally occurring seasonal wetlands that were formed during the Ice Age. Ten million migratory birds used the area until the early 1900s, when the process of reclaiming the land to cultivate crops began in earnest. Today, less than 25 percent of the historic wetlands remain and the Klamath Basin is deeply troubled by disagreements over water supplies between environmental interests, American Indians, farmers, and others. This problem is particularly aggravated during drought years, when the demand for water greatly exceeds the supply.

Lower Klamath was the nation's first waterfowl refuge, established by President Theodore Roosevelt in 1908. It is one of the premier birding areas in the country. If a solution to the water issue is not found soon, this incredible treasure could be lost.

The fun: This is driving and canoeing country! The Klamath Basin's lush wetlands, lakes, and farms form a patchwork of valuable wildlife habitat in an arid, high-desert landscape. Sagebrush, chaparral, and juniper dot the open landscape, broken by rocky cliffs, forested ridges, and Lava Beds National Monument—a fantastic landscape of desert plateaus, rugged craters, and lava tubes.

Spend part of the day or more right in your vehicle! You can easily see dozens of bald eagles and thousands of other water birds from two 10-mile auto tours—one at Lower Klamath NWR and the other at Tule Lake NWR. There are park and stretch areas and trails to wander. Pick up auto tour booklets at the complex headquarters on Hill Road near Tule Lake. Take some time to bird along the pockmarked cliffs surrounding Tule Lake to view roosting and nesting great horned and barn owls. The base of each cliff is littered with the fur and bones of deer mice and meadow voles consumed by the owls.

If you want to take home photo memories of your trip, plan ahead and rent one of eight photo blinds located at Lower Klamath or Tule Lake. A fee of $5.00 per person per day will buy you the chance to capture the drama of the marsh or a spectacular sunrise or sunset. The best time to use the blinds for eagles and other birds of prey is late winter; viewing waterfowl, shorebirds, and marsh birds is best during spring and early summer. Blinds are set up for morning photography with a minimum of a 300 mm telephoto lens. Both auto tour routes offer great photography opportunities right from your vehicle.

Make time for at least one early-morning start. The eagles feed and spend the night roosting in large, open-crowned conifers on northeast-facing slopes that protect them from the prevailing wind and can accommodate their huge wingspread. Early risers often gather just outside the Bear Valley Refuge (which is closed to the public) to sip their coffee and witness the pre-sunrise "flyout," where a hundred eagles or more lift off at once and fly overhead on their breakfast hunt.

BALD EAGLE—TITAN OF THE SKY

He is a titan—his speed, accuracy, and hunting prowess giving him unrivaled command of the sky. The bald eagle rides on thermal currents that guide him on lazy spirals into the clouds. When he planes out, his powerful 7-foot wingspan can effortlessly carry him over great distances. Without flicking his tawny eyes he can change course in an instant, plummeting at speeds of 100 miles per hour to snag a fish barely glimmering beneath the water's surface a mile distant.

Among the ancient peoples of Babylonia and Egypt, the bald eagle was a symbol of divine right. American Indians honored (and still honor) its power, revering even its feathers as sacred. In 1782 the people of a young nation also acknowledged its great energy and prowess, choosing this monarch of the wind as a national symbol. In colonial days, wintering bald eagles were found in the East from Labrador to Florida's Gulf Coast and in the Pacific from Alaska to Baja California. There may have been 25,000 to 75,000 in forty-five of the lower forty-eight states, congregating in huge groups at rivers and lakes. And then they were slaughtered and poisoned. Only bald eagle populations in Alaska, their predominant breeding grounds, remained fairly stable.

In the lower forty-eight states, their power and majesty were no match for decades of wanton killing. Even after the Bald Eagle Protection Act of 1940 made it illegal to harass, possess without a permit, or kill bald eagles, western ranchers continued to slaughter them by the thousands. DDT poisoning caused eggshell thinning that decimated their numbers. The banning of DDT, protection under the Endangered Species Act, and a concerted recovery program involving captive breeding and reintroductions have led the threatened bald eagle to the eve of delisting.

In the 1960s very few bald eagles could be counted at Klamath Basin, once known to attract 1,000 eagles that followed and feasted on wintering waterfowl. Discovery and protection of their night roosts and establishing Bear Valley National Wildlife Refuge as the first refuge to protect night roosting areas have allowed the Klamath Basin to once again claim the largest bald eagle wintering population in the lower forty-eight states.

You can see wintering bald eagles in many other California locations. Some prominent gatherings occur at Lake San Antonio (see Weekend 6), on Packers Bay at Shasta Lake (see Weekend 20), Eagle Lake, Cache Creek, Hawk Hill at Golden Gate National Recreation Area (see Weekend 39), and Millerton Lake near Fresno.

Special tips: Unless you live in Redding, this is a long trip, so plan on at least a full weekend or more. January snow can be a factor in timing your visit. Check on winter road conditions at (800) 427–ROAD or www.dot.ca.gov/hq/roadinfo. If you can't make it to the refuge for winter viewing, plan a trip when it is warmer and you can see portions of the refuge by canoe. Upper Klamath NWR, just over the Oregon border, has a self-guided canoe trail open year-round. If you don't have a canoe, you can rent one at nearby Rocky Point Resort. The Tule Lake and Klamath Marsh canoe trails are open from July 1 to September 30 (no rentals nearby). Tour information is available at the complex headquarters.

Food and lodging: Klamath Falls, Tulelake, Merrill; or camp in a nearby RV park or national forest or at Lava Beds National Monument. Contact the Klamath County Department of Tourism at (800) 445–6728 or the chamber of commerce at www.klamath.org for lodging information. This is scenic but remote country and not close to many amenities. Plan ahead.

Next best: Make time to visit some of the other refuges in the complex. Come in mid-February to the annual Klamath Basin Bald Eagle Conference, one of the oldest festival-like gatherings in the state; check www.eaglecon.org. Use another day of your weekend to visit Lava Beds National Monument, where volcanism has shaped a rugged landscape of caves, lava tubes, cones, and chimneys. The area was the site of a famous Indian battle, where the famous chief Captain Jack made his last stand. On the drive back to Redding on California Highway 299, take a 6-mile detour on California Highway 89 to visit McArthur Burney State Park and its beautiful 129-foot waterfall. If you travel CA 89, you can also take in the McCloud River Preserve near the town of McCloud.

For more information:
Klamath Basin National Wildlife Refuge Complex
4009 Hill Road
Tulelake, CA 96134
(530) 667–2231
http://klamathbasinrefuges.fws.gov/

Festival at Former Navy Shipyard Celebrates Wildlife

Rafts of waterfowl, historic buildings, and guided tours are just a few of the highlights of the San Francisco Bay Flyway Festival. This once-a-year peek into the Navy's first installation on the West Coast and some of the most unspoiled salt marsh habitat and scenic vistas in the San Francisco Bay Area is a January must.

Site: Mare Island, eastern edge of San Pablo Bay in Vallejo.

Recommended time: Most of Mare Island is off-limits to visitors except during special events. The San Francisco Bay Flyway Festival occurs on the fourth weekend in January and offers guided tours of some of the best cultural and natural history locations on the Island and surrounding bay marshlands.

Minimum time commitment: Plan on a full day at the festival to take in a number of field trips.

What to bring: Sturdy walking shoes, water, layered warm clothing, rain gear, your favorite bird guide, binoculars, and spending money. Lunch and snack items are available at the festival headquarters, as are wildlife-related equipment and gifts.

Hours: Festival hours 9:00 A.M. to 4:00 P.M. Saturday and Sunday.

Admission fee: None.

Directions: From the San Francisco Bay Area or Sacramento, take Interstate 80 to Vallejo. Exit on Tennessee Street and follow the signs to the waterfront, ferry terminal, and Touro University on Mare Island. At the waterfront, Tennessee Street continues over the large blue bridge and onto Mare Island. Follow the signs to the festival headquarters.

The background: Mare Island was the first U.S. naval station built on the West Coast, in 1853. Huge dry docks, the first constructed with Sierra granite, were used to build and refit wooden steam and sailing ships and later, steel ships and submarines. The last ship assembled at Mare Island was the nuclear submarine U.S.S. *Drum,* launched in 1970. The base was decommissioned in 1996.

For architecture fans, buildings on the base range from the industrial docks, with their historic brick warehouses and modern cranes, to the

Tidal marshes and an unobstructed view of Mount Tamalpais across San Pablo Bay from Mare Island. Robert W. Garrison

stately mansions on officer's row. The adjoining craftsman-style chapel displays the largest number of Tiffany Studio stained-glass windows in the West. Plans are under way to redevelop the industrial and residential portions of the island, and most of the area is closed to the public except during special events.

The shipyard was built on San Pablo Bay at the mouth of the Napa River. The river and nearby Carquinez Strait deposit hundreds of tons of silt into the shallow bay each year. The nutrient-rich mud and bay waters, in turn, attract tens of thousands of waterfowl and shorebirds in winter. Along the edge of the bay, some of the best remaining salt marsh habitat supports a number of endangered species, including the salt marsh harvest mouse and California clapper rail. The San Pablo Bay National Wildlife Refuge manages most of the salt marsh habitat along the eastern edge of

San Pablo Bay, including Mare Island. In addition to the salt marsh habitat, settling ponds on Mare Island, used to deposit bay mud dredged from the harbor, attract waterfowl and shorebirds during the rainy winter season. Birds of prey are also common throughout the marshlands.

The fun: Start your visit at the festival headquarters. Sign up for a number of free field trips, and use the balance of your time to walk the western levee trails along the edge of San Pablo Bay. On a clear day the vistas across to Marin County and along the East Bay hills are spectacular. Bring your binoculars and field guide to identify the rafts of ducks floating on the bay and ponds and the shorebirds at the water's edge.

If you miss one of the historic tours of the island, drive through the shipyards and officer's row. Stop at the park where the chapel is located and use your binoculars to search the eucalyptus trees for monarch butterflies. The butterflies over-winter in large eucalyptus trees throughout the central coast region.

Special tips: Be prepared for cold, rainy weather. Levee trails can be slick and muddy, so wear good walking shoes and carry a clean pair of shoes to change into after your hike.

Food and lodging: Limited food services are available at festival headquarters. A variety of dining options can be found in the marina complex near the ferry terminal across the channel from Mare Island and in the downtown area. Accommodations are located along the I–80 corridor in Vallejo. The festival Web site provides a list of local accommodations, or contact the Vallejo Convention and Visitors Bureau at (800) 4–VALLEJO or www.visitvallejo.com.

Next best: The festival offers a variety of field trips to locations throughout the San Pablo and San Francisco Bay region. Led by local experts, the trips offer access to areas often closed to the public. The times and destinations will change from season to season, so check out your options as soon as you arrive at festival headquarters, or preregister on the festival Web site. For a nonfestival option, take the BayLink ferry from Vallejo to the San Francisco Ferry Building and Fisherman's Wharf. The ferries run on a regular basis throughout the day and provide a unique perspective of San Pablo and San Francisco Bays.

Historic buildings and wetlands are side by side on Mare Island. ROBERT W. GARRISON

For more information:
San Francisco Bay Flyway Festival
(707) 649–9464 or (707) 557–9816
www.sfbayflywayfestival.com

San Pablo Bay National Wildlife Refuge
(707) 562–3000
http://refuges.fws.gov

BayLink Ferry Service
www.baylinkferry.com

Salt Marsh Heaven in a Sea of Humanity

Often exploited and buried as bayside cities grew beyond their boundaries, the salt marsh habitats of San Francisco Bay have been reduced to less than 15 percent of their original size. The Palo Alto Baylands reflect both the early exploitation of the marshlands and the best preserved habitat remaining in the South San Francisco Bay.

Site: Palo Alto Baylands Nature Preserve is located on the southwest edge of San Francisco Bay in the city of Palo Alto.
Recommended time: Winter is the best season for viewing waterfowl, shorebirds, and raptors in the South San Francisco Bay. Plan your visit to coincide with a high tide for the best chance of seeing the endangered California clapper rail.
Minimum time commitment: Set aside half a day to hike some of the marsh trails or take a guided nature walk.

What to bring: Binoculars, a spotting scope to view birds on the bay, and a favorite bird guide. Dress for the weather. During winter bring layered clothes and rain gear. Consider a spare pair of shoes: The longer trails can get muddy after a rain. (There are a number of shorter boardwalks and paved trails if the unpaved trails are in poor shape.)
Hours: Open daily 8:00 A.M. to sunset.
Admission fee: None.

Directions: From Palo Alto on U.S. Highway 101, take the Embarcadero Road East exit. Drive 1.5 miles to the T-junction, turn left, and continue to the Lucy Evans Nature Interpretive Center.

The background: The Palo Alto Baylands Nature Preserve contains pristine and restored salt marsh habitat, miles of hiking trails, boardwalks, a nature center, a boat launch, and an art park. The salt marsh habitat, muddy-banked sloughs, open water, and grassy fields attract more than 150 species of resident and seasonal wildlife. Birds of prey hunt in fields and marshes, and shorebirds line the water's edge, probing the water and mud for food. Extensive beds of pickleweed and cordgrass salt marsh support some of the largest populations of endangered California clapper rails and salt marsh harvest mice in the south bay.

The preserve's current configuration reflects a history of both preservation and abuse of the marshlands. Much of the present salt marsh has been protected since the 1920s, but the area also contains a municipal golf course and airport built on landfill, a wastewater treatment plant that discharges into the bay, and a garbage dumpsite that is being restored. The city of Palo Alto is a leader in the restoration and reuse of the baylands for wildlife and habitat protection and passive recreational use. This area is one of the best birding locations in the San Francisco Bay Area, thanks to the combination of resource protection and enhancement and recreational access.

The fun: Follow the signs to the interpretive center and park in the adjoining parking lot. If the visitor center is open, stop by and inquire about guided tours and check for any sightings of rare birds in the marsh. The short 0.2-mile boardwalk leaves from the visitor center and is a good place to start your visit. Carefully scan the pickleweed and cordgrass marsh for the elusive and well-camouflaged California clapper rail. This is often the best place to see this endangered bird as it moves through thick vegetation in search of invertebrates. Depending on the condition of the trail, venture farther along the perimeter trails adjoining the sloughs leading to the bay to view ducks, shorebirds, and raptors.

Stop by Byxbee Park, an unusual combination of nature and landscape art built on a former landfill. The artistic components of the park have definitely generated controversy in the community, but the raptors and jackrabbits seem to appreciate the habitat it provides. The Emily Renzel Wetlands, adjoining US 101 and East Bayshore Road, is a great place to view waterfowl and other shorebirds attracted to the nutrient- and food-rich wastewater, which is first cleaned and then discharged, from the nearby Regional Water Quality Control Plant.

Special tips: Winter weather can be hard to predict, so plan for cold, wet conditions just to be safe. This is an urban park, so lock your car and don't leave valuables behind.

Food and lodging: Palo Alto has numerous restaurants and accommodations. Contact the Palo Alto Chamber of Commerce at (650) 324–3121 or www.paloaltochamber.com/visitors.

Next best: If you are traveling with children, a stop at the Coyote Point Museum in San Mateo is a great way to introduce children to the natural history of the bay and general environmental concepts such as food webs.

Live, nonreleasable native wildlife provide close-up views of some of the south bay's more hard-to-see residents. Contact the museum for direction at (650) 342–7755 or www.coyoteptmuseum.org/index.htm.

For more information:
City of Palo Alto
250 Hamilton Avenue
Palo Alto, CA 94301
(650) 329–2506
www.city.palo-alto.ca.us/ross/naturepreserve/baylands.html

Eagle Watching by Boat

Our nation's symbol is back from the brink of extinction. Lake San Antonio has the largest wintering population of once-endangered bald eagles in central and southern California. Watch from shore, or take a guided boat tour. Camp out, rent a cabin—and bring a bike or your favorite water sport equipment for a relaxing weekend.

Site: Lake San Antonio, 39 miles south of King City (about one hour).
Recommended time: December to mid-March for eagle viewing; eagle boat tours January through the first weekend in March. Lots to do year-round.
Minimum time commitment: Full day, plus driving time.
What to bring: Binoculars, warm jacket, beverages and lunch, your favorite bird guide, and camera.
Hours: Open twenty-four hours, 365 days. Eagle tour boat leaves from South Shore Marina Saturday and Sunday at 11:00 A.M. and returns at 2:00 P.M. Bring a lunch to eat on board.
Admission fee: $6.00 entry fee. Camping, RV, equestrian, boat launch, and eagle boat tour fees are separate. Call (805) 472-2311 to make eagle tour reservations. Boat tour is $10.00 adults, $8.00 for seniors and children, and includes a park entry fee. Children must be age six or older, or weigh at least forty pounds. There is also a $3.50 reservation fee per person.

Directions: Directions provided from King City to the South Shore. Call contact below for directions to North Shore and for Morro Bay access. Take U.S. Highway 101 south toward King City. Just north of the city, take the Jolon Road (G–14) exit. Go south on Jolon Road for 20 miles to Lockwood. Turn right onto Interlake Road (G–14). Continue for 13 miles to San Antonio Lake Road and turn left. Proceed 3 miles to the South Shore entrance.

The background: If you're itching for an easy getaway, put Lake San Antonio on your list. This 16-mile-long lake set in an oak woodland and located about 20 miles inland from the Central Coast offers something for everyone who loves the outdoors. One of its big claims to fame is the international crowd it draws. Bald eagles traveling the Pacific Flyway from cold northern regions pass the winter here, forming the largest gathering of

Eagle Watching by Boat

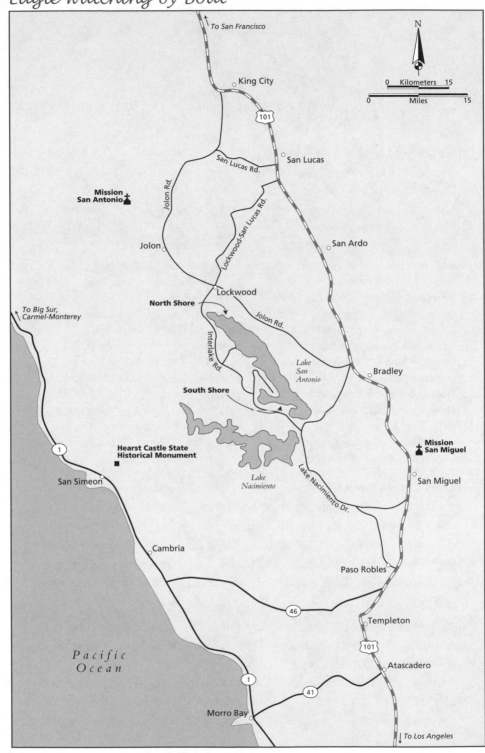

To San Francisco

King City

101

San Lucas Rd.

San Lucas

Jolon Rd.

Mission
San Antonio

Lockwood-San Lucas Rd.

San Ardo

Jolon

Lockwood

North Shore

To Big Sur,
Carmel-Monterey

Jolon Rd.

Interlake Rd.

Lake
San
Antonio

Bradley

South Shore

Hearst Castle State
Historical Monument

Lake
Nacimiento

Lake Nacimiento Dr.

Mission
San Miguel

San Miguel

1

San Simeon

Cambria

Paso Robles

46

Templeton

101

Pacific
Ocean

Atascadero

1

41

Morro Bay

To Los Angeles

N

0   Kilometers   15

0   Miles   15

eagles in central and southern California. The big, majestic birds attract visitors from around the world.

Like the avid human anglers who frequent the lake, eagles feast on the stripers, catfish, crappie, and bluegill the lake supports, as well as wintering waterfowl that travel the flyway.

The bald eagles are unmistakable: The adults have dark chocolate bodies, a white head, one of the largest beaks among birds of prey, and long, powerful wings. Bald eagles were slaughtered during the early 1900s. Their numbers plummeted even further from ingesting the pesticide DDT, which caused deformities and eggshell thinning. Following protection under the Endangered Species Act, captive breeding programs, and protection of habitat, bald eagles have rebounded. They are currently considered "threatened," but delisting may soon become a reality. See the bald eagle sidebar on page 20.

There are more than 500 campsites in three campgrounds, a marina with boat rentals, tackle, grocery store, and lodges for rent on the South Shore. The North Shore offers 307 campsites, 4 miles of shoreline camping, plus a store and marina.

The fun: If you think modern anglers have *the* fishing gear, you haven't watched an eagle fish! Outfitted only with sharp eyes and lethal talons, the eagle perches on a shoreline snag or cruises above the lake watching for a silvery flash at the water's surface. He may drop from heights of dozens of feet, plunging into the water to grab his prey, or he may cruise near the surface and grab his prize without missing a wingbeat.

You can witness this from the shoreline, or treat yourself to a guided tour aboard Monterey County Park's 56-foot eagle watching boat, complete with binoculars. Be sure to bring a warm jacket and a bag lunch (you can eat on the boat). Before you leave you'll view a thirty-minute movie presentation about the eagles; your guide will assure that the learning will continue on board the boat. The tours are popular, and reservations are required. The boat and other facilities are accessible to those with disabilities.

Don't leave your binoculars or camera at home. The lake supports a bonanza of other wildlife as well. Migratory waterfowl winter here, including Canada geese, Clark's and western grebes, and white pelicans. Among the many resident species is a herd of more than 200 black-tailed deer, normally visible in the campgrounds.

When you're done watching wildlife, spend the rest of your weekend hiking or biking on 25 miles of trails. Explore the campgrounds and the activities they offer. Come in the spring to enjoy the wildflowers (there is a Wildflower Festival and Triathalon in May) and during summer and fall to swim, fish, water-ski, or ride personal watercraft on the lake.

Special tips: The boat tours are popular; make reservations in advance.

Food and lodging: Groceries are available at resort. Restaurants and lodging in King City and Paso Robles. Contact the Monterey County Convention and Visitors Bureau at (831) 385–3814 or www.montereyinfo.org. Contact the Paso Robles Chamber of Commerce at (805) 238–0506 or www.pasorobleschamber.com.

Next best: Nearby Lake Nacimiento offers water sports and camping. Pinnacles National Monument (see Weekend 38) is east of King City, and Monterey Bay is only a few hours away.

For more information:
Monterey County Parks
2610 San Antonio Road
Bradley, CA 93426
(805) 472–2311
www.co.monterey.ca.us/parks/sanantonio.htm

Tranquility on Suisun Bay

Walk on secluded paths, canoe down quiet waterways, fish on a lazy afternoon, savor a wetland view... leave urban life behind and allow the serenity of one of the state's premier wildlife areas to replenish your spirit.

Site: Grizzly Island Wildlife Area, about 13 miles (less than a half hour) east of Fairfield.

Recommended time: Late September and spring for water birds (closed during waterfowl season, October to February). Peak waterfowl viewing in February. Elk rut is in fall, and calves are born in spring. Often a nice place to cool off during the hot summer, when Delta breezes are blowing.

Minimum time commitment: Half day.

What to bring: Binoculars, day pack, insect repellent, food and water; rain gear for winter viewing.

Hours: Daily, twenty-four hours. Field office may be staffed weekdays from 8:30 A.M. until 4:30 P.M.

Admission fee: $2.50 day-use fee (self-register in front of park office) or valid California hunting or fishing license.

Directions: From Interstate 80 in Solano County, take California Highway 12 east. Drive about 4 miles on CA 12; turn right onto Grizzly Island Road and drive about 9 miles to the field office.

The background: Where the Sacramento and San Joaquin Rivers blend with ocean tides, a great marsh was formed. Millions of migrating birds sought its tranquil ponds. Tule elk, pronghorn, and deer foraged in its uplands. For a long time it has been called Grizzly Island, a name some think came either from the grizzly bears that used to swim across the bay from Mt. Diablo to feast on the area's blackberries and rosehips, or perhaps it's a reference to grisly murders and other treachery that once occurred in this remote, swampy place.

From 1875 until 1950, farmers built and maintained levees to keep the salty tidal water from their grazing pastures and fields planted with beans, grains, beets, and asparagus. Nature eventually won; the salt water kept encroaching, ruining the fields and deteriorating the levees. Although the elk, pronghorn, and bears had disappeared, waterfowl and shorebirds continued to come by the millions. In 1931 the Department of Fish and Game

Heavily antlered male tule elk spar each fall for the right to breed, producing a new generation of spotted calves the following spring. WILLIAM E. CLARK/CALIFORNIA DEPT. OF FISH AND GAME

purchased a parcel called Joice Island, which became one of the first state-owned wildlife refuges. Since then the complex has grown to more than 15,000 acres, encompassing a patchwork of eleven parcels that offer outstanding outdoor experiences.

The wildlife area protects natural tidal wetlands, and its staff maintains more than 8,000 acres of diked seasonal ponds, which are managed for geese, ducks, shorebirds, and other migratory birds. There are more than 225 species of birds, from secretive California clapper rails and ubiquitous mallards to legions of shorebirds, songbirds, and hawks.

Tule elk were relocated to the area in 1977, and some of the area's more than one hundred elk are often visible, from sparring bulls in fall to spotted calves in spring. Hundreds of tule elk have been captured here and relocated to other historic elk ranges in the state to start or augment herds. Grizzly Island is one of the premier places for seeing river otters, supporting perhaps California's largest population. You may even catch a glimpse of a plucky, endangered salt marsh harvest mouse clinging to its home in a swaying clump of pickleweed bobbing in the high tide. There are more than 75 miles of hiking trails and a viewing platform. Boaters, anglers, and hunters can enjoy seasonal access to some of the tidal sloughs (check before launching, as interior sloughs are closed to boats).

The fun: The 9-mile drive into the wildlife area on Grizzly Island Road allows you to leave the buzz of highway traffic and stresses of urban life behind as you parallel the Potrero Hills, pass shimmering wetlands, cross over sloughs, and wind past weathered duck clubs. When you arrive at the welcome kiosk and register, stop by the field office for an area map.

You can experience portions of the largest contiguous estuarine marsh in the lower forty-eight states right from your vehicle. If it hasn't recently rained, the gravel roads can be dusty; you'll want to drive slowly, anyway, to savor the scenery and wildlife. Be sure to stop at the new viewing platform located at Parking Lot 1a, where you may see hunting birds of prey and grazing tule elk. A seasonal pond is adjacent to the platform.

The wildlife area is a hiker's paradise. Nine staging areas lead to paths that meander for miles through the marshes and fields. The trails are flat and easy to follow. Some cut through fields, but most are on levees. Winter visitors will be sure to find some mud, so wear appropriate shoes. Kayaks, canoes, and boats are allowed on some tidal sloughs.

In February, waterfowl populations will be at their peak. The huge American white pelicans are conspicuous, often teaming up to drive fish into the shallows, where the birds can easily catch a meal. Noisy flocks of geese move from pond to pond. Many male ducks wear bright breeding plumage, and you may even see early signs of breeding. The mudflats are prowled by least sandpipers and dunlins. Graceful herons and egrets may be spotted commuting between the marshes and their rookeries. As you watch the big birds, keep your binoculars handy for the smaller ones. Marsh wrens, common yellowthroats, and other songbirds are common. There are also large numbers of ground-nesting owls, including short-eared owls near Parking Lot 1. Anytime you're close to water, watch for playful river otters. You'll notice slide marks along the slough and pond banks where they toboggan into the water.

Very few places in the state offer fairly reliable views of tule elk, and this Central Valley wildlife area is one of them. The field office staff may be able to tell you where the elk have been seen recently. If you hear loud grunts and high-pitched squeals, you know that elk are near. In February the bulls and cows are usually separate, and the bulls may be just beginning to shed their massive antlers. These elk are eating "good groceries," so some of the males weigh more than 800 pounds and can grow record-sized antlers. The cows may be more wary as they await the birth of their calves in spring. If you come in March or April, it is not unusual to see wobbly calves near Parking Lot 3 or 4.

Special tips: Many areas within the complex are closed August to February, during hunting and dog training season. However, Hill Slough Wildlife Area is open year-round for wildlife viewing. Call to check before you visit during these times, or visit Grizzly Island on the Department of Fish and Game Web site.

Food and lodging: Many motels are located in Fairfield. There are no services available on Grizzly Island Road, but Main Sreet and Sunset Avenue in Suisun have several fine restaurants. Contact the Fairfield-Suisun Chamber of Commerce, 1111 Webster Street, Fairfield, CA 94533; (707) 425–4625 or www.ffsc-chamber.com.

Next best: In Solano County, visit Lake Solano Park or Rockville Hills Park. If you're heading back to the Bay Area, consider the Martinez Shoreline and Point Pinole, both managed by the East Bay Regional Park District. Closer to Sacramento, stop at the Department of Fish and Game's Yolo Bypass Wildlife Area in Davis or Jepsen Prairie Preserve (see Weekend 15).

For more information:
Department of Fish and Game
2548 Grizzly Island Road
Suisun, CA 94585
(707) 425–3828
www.dfg.ca.gov/lands/

WEEKEND 8
February

Elegant Plumes and Fuzzy Youngsters

A great egret flies, gliding on air currents with his powerful wings. He calls, stretches his neck skyward, and then raises the elegant nuptial plumes on his back. You are there—apart from this courting ritual to win a mate but also part of a moment that is timeless.

Site: Audubon Canyon Ranch's Bolinas Lagoon Preserve, about 3 miles north of Stinson Beach.
Recommended time: Preserve is open mid-March through mid-July.
Minimum time commitment: A few hours to hike and see the rookery. Add more time to explore the lagoon.
What to bring: Binoculars (mounted spotting scopes are provided), warm clothes, rain gear for winter viewing, day pack, picnic lunch, and your favorite bird guide.
Hours: Weekends and holidays, mid-March through mid-July, 10:00 A.M. to 4:00 P.M.
Admission fee: None, but a donation is requested.

Directions: From Stinson Beach in west Marin County, take California Highway 1 north 3 miles to preserve/rookery entrance. Bolinas Lagoon borders CA 1; look for pullouts.

The background: The rugged southern flank of Mt. Tamalpais includes Bolinas Ridge, where four steep canyons forested with redwoods overlook a sweep of sandy beach and a tidal lagoon. More than just pretty coastal scenery, this thousand acres of canyon forest and shoreline offer nesting and nearby feeding areas to some of nature's most dramatic wading birds: great blue herons and great and snowy egrets.

Bolinas Lagoon Preserve is one of three preserves owned and operated by the nonprofit Audubon Canyon Ranch. The site preserves a rookery of towering redwoods, often with more than a hundred nests reused annually while the couples court, breed, nest, and fledge their young. The trails, lookouts, and facilities at Picher Canyon's Schwartz Grove have been developed to allow visitors a bird's-eye view of the action without harming or disturbing the birds. Even spotting scopes are provided, and there are always volunteer ranch guides and knowledgeable visitors at the observation deck to share information about the nesting activity.

The birds knew what they were doing when they established the rookery here. The canyon's redwoods, Douglas fir, and California bay provide protection from harsh weather, and the lofty tree nests discourage ground predation. A quick flight over CA 1 brings the hungry birds to Bolinas Lagoon, where silted tidal channels and salt marsh habitat provide shallow feeding areas during low tides for the egrets and herons and about sixty other water-associated birds, from ospreys to pelicans. Patient visitors may even spot harbor seals and their pups playing in the surf.

The fun: You will be greeted by ranch guides with information and maps at the parking area located near a white Victorian farmhouse. The self-guided Kent Trail lined with Douglas iris and other spring wildflowers is an easy 0.5-mile walk. It leads to Schwartz Grove, where an overlook offers bench seating and a quiet place to observe the birds. Dramatic courtship dances and displays occur into June, though by April most birds will be sitting on nests. You can watch parents feeding their nestlings during late spring, or be on hand in the early summer to see their first flights. This is one of the few places in California where you can observe a large rookery in action.

If you'd like a longer walk, there are 8 miles of trail (some with benches overlooking the grove). During spring you'll find Douglas iris, California poppies, and other wildflowers. You'll also enjoy the quiet, sod-roofed bird-watching structure, picnic area, restrooms, drinking water, and bookstore. All but the hillside trails are accessible to those with disabilities.

Be sure to save time to enjoy the Bolinas Lagoon. Whether beaten by winter storms, cloaked in fog, or bathed in sunshine, the lagoon offers excellent views year-round. During fall, it is home to thousands of migratory birds. Local trees also harbor other autumn travelers, including monarch butterflies.

Special tips: Some trails may be slippery during winter. Refrain from talking loudly so that others can enjoy this outstanding viewing experience.

Food and lodging: Stinson Beach and Bolinas have some lodging and restaurants. Mill Valley is only a half hour distant. Contact the Marin County Visitors Bureau at (415) 499–5000 or www.visitmarin.org.

Next best: You could spend a month here! Mt. Tamalpais State Park, Muir Woods National Monument, Samuel Taylor State Park, and Wheelright

A great blue heron stands in the shallows at Bolinas Lagoon and waits, ready to grab fish in its bill with lightning speed. CLERIN W. ZUMWALT

STANDING TALL:
THE GREAT BLUE HERON

Whether you're at a freshwater marsh, an inland pond, or a coastal wetland, the largest heron in North America is unmistakable. This elegant, slate-blue bird is 4 feet tall with a wingspan of nearly 7 feet. His white head has a trailing black crown, yellow eyes, and a long yellow bill.

Herons and their egret cousins are known for the incredible courtship dance they perform to win a mate. The male circles in flight with his long neck stretched skyward. Once a mate is chosen, he greets her with plumes erect and wings extended. These extravagant and delicate plumes, called nuptial feathers, reach beyond the tail and add to the drama and beauty of the dance.

The birds build their big branchy nests within a colony of other egrets and herons called a rookery, often in the same group of trees year after year. Eggs are carefully incubated by both parents, each spelling the other to hunt for food. Breeding may vary throughout the state, though hatching may occur as early as late spring, an excellent time to see the parents fly in and out with food for the fuzzy youngsters. By late June or early July, the young birds are usually ready to make their first awkward flights.

The hunt for food takes the birds to the nearby wetland or pond. Here herons and egrets stand statuelike in the shallows, waiting for fish to swim within striking range. With a laser-fast movement, the prey is impaled or seized in the bird's rapierlike bill.

Nature provided herons with elegant nuptial feathers to help attract a mate. Some thought if it worked for birds, it would also work for people. During the nineteenth century, heron and egret populations were nearly decimated as birds were shot and their elegant courtship plumes taken to adorn fashionable hats.

In 1918 the Migratory Bird Treaty gave legal protection to their rookeries, allowing populations to recover. California rookeries are still protected to safeguard the wetland habitat upon which they depend, and rookeries are normally closed to the public to prevent disturbance of the nesting birds. The views at Bolinas Lagoon Preserve are outstanding. Stone Lakes National Wildlife Refuge (916–775–4420) near Sacramento normally offers a guided rookery tour in late winter or early spring.

Chances are good that you will spot a song sparrow as you walk the trail to the rookery viewing platform. These small streaked birds announce their presence with bold songs and can often be found foraging in bushes. WILLIAM E. GRENFELL

Center/Green Gulch Farm are all very near. Point Reyes National Seashore (see Weekend 13) is only a short distance to the north on CA 1. If you want to explore the nearby town of Bolinas, don't count on finding directional signs to the town; they have mysteriously disappeared for many decades!

For more information:

Audubon Canyon Ranch/Bolinas Lagoon Preserve
4900 Highway 1
Stinson Beach, CA 94970
(415) 868–9244; fax: (415) 868–1699
www.egret.org

Whale Watching from the San Andreas Fault

A dome of granite swept north by the San Andreas Fault protects the fishing harbor of Bodega Bay and provides the perfect perch to watch Pacific gray whales migrating south from Alaska to their calving grounds in Baja California.

Site: Bodega Bay and Bodega Head, about 25 miles from Santa Rosa (half hour).

Recommended time: Gray whales migrate along the California coast between December and March. The southern migration peaks in early January.

Minimum time commitment: Six hours.

What to bring: Warm clothes, waterproof boots, rain pants, rain parka with hood, gloves, water and snacks, sunglasses, camera, binoculars, and your favorite bird guide.

Hours: Three-hour boat trips generally leave at 9:00 A.M. and 1:00 P.M.

Admission fee: Boat trips run around $25 for adults; $15 for children under age sixteen.

Directions: The town of Bodega Bay is located 68 miles north of San Francisco on California Highway 1 or about 25 miles west of Santa Rosa on the Bodega Highway, which intersects with CA 1 east of the bay. To reach Bodega Head, turn west on East Shore Road on the north end of town. At the bottom of the hill, turn right onto Westside Road and follow along the edge of the bay to the parking lot at the end of the peninsula.

The background: Pacific gray whales pass the California coast twice a year on their annual migration between their feeding grounds in the arctic seas surrounding Alaska and their calving grounds in the lagoons of Baja California. From December through March, the whales travel more than 12,000 miles south, with the pregnant females leading the migration. The shallow southern lagoons offer protection from predators and warm, calm water for the calves to be born. By mid–February, the whales begin their return journey north. Last to leave are the females with their calves.

Beyond whale watching, Bodega Bay and Bodega Head offer a unique glimpse of California's geologic past. The infamous San Andreas Fault runs

The rugged Sonoma County coast near Bodega Bay provides breathtaking scenery, good vantage points for whale watching, and great birding. ROBERT W. GARRISON

directly underneath the western edge of the bay and the town itself. The land to the west of the bay, including Bodega Head, is moving north along the fault. During the 1906 earthquake, the harbor and bay shifted 15 feet north of the town. In the 1960s the construction of a nuclear power plant on Bodega Head was stopped when geologists found secondary faults underneath the site of the foundation. The foundation pit, "Hole-in-the-Head," is now filled with fresh water and attracts water birds. Bodega Head is part of Sonoma Coast State Beach.

The fun: The Bodega Bay area offers a variety of whale watching adventures. For the landlubbers in the crowd, Bodega Head, located on the southwest end of the bay, provides a perfect whale lookout point from the parking lot at the end of the road. Chances are good that there will be other whale watchers in the parking area. For whale watching, the more people the better. While whales are huge in comparison to other animals, they remain hidden beneath the water. You are looking for their 15-foot spouts, the steamy jet of air they exhale before taking another breath and diving. On a calm day, the spouts are easy to see. When the water is choppy, the spouts readily blend with the whitecaps. The best way to find whales is without binoculars or spotting scopes. Scan the horizon for spouts and when you spot one, switch to your binoculars for a closer look. The whales generally travel in groups of two to six, so you may see other spouts. If you are lucky, you may see more than just spouts. Gray whales occasionally lift their flukes (tail fins) out of the water before a deep dive (sounding) and may spyhop, lifting their head out of the water to look around.

For the more adventurous, a boat trip is a great way to view the whales. Two commercial fishing boat charters offer whale watching tours January through April from Bodega Harbor. The morning and afternoon tours are generally three hours long. Call ahead to reserve a spot and to check their current trip schedules.

Boat viewing offers a different vantage point than the coastal bluffs. First, you will be much closer to the whales. You could be as close as 100 yards, the minimum suggested distance boat operators should maintain from any marine mammal. Even at 500 yards, these animals are awesome. The forceful sound of their blows and the view of their mottled backs skimming the surface as they breathe is a sight to behold. Second, when you view whales from the water, you realize how big they are and how small (and vulnerable) you are.

Special tips: Consider taking seasickness medication before your boat trip if you are susceptible to motion sickness. You will be exposed to the weather, so dress warmly and wear wind- and rain-resistant clothing.

Food and lodging: Bodega Bay offers a number of restaurant and motel options. Contact the Sonoma County Visitor Center at (707) 875–3866 or www.sonomacounty.com.

Next best: Bodega Bay is also a birding hot spot for pelagic (open ocean) birds that can be seen from Bodega Head and waterfowl and shorebirds that use the bay. Take some time to bird along Westside Road as you drive out to Bodega Head and while you are whale watching from the Bodega Head parking area.

For more information:
Sonoma Coast State Beach
(707) 875–3483
www.parks.ca.gov

Wil's Fishing Adventures
1580 East Shore Road
Bodega Bay, CA 94923
(707) 875–2323
www.bodegabayfishing.com

Bodega Bay Sport Fishing
1410 Bay Flat Road
Bodega Bay, CA 94923
(707) 875–3344
http://usafishing.com/bodegabaysportfishing.html

Waterfalls and Spring Flower Displays

View the spectacle of Feather Falls, the seventh highest waterfall in California, as it plummets more than sixty stories down a sheer rock face. Wildflowers blanket the foothills on this 9-mile hike. Then make time to see the wildflowers display at nearby Table Mountain.

Site: Feather Falls, in the Plumas National Forest, about forty-five minutes east of Oroville.

Recommended time: Spring is the best time to take this trip. Hot summer temperatures bake the hills to a golden brown and reduce the falls to a trickle.

Minimum time commitment: The site has two trails. Allow about four hours for the shorter 9-mile loop trail. An additional 2-mile spur trail leads to the top of the falls.

Plan on a day and a half to fully explore Feather Falls, Table Mountain, and the area around Oroville.

What to bring: Plenty of water, lunch and trail snacks, day pack, sunscreen, hat, insect repellant, good hiking boots, bird and flower guides, and binoculars.

Hours: Year-round, unlimited access.

Admission fee: Free camping available at trailhead; no entrance fees.

Directions: From California Highway 70 in Oroville, take Oro Dam Boulevard east to California Highway 162 (Olive Highway). Turn right and travel approximately 8 miles to Forbestown Road; turn right and travel 6 miles to Lumpkin Road; turn left and travel 10.5 miles to Bryant Ravine Road. Turn left for 1.5 miles to parking area. To reach Table Mountain, return to Oroville. At the intersection of CA 162 and Oro Dam Boulevard, continue straight ahead on Washington Avenue through town. Washington Avenue becomes Table Mountain Boulevard. Turn right onto Cherokee Road and continue to top of plateau.

The background: Feather Falls is the state's seventh highest waterfall, cascading more than 640 feet down a sheer rock face. Located at an elevation between 1,600 and 2,400 feet, Feather Falls and the loop trail are located in the Sierra Nevada foothills in the transition between blue oak/foothills pine forests and higher-elevation black oak/ponderosa pine forests. A few

In early spring Feather Falls roars into the canyon below. ROBERT W. GARRISON

seasonal and year-round streams support water-loving plants, but the majority of the plants at this elevation must adapt to the hot, dry summers and occasional wildfires that sweep through the area. Many of the smaller plants are either annuals, which sprout, flower, and seed in one season before dying, or perennials that die back to underground bulbs in summer. Deciduous shrubs and trees survive the heat by either sending taproots deep into the soil to reach year-round water or shedding their leaves as the water disappears. Evergreen plants tend to have small, leathery leaves that reduce water loss during the heat of the summer.

Animals must also adapt to these hot, dry conditions. They tend to migrate to higher elevations where food and water are plentiful, sleep during the heat of the day, or enter into a summer "hibernation" called estivation until the winter rains return. However, during spring, when water and food are plentiful, the area's wildlife will be actively feeding and raising their young.

The fun: Feather Falls is one of those must-do hikes in early spring, when the falls are roaring and the wildflowers sweeten the air. The 9-mile loop trail is moderately difficult, primarily due to the last mile, which is entirely uphill and in the full sun. Don't let the trail's difficulty keep you from going. This is a great family outing, and walkers of all ages complete the trip in spring, when the weather is cool. The loop trail ends at a viewing platform that overlooks the falls and offers views down Lake Oroville. A 1-mile spur trail continues to the top of Feather Falls and along the lush Fall River. Watch for bedrock mortar holes in the granite slabs adjoining the creek. The mortar holes identify the sites of seasonal villages where generations of Maidu women ground acorns into flour for their families.

After the first half mile, the trail splits; hikers are advised to take the left (lower) trail. It is shorter, about 3.5 miles, but more difficult due to occasionally steep elevation changes. The two trails merge 0.5 mile before the falls viewing platform. Heading back, hikers again can take a left at the split onto the longer trail (about 4.5 miles). It has a more even grade, is better for mountain bikes, and reduces the final uphill climb to 0.5 mile.

The floral display changes weekly as the weather warms and the soils dry. It is impossible to predict what flowers will be on display, but you are guaranteed of seeing a nice variety of blooms from the treetops to the ground. White-flowering dogwoods and California buckeyes decorate the canopy, fragrant blooms of the California snowdrop bush and deerbrush mix with the blossoms of other shrubs, and a multicolored carpet of flowers compete with the green grass in the open meadows. Don't forget your flower guide if you like identifying the plants you are viewing.

While the waterfall and flowers are the big draws, wildlife viewing is also outstanding. Look around for surprises, such as a northern pygmy owl sitting in the tree above your head. These uncommon birds are completely fearless and often let you get within feet of them. Listen for the raucous calls of acorn woodpeckers, and watch for birds of prey, swifts, and swallows circling overhead. Lizards and snakes are common, including the western rattlesnake, so watch where you walk. Millions of ladybird beetles (ladybugs) hibernate in the area and can often be seen around the bases of rocks and shrubs.

Special tips: Warning: Do not leave valuables in your car. The hot afternoon sun beats down on the uphill portion of the return trail, so start hiking early and take plenty of breaks. There is loads of poison oak along the trail, so know what it looks like (see sidebar on page 160). Depending on the weather, mosquitoes and ticks may be bothersome.

Food and lodging: Oroville has a fair selection of food and lodging. Chico, 22 miles to the north on California Highway 99, offers more choices. Contact the Oroville Area Chamber of Commerce at (530) 538–2542 or (800) 655–4653; www.orovillechamber.net or www.experiencebuttecounty.com.

Next best: A trip to the Oroville area in the spring is not complete without a drive up Cherokee Road to the top of Table Mountain. The steep bluffs that surround Oroville to the northeast are the remnants of an ancient lava flow. The relatively flat-topped Table Mountain supports massive fields of blue lupine, yellow owl clover, and dozens of other native flowers during the very short spring season before the rocky soil bakes to a hard crust. Continue on Cherokee Road, take a brief detour to see a covered bridge, and then continue past the gold rush town of Cherokee before returning back to Oroville on CA 70.

For more information:
USDA Forest Service
Feather River Ranger District
(530) 534–6500
TTY: (530) 534–7984
www.fs.fed.us/r5/plumas/

Down by the Riverside

Ride a bicycle, hike the trails, and bring a picnic to enjoy at a scenic park while you experience Sacramento's American River Parkway. The lush green corridor of shady trees hugging the American River will help you forget that you are really in the midst of a busy urban area.

Site: American River Parkway, which follows the river in Sacramento and Placer Counties for 32 miles.
Recommended time: March through April for wildflowers. Fall through spring for waterfowl and spawning salmon. A great experience any time of year.
Minimum time commitment: One hour.

What to bring: Backpack, food, water, sturdy walking shoes for hiking. You can bring or rent bikes and horses.
Hours: Daily, sunrise to sunset.
Admission fee: No charge for activities; self-paid parking fees required in some areas.

Directions: There are many access points to the parkway, all from U.S. Highway 50. The best way to make a selection is to go to www.bikewaymap.com. This site provides a detailed map of parking and access sites along the entire parkway.

The background: Considered by many to be the true jewel of Sacramento, the American River Parkway is a 32-mile protected greenbelt flanking the river from Old Sacramento, where it joins the Sacramento River, to Nimbus Dam in Rancho Cordova and beyond to the town of Folsom. Although some land had been purchased before this, the County of Sacramento had the wisdom to protect this highly coveted river frontage beginning in the 1960s, safeguarding this natural riparian corridor from development and for enjoyment. The Jedediah Smith Memorial Trail runs its entire length and was named for the famed explorer, who was the first American to reach California overland by crossing the Sierra Nevada Range.

The parkway is probably the most visited destination in the state's capital, drawing more than five million visitors annually. Ancient oaks and cottonwoods shade winding shrub-lined trails, which are a recreational haven for workers taking a lunchtime stroll and people hiking, skating, bicycling,

The American River Parkway offers outstanding recreation opportunities in one of Sacramento's most stunning settings. GARY KUKKOLA/COUNTY OF SACRAMENTO

and horseback riding. More than 32 miles of paved and dirt trails provide an easy way to explore the parkway, which is dotted with historic gold rush sites and evidence of Maidu Indians, who once lived along the river's banks. Numerous riverside parks and recreation areas border portions of the trail and provide both access points and places to rest, picnic, and enjoy the abundant wildlife and tranquility. Some picnic areas can be reserved for groups. While asphalt and homes crowd its borders, the parkway has become a magnet and transportation corridor for urban wildlife, from deer, raccoons, river otters, and numerous small mammals to a variety of birds enjoyed by avid birders and novices alike. Mountain lion sightings are rare, but they also use the parkway, normally between dusk and dawn.

The river itself is also a magnet, providing postcard views and rich opportunities for fishing, canoeing, kayaking, and rafting. The water can be refreshingly cold to frigid; enter where there is sanctioned access, wear a life vest, and always avoid the middle portions of the river, where the current can be extremely strong. Just look along the banks and you'll see areas where the scouring water has left its mark. Caution: Sacramento County Parks does not recommend swimming anywhere along the American River due to cold water, currents, underwater obstructions, and the lack of lifeguards; an average of six drownings occur each year.

The fun: Whether you like golf or fishing, hiking or bicycling, the parkway is rich with recreational opportunities. Start by visiting the previously mentioned bikeway Web site to decide where you want to begin your parkway adventure. If you didn't bring your own bike, you can rent one in Old Sacramento just blocks from the state capitol in the downtown area and then pedal on the mile-long connector to the parkway trailhead at Discovery Park. Another excellent access point is Ancil Hoffman Park's Effie Yeaw Nature Center. Start out by learning about the parkway's resources at the visitor center, visit a re-created Maidu Indian site, or just enjoy hiking some of the loop trails that wind through the old river floodplain forest. The nature center is a great stop for children; exhibits and guides help them appreciate this incredible riverside jungle.

If you're looking for a good sweat, there's a par course for exercising at Bannister Park in Fair Oaks. You can also access the San Juan Rapids here, the only rapids on this stretch of the river. Goethe Park (pronounced *gay-te*) in Rancho Cordova offers a little of everything, from trails for walking, running, and bicycling to shoreside access and river contemplation.

A highlight of the parkway are two Department of Fish and Game–operated fish hatcheries located just below Nimbus Dam in Rancho Cordova. Chinook salmon and steelhead can no longer bypass the dam to reach their native spawning habitat, where they would normally die after spawning. Instead, a weir helps to guide them up the fish ladder to Nimbus Hatchery. The hatchery spawns the fish and raises millions of them in a dozen holding ponds. Salmon spawning occurs in fall and is celebrated at an annual hatchery festival (see Weekend 42); steelhead spawn during winter. The adjacent American River Hatchery raises several species of trout. At either hatchery, you can buy some fish food for 5 cents and watch the fish boil to the surface when the food hits the water. You can also learn about them, and the river, at the new Nimbus Hatchery Visitor Center.

Special tips: A hint about trail use protocol from Sacramento County Parks: To avoid accidents, people on foot should remain on the soft shoulders of the trail; bikers and skaters should remain on the asphalt path, to the right of the yellow line. Bicycle passing should only be done on the left, with a verbal warning, like "on your left." A 15 mile per hour speed limit is enforced. Horses are not allowed on the paved trail surface, except at trail crossings and bridges. Please yield to horses. An equestrian trail parallels much of the parkway, and there are numerous staging areas and watering troughs.

Food and lodging: Available from downtown Sacramento to Folsom in numerous suburban communities. Contact the Sacramento Convention and Visitors Bureau, 1303 J Street, Suite 600, Sacramento, CA 95814; (916) 264–7777 or www.sacramentocvb.org.

Next best: Nothing compares with the American River Parkway when it comes to size and diversity of recreational opportunities, all in an urban area. However, the River City offers numerous other adventures to add to your parkway experience. In Old Sacramento you can take a horse-drawn carriage ride, cruise down the Sacramento River on a riverboat, or ride a steam train along the river. Before or after the train ride, be sure to explore the California State Railroad Museum. If you're interested in American Indian culture, visit the Maidu Interpretive Center in Roseville. Folsom Lake is also just a short drive distant.

For more information:
Sacramento County Regional Parks, Recreation, and Open Space
4040 Bradshaw Road
Sacramento, CA 95827
American River Parkway Information: (916) 875–6672
Effie Yeaw Nature Center: (916) 489–4918
www.sacparks.net

Celebrate the Return of the Aleutian Canada Goose

Crescent City celebrates the recovery of the Aleutian Canada goose population, which expanded from near-extinction to more than 50,000 strong, at a five-day wildlife festival. The geese arrive in the area to refuel before flying nonstop over 2,000 miles to their breeding grounds in the Aleutian Islands of Alaska.

Site: Festival headquarters, located in Crescent City.

Recommended time: The geese remain in the Crescent City area for a few weeks in late winter and early spring. The festival occurs when the geese are at their highest concentrations.

Minimum time commitment: Two days to take in a sampling of festival field trips and programs.

What to bring: Rain gear, warm clothes, waterproof boots, day pack, binoculars, and your favorite bird guide.

Hours: The festival starts at 7:00 A.M. on Friday morning and concludes at 8:00 A.M. on Monday morning as the last field trips depart from festival headquarters.

Admission fee: $40 festival registration fee to participate in more than eighty field trips and workshops. Additional fees for some events and excursions.

Directions: Crescent City is located on U.S. Highway 101, 20 miles south of the Oregon border. The festival headquarters is located at the Crescent City Cultural Center, 1001 Front Street. Heading north into town on US 101, turn left onto Front Street and proceed 3 blocks to the intersection of Front and Play Streets.

The background: For nearly twenty-five years, the Aleutian Canada goose was thought to be extinct. The birds nest on the Aleutian Islands in Alaska, and the release of nonnative arctic foxes on many of the islands in the nineteenth and early twentieth centuries destroyed most breeding colonies. In 1963, 200 to 300 geese were discovered on isolated Buldir Island. Eighteen were captured and formed the basis of a recovery program. The bird was officially listed as endangered in 1967. With help from some of their wild relatives, captive-reared geese finally learned the migration

SELECTING A FIELD GUIDE

You don't need an in-depth knowledge of the environment to appreciate nature. But for many, curiosity and familiarity lead to a desire to learn more about the plants and animals we see on our outdoor adventures.

Over the past decade, the number of regional, state, and national natural history field guides has skyrocketed. Some are good, others great, but the choice can be daunting. Amazon.com lists more than 2,600 bird field guides alone. They range from very specific local or species guides to very broad natural history texts. Finding the right balance of specific details and broad coverage can be difficult.

Field guides, as their name implies, should help you identify subjects while you are in the field, whether they are rocks, birds, flowers, or trees. They should be easy to carry and offer information and illustrations that are easy to find and use in the field. Bird guides rely on a series of field characteristics, such as color, size, shape, habitat, range, and song to help you narrow your choices. Since plants can't run or fly away from you, flower and tree guides tend to use identification keys that take you systematically from one characteristic to the next until you reach the family or genus. Due to the large number of California native plants, more than 6,000 species, most wildflower guides focus on the most commonly seen species, or key plants, only to the family level.

Look for these characteristics when shopping for a field guide:

route to their wintering habitat in California. The geese have made a remarkable comeback, thanks to extensive recovery efforts that included removing foxes from previous nesting islands; captive breeding and reintroducing the birds to the islands; establishing national wildlife refuges in their California habitat; and hunters' support of hunting bans in Alaska, Oregon, and California. Now more than 50,000 strong, the Aleutian Canada goose was removed from the Federal Endangered Species List in 2001.

The area around Crescent City plays an important role in the annual migration of the geese from their wintering grounds in the Central Valley of California to their breeding grounds. In late winter and early spring, the geese gather in the area to feed and rest before making their nonstop, 2,000-mile journey back to the Aleutian Islands. For a few weeks the birds

Size and construction. The guide should fit into your favorite pants pocket or knapsack, have a well-constructed binding, and have pages that will stand up to wear and rain.

Geographic area covered. Local and regional guides are often the most detailed, but they tend to lack high-quality, full-color illustrations or photographs. Start with a national or western states guide. As your interest grows and identification is less of a concern, purchase regional guides for more detailed information. Rely on locally produced checklists to help you watch for and identify local specialties.

Illustrations. High-quality, full-color illustrations are a must. Generally illustrations are preferred over photographs because they can emphasize key identifying markings and variations by season or gender.

Layout. Look for guides that place the text, illustrations, and range maps all on the same page so that you don't have to hunt for information.

Range maps, vocalization charts, silhouettes. The better guides offer a variety of tools to help you easily narrow down your subject. Read the introduction to the guide to learn about these identification aids before you buy the book.

Price. Remember that you are building your field library for the long haul. But because you're using them, these books will wear out over time. A good guide should run between $15 and $40.

gather on the offshore islands to sleep at night and fly en masse at dawn to mainland pastures to graze during the day. The entire population is concentrated in a very small area, and the birds are easily viewed from coastal bluffs. The sight and sound of tens of thousands of geese flying overhead at daybreak is a remarkable spectacle that everyone should experience.

The fun: The Aleutian Goose Festival was created in 1998 to celebrate the annual return of the geese to the north coast. While field trips to see the "dawn fly-off" and "fields of geese" are the centerpiece of the festival, more than eighty other field trips and workshops have been crafted to highlight the diversity of wildlife, habitats, and cultural history along the north coast. From the tidepools of the rocky shoreline to the towering redwood forests, the trips are designed for both beginners and advanced viewers. Each trip

The world's entire population of Aleutian Canada geese stops off near Crescent City before returning to nest on the Aleutian Islands off Alaska. WILLIAM E. GRENFELL

is led by a local expert who can teach you how to use binoculars or help you find a rare bird for your life list.

The festival offers a nice blending of recreational activities and educational programs. Take a deep-sea boat trip to view seabirds and marine mammals, kayak on coastal lagoons, or glide down the Smith River in a driftboat. Learn how to sketch or photograph wildlife, identify birds by sound, or select your next pair of binoculars. Some activities are covered under the cost of registration; others require an additional fee. Preregistration is strongly encouraged. Visit the festival Web site for more information on the upcoming festival or to request a registration packet.

Special tips: Plan for wet, cool weather. Waterproof rain gear and boots are a must. A wide-brimmed rain hat with a chin strap works best when using binoculars and listening for wildlife.

Food and lodging: Crescent City has a good selection of accommodations and restaurants. Contact Crescent City—Del Norte County Chamber of Commerce Visitor Center at (800) 343–8300 or www.northerncalifornia.net.

Next best: While this is not the only place in Northern California to see Aleutian Canada geese, the northwest corner of the state offers some of the most spectacular scenery and diversity of public lands found in California. Redwood National Park and the various redwoods and coastal state parks (see Weekend 33) and surrounding national forests provide access to hundreds of miles of driving routes and trails. Travel south on US 101 between Crescent City and Arcata to view old-growth redwood groves, elk herds, and coastal lagoons. From Arcata, California Highway 299 east to Redding follows the rugged Trinity River Canyon through the Trinity Alps (see Weekend 35) and thousands of acres of national forestland. U.S. Highway 199 north to Grants Pass follows the wild and scenic Smith River through Jedediah Smith Redwoods State Park and the Smith River National Recreation Area. At this time of year, you are likely to find solitude no matter which route you take. Stop often and soak up the sights, sounds, and smells of the wild north coast.

For more information:
The Aleutian Goose Festival
(800) 343–8300 or (707) 465–0888
www.aleutiangoosefestival.org

Whales, Wildflowers, and Elk

There aren't many places where you can see elk (California's largest land mammal), whales (the world's largest sea mammals), and the delicate blooms of hundreds of wildflowers all in one visit. A little luck, combined with an early spring visit to Point Reyes National Seashore, can yield all three experiences, and much more!

Site: Point Reyes National Seashore, about 20 miles (forty-five minutes) from Petaluma.

Recommended time: April and May for peak wildflowers. Whales in late January to February and March to April. Tule elk any time.

Minimum time commitment: One full day, but a weekend would be best.

What to bring: Layered clothing, binoculars, water, picnic lunch, and wildflower book (you can purchase one at the Bear Valley Visitor Center).

Hours: Sunrise to sunset. Bear Valley Visitor Center open daily 9:00 P.M. to 5:00 P.M.

Admission fee: None.

Directions: From the Bay Area, take U.S. Highway 101 north. Take the Sir Francis Drake Boulevard exit west to California Highway 1. Follow signs at Olema to Bear Valley Visitor Center. Or you can exit US 101 at Petaluma and follow D Street west. It becomes the Point Reyes/Petaluma Road, ending at the town of Point Reyes Station. From there take CA 1 south and follow the signs to the national seashore.

The background: Along California's more than 1,000 miles of coastline, the rocky headlands and outcrops that define Point Reyes National Seashore are among the state's most dramatic scenery. On one side of this fingerlike peninsula lies protected Tomales Bay; on the ocean side, ferocious Pacific waves pummel the rock-armored cliffs along miles of sandy beaches.

Located in a remote corner of Marin County dotted with family farms and ranches, the area is largely undeveloped and has a timeless quality about it. The area bristles with early California history. Point Reyes (La Punta de Los Reyes), Drakes Estero, Tomales Bay, and other names originate from the visits by their namesake Spanish and English explorers more than 500 years ago.

Dozens of miles of trails yield views of scenery much as it must have appeared to the local Miwok Indians hundreds of years ago. A Miwok village has been re-created near the Bear Valley Visitor Center and often includes demonstrations of flintknapping, fire starting, and other native arts.

One of the trails located along a rift zone parallels a portion of the San Andreas Fault. This is earthquake country, and geology lessons abound: The 1906 trembler that devastated San Francisco also moved the entire peninsula 16 feet to the north.

Opportunities to learn and explore are everywhere. You can observe ocean tidepools, go clamming (in season), see a famous lighthouse, watch whales, observe one of the few captive populations of tule elk, visit a Morgan horse facility, view some of the more than 470 bird species that migrate or reside here (representing 45 percent of North America's bird species), or savor spring views of wildflowers. The park boasts 900 wildflower species— 17 percent of all species that occur in the state!

The fun: A stay at Point Reyes National Seashore is almost like a visit to many parts of the state all rolled into one. In a single day you can move from craggy ocean headlands and wide sandy beaches to pastures, chaparral-dotted ridges, hillside meadows, and dense forests. You can drive on well-maintained paved roads, boat on the bay and lagoon, or hike, bike, and ride horses on trails set aside for those purposes.

Wildflowers often appear in late March, from common California poppies, lupines, and wild radish to less common beach primrose and checkerbloom. Time your visit for a weekend to take advantage of wildflower walks led by a park naturalist, or bring a field guide and explore on your own. Chimney Rock is probably the most popular site, with up to thirty different species to appreciate. From the last weekend in December until mid-April, the road to Chimney Rock is closed. Weekends and holidays, weather permitting, a shuttle will take you to a 0.5-mile hiking trail (round-trip) to view the flowers. Be sure to look for elephant seals in the surf and hauled out on the rocks below. Wildflowers and wildlife also abound at Abbotts Lagoon, along trails at Tomales Point, and along Limantour's Muddy Hollow Trail.

Migrating gray whales pass Point Reyes in late December through January and then return on their northward trek from mid-March to early

The view is spectacular en route to the Point Reyes Lighthouse—a great place to watch whales, taste the salt air, and ponder the immensity of the ocean.
ROBERT W. GARRISON

May. If you visit during the March wildflower bloom, you may still see some stragglers during April from any coastal viewpoint.

No matter when you visit, there is always a good chance of seeing tule elk. Prior to the 1860s, thousands of tule elk inhabited the area. Throughout the state, their numbers dwindled because of market shooting during the gold rush, loss of habitat, and disease from interacting with domestic livestock. The elk you'll see are descendants of a small group moved to Point Reyes during the 1970s as part of a program to restore tule elk populations in their historic California range. The elk are in a 2,600-acre enclosure just north of Historic Pierce Point Ranch near Tomales Point. They often blend with the dun-colored landscape, so watch for their white rump patches and listen for their squeals and bugling.

Many areas are accessible to those with disabilities. Horses can be rented at Five Brooks Stable (415–663–1570). You can see that it will be hard to fit all of this into one day. Take advantage of some of the charming lodging or camping opportunities, and stay for the weekend. There are also local artists, charming shops, and fresh oysters to purchase and feast on from Tomales Bay!

Special tips: There are very strong winds at the lighthouse. The surf can be heavy and dangerous; many beaches are not suitable for swimming. If your interest is wildflowers, call in advance—the exact blooming season varies annually.

Food and lodging: Excellent food and a selection of motels, bed-and-breakfasts, and lodges at Point Reyes Station and Inverness. Contact the Point Reyes Lodging Association at (800) 539–1872 for suggestions. Camping in the park (backpack and boat-in beach camping only), Olema Campground, and nearby Samuel P. Taylor State Park. Horse camping at Stewart Horse Camp (415–663–1362). Contact the San Rafael Chamber of Commerce at (415) 454–4163 or www.sanrafael.org or the Petaluma Chamber of Commerce at (707) 762–2785 or www.petaluma.org.

Next best: You can easily spend your entire weekend at the seashore. If you have more time, Bodega Bay and Sonoma State Beaches are to the north. Bolinas Lagoon is south (see Weekend 8). If you're interested in birds, make time to visit the Point Reyes Bird Observatory, located in Bolinas, to learn about their amazing programs and research.

For more information:
Point Reyes National Seashore
Point Reyes, CA 94956-9799
Prerecorded information: (415) 464–5100
Bear Valley Visitor Center: (415) 464–5137
Camping Reservations: (415) 663–8054
www.nps.gov/pore/index.htm

March

Rare Wildflowers and Bay Views

Enjoy some of the finest vistas of San Pablo Bay, the Tiburon Peninsula, and San Francisco from a serpentine summit studded with wildflowers found nowhere else in the state. Toss in a prehistoric rock art site, Pacific tree frogs calling from seasonal streams, and wind-sculpted thickets of live oaks and bays if you need additional reasons to visit this magical place.

Site: Ring Mountain Open Space Preserve, nestled along San Francisco Bay between Corte Madera and Tiburon.
Recommended time: April is usually the best month for wildflowers, but the peak bloom can begin in March and vary over a number of months, depending on seasonal rainfall and drying winds. Start your hike midmorning to avoid the wind that generally picks up in the afternoon.
Minimum time commitment: Four hours.
What to bring: Sturdy walking shoes, water, sunscreen, and a hat. Add a copy of your favorite wildflower guide (*Pacific States Wildflowers* is a good general guide for California), binoculars, and a camera. Pick up the fixings for a gourmet picnic lunch at any of the local markets or delis in Corte Madera or Tiburon, and dine in style at the summit. Note: There are no restrooms, garbage cans, or other developed facilites in the preserve.
Hours: Sunrise to sunset daily.
Admission fee: None.

Directions: From U.S. Highway 101 near Corte Madera in Marin County, take the Paradise Drive exit east toward Tiburon. Follow Paradise Drive 1.75 miles and look for the fire road and gate with a sign on the right-hand (west) side of the street just past Westward Drive. Park on the side of the road, and watch out for traffic.

The background: This site offers the novice hiker scenic vistas and a diversity of terrain and wildflowers usually available only to the most hardy hikers.

Wildlife viewing takes a back seat to the spring wildflowers and scenic vistas, but watch for birds of prey soaring above the hillsides and scrub jays, bushtits, and small songbirds in the thickets. Western fence lizards bask on the rocks, and Pacific tree frogs call from the seasonal streams.

The terrain and habitats in this small preserve are quite diverse. Even novice naturalists can readily observe the differences. Rocky outcroppings shelter groves of coastal live oaks, California buckeyes, and California bays. On the south and west sides of the hill, prevailing winds from the ocean have sculpted the trees into beautiful shapes. On the moist, leeward side of the hill facing the parking area, coyote bush, poison oak, and other chaparral plants form dense thickets in the protected swales. Open grasslands cover the balance of the reserve. Here, nutrient-poor serpentine soils favor native plants over the exotic grasses that have taken over most other grasslands in California. The rare and endemic Tiburon mariposa lily, Tiburon paintbrush, and other rarities can be found growing here. Also look for blue-eyed grass, California poppies, and tidytips, to name just a few.

The area is so beautiful that it is easy to ignore the new houses lining the borders of the preserve or that you're sharing the area with hikers, bikers, and rock climbers. When you remember that you are in the heavily populated Bay Area, it is easy to overlook these distractions and be thankful that The Nature Conservancy and the Marin County Open Space District had the forethought to protect this beautiful and unique "mountain."

The fun: Topping out at about 600 feet Ring Mountain really isn't much of a mountain. But the scenic vistas and diversity of wildflowers found on its slopes rival many of the West's tallest peaks. The 1.5-mile hike begins across the street from the rich salt marsh and mudflats of the Corte Madera Marsh. (A self-guided nature trail brochure is available from the Marin County Open Space District.) The trail parallels a seasonal stream as it winds its way toward the summit. The first part of the hike is steep and the trail a bit rough, so take your time and enjoy the flowers and views of the marsh and bay. A number of bisecting trails cross the hillside, but eventually all lead to the summit. The private residences along the west edge of the reserve make this the least scenic portion of the hike. Focus on the flowers, rocky outcroppings, and hidden gardens tucked along the stream.

At the top of the hill, you will reach a grassy saddle. Head south to the summit and continue on to enjoy spectacular views of the Golden Gate Bridge, Richardson Bay, and San Francisco. Work your way around the southwest side of the hill, and loop back to the saddle where you started. To find the prehistoric rock art, from the saddle look west down the hill for a large boulder with a short rail fence on the right side. There you'll see the worn impressions of concentric circles carved on the rock face. To return, retrace your steps and proceed back to the parking area.

Special tips: Poison oak is found everywhere but in the grasslands. Make sure you can identify the plant, and stay on the trail to avoid contact (see the Poison Oak sidebar on page 160). The serpentine soils can be very slippery when wet. Watch you step.

Food and lodging: Corte Madera, Tiburon, and the communities adjoining CA 101 offer many options for food and lodging. For more information contact the Marin County Conference and Visitors Bureau at (415) 499–5000 or www.visitmarin.org.

Next best: The Army Corp of Engineers' Bay Model in Sausalito provides another view of the San Francisco Bay and Delta—this time from a scale model stretching throughout a two-acre building. Learn about the hydrology and geology of the San Francisco Bay and Delta at the Bay Model, then rent a sea kayak from Sea Trek and experience the bay from the water. Sign up for a guided tour from their Web site (www.seatrekkayak.com), or drop by their office at the end of Liberty Ship Way behind the two-story harbor master's office.

For more information:
The Marin County Open Space District
3501 Civic Center Drive, Room 415
San Rafael, CA 94903-4155
(415) 499–6387
www.marinopenspace.org

Pioneer Prairies and Ephemeral Ponds

Leave the interstate and its gas stations and fast food behind, and explore a place that time—and the plow—have not touched. Experience California as it was during its pioneer days, when native grasses were as tall as a horse's back and lovely springtime pools dotted the land.

Site: Jepson Prairie Reserve, about 10 miles from Dixon.
Recommended time: Mid-February through mid-May, when flowering ends; waterfowl present February and March.
Minimum time commitment: Two to three hours.
What to bring: Rain gear early in the season, binoculars, sturdy walking shoes, hat, and insect repellent.

Hours: Parts of the reserve are open for hiking and wildlife viewing daily, sunrise to sunset. Docent-led tours are available, but you need to reserve a space in advance by phoning (530) 758-5093. Check the Web site for the tour schedule.
Admission fee: Free, but the docents leading tours request a $5.00 donation to the Solano Land Trust, to be used to benefit the reserve.

Directions: From San Francisco, take Interstate 80 east to California Highway 113. From Sacramento, take I–80 west to CA 113. Drive south on CA 113 for 14 miles. The road turns toward the left and becomes Cook Lane at the flashing yellow lights. Drive on the dirt road for 0.75 mile and park off the road, on the shoulder.

The background: In California's pioneer days, one-fourth of the region was covered with native bunchgrasses that often grew taller than a horse's back. These quickly disappeared as European annual grasses edged out the California natives during years of drought and constant overgrazing. Over time, almost all the open grasslands of the Central Valley were cultivated or cleared for residences and businesses.

During the same era, more than one-third of the state was dotted with vernal pools. These shallow depressions are lined with impervious soil that holds winter rainwater. By spring these temporary ponds sustain a bonanza of unusual flora and fauna, from imperiled fairy shrimp and tiger salamanders to northwestern pond turtles and ducks. The ephemeral ponds may be just a few feet to a few acres in size but are rarely more than 2 feet deep. As the weather warms, the water slowly evaporates, and rings of bright, delicate wildflowers appear. By summer the incredible scenery has disappeared, leaving behind land that is dry and cracked but holding seeds and larvae for a new round of life the following spring.

Less than 1 percent of California's native Central Valley grasslands and only a fraction of its vernal pools remain. Jepson Prairie, named for the famous local botanist Willis Linn Jepson, may be one of the state's finest remnants of this piece of Old California. It is owned by the Solano Land Trust and managed as part of the University of California—Davis Nature Reserve System.

The fun: While you must make reservations to explore this fragile habitat on a guided weekend tour, the two-hour docent-led walk is a "must do" experience. These knowledgeable people share fascinating information about the wildflowers and vernal pool life. If you go when the pools are full, you'll learn about fairy shrimp and their fascinating life cycle. You'll see the incredible range of insects that make the pools so productive.

Go a few weeks later and the pools may be drying. You'll see gorgeous bands of yellow, white, and blue wildflowers, each growing in a special zone of the pond, with names you'll barely be able to pronounce—Mason's lileoposis, fragrant fritillary, and dwarf downingia. Shorebirds will be probing the mudflats for a meal. A brood of ducklings may be tipped up, dabbling for edibles along the bottom. Olcott Pond, one of the largest vernal pools in the country, is preserved at Jepsen Prairie. The trail takes you past trees festooned with loggerhead shrikes and flycatchers and pools teeming with waterfowl. You'll see narrow pathways made by rodents scurrying through the tall grasses and notice hawks cruising above, watching these openings for their next meal. You'll have the chance to see the mima mounds and develop your own speculations as to how these humps of soil occurred. If you arrive when Olcott Pond is drying, you may see rare Colusa or Solano grass emerging in scattered stands and be able to imagine the Patwin tribe camped along its shores. You'll also hear how The Nature Conservancy, University of California/Davis, and other partners are tending the land, using carefully controlled burns and sheep grazing to maintain the vitality of the grasslands.

VERNAL POOLS

They have been called potholes, springtime pools, rain pools, and hog wallows. The most common name, vernal pool, describes a small pond that flourishes in late winter and spring. In North America, these springtime pools are found in the western United States in areas that have a Mediterranean climate, particularly California and southern Oregon. Almost two dozen species of plants and wildlife found at California pools are considered rare, threatened, or endangered, some of them flora and fauna that are found nowhere else on earth.

A vernal pool is a complete world in miniature, with species that have adapted to a changing environment. A pool's life is brief, enduring just a few months. If you look during the summer, there are no signs of water, only dry, cracked low spots on the ground. When it rains during winter, water collects in these shallow depressions because they are lined with impermeable clay or hardpan. As rain fills the shallow basin, it awakens dormant seeds and larvae surviving in the alkali soil, waiting for fresh water to begin their life cycles.

Several hundred delicate aquatic plants bloom, breed, and die in and near the water. Estivating (summer hibernation) snails, toads, and tiger salamanders emerge from the mud and reproduce in the shallow water. Imperiled delta green ground beetles scuttle across the damp soil. At least five species of tiny fairy shrimp inhabit the nutrient-laden pools; they survive the summer in a drought-resistant egg state, living only briefly when water is present. Other visitors are more obvious: amphibians and ducks zigzag across the pools, great blue herons wade in the shallows, and mice, jackrabbits, and squirrels drink at the water's edge.

As the weather warms, stunning narrow bands of white, gold, purple, and blue vernal pool flowers form concentric circles around the pool where the water has receded, then slowly die as the water disappears. Long after the ponds are dry, colorful lupines, brodiacas, and other flowers appear among the grasses.

Some vernal pools are dozens of feet across and up to 2 feet deep; others span only a few feet, with a depth of just inches. The Olcott Pool at Jepson Prairie Reserve is one of the nation's largest, more than 2,600 feet in diameter. No matter what the size of the pond, a remarkable mixture of plants have closely adapted to and flourish in this changing environment.

Beer lovers who develop a big thirst after savoring this gem of a reserve can head to Davis to sample some of the local brews available at Sudwerks.

Special tips: If you visit the reserve on your own, please remain on the designated trails and refrain from using nets to explore or disturb the delicate vernal pool life.

Food and lodging: Food is available in Dixon, and a wide variety of food and lodging are available in Davis. Contact the Dixon, California, Chamber of Commerce, 10 East Mayes Street, Dixon, CA 95620; (707) 678–2650; www.dixonchamber.org.

Next best: There are vernal pools at several other locations, including the Vina Plains (south of Los Molinos) and Cosumnes River Preserve (Galt), both Nature Conservancy sites, and Phoenix Park (Orangevale, near Sacramento). You can explore other Coast Range habitats that are part of the University's Natural Reserve System at Stebbins Cold Canyon Reserve near Lake Berryessa.

For more information:
University of California—Davis Natural Reserve System
DESP/Wickson Hall
University of California
Davis, CA 95616
(530) 752–6949
http://nrs.ucdavis.edu/jepson.html

Solano Land Trust
www.solanolandtrust.org

Backpacking in the Historic Ranchlands of the East Bay Hills

A short drive from suburban communities, but a century back in time, Sunol Regional Wilderness preserves the historic ranchlands of the East Bay hills, where cattle still graze on the open hillsides and wildlife thrive along meandering Alameda Creek.

Site: Sunol Regional Wilderness is nestled in the East Bay area hills between Fremont and Pleasanton, near the town of Sunol.

Recommended time: Sunol Regional Wilderness is at its best in spring, when wildflowers carpet the green hills and the streams run full. Summers are hot and dry, but pockets of water along Alameda Creek tend to concentrate wildlife along the riparian woodlands. In fall the acorn-ladened oaks attract many species of birds and mammals. Winters can be cool and wet, but on days between storms the crisp, clear air and empty trails make hiking a joy.

Minimum time commitment: Two days to backpack, four hours for a day hike.

What to bring: Backpacking supplies, good hiking boots, backpacking permit, mosquito repellent, binoculars, and water filter.

Hours: 7:00 A.M. to dusk year-round. Gates are locked at dusk.

Admission fee: $4.00 parking fee; $5.00 per person per night for backpacking.

Directions: From Interstate 680 between Fremont and Pleasanton, take the Calaveras Road/California Highway 84 exit. Or from Fremont, turn right (turn left from Pleasanton) onto Calaveras Road. Once on Calaveras Road, turn onto Geary Road and proceed to park entrance.

The background: Sunol Regional Wilderness lies in the rugged East Bay hills, surrounded by San Francisco Water Department lands that link Del Valle Regional Park to the northeast and Mission Peak Regional Park to the west. These public lands protect important wildlife corridors and watersheds and offer miles of hiking and equestrian trails. The Ohlone Wilderness Trail extends 28 miles from Del Valle through Sunol to Mission Peak, where it connects to the Bay Area Ridge Trail running along the crest of

Bobcats are a common but rarely seen predator in the historic ranchlands of the East Bay hills. JOSEPH E. DIDONATO

the East Bay hills. The Bay Area Ridge Trail is an ongoing effort to create 400 continuous miles of trails along the ridgetops surrounding the bay.

Before the park was established or water was piped across the area from Hetch Hetchy in Yosemite to the City of San Francisco, the oak-studded foothills and sycamore creek bottoms supported cattle ranches. With roots dating to the Mexican Rancho period prior to California's statehood in 1850, the region's rich ranching history is reflected in the old barns, pastures, and homesteads that still survive in the area. Cattle continue to graze the parklands, in part to reduce the threat from wildfires.

Sunol Regional Wilderness is known for its great hiking trails and diverse topography and habitats. Lush Alameda Creek traverses the southern boundary of the area. Huge sycamores, cottonwoods, alders, and bigleaf maples line the stream banks. In a popular hiking area known as Little Yosemite, the water from Alameda Creek cascades over boulders and into shallow pools as it courses through a narrow gorge. Away from the streambed, the steep-sided canyons and rolling hills support blue and live oak woodlands and open grasslands. Dry, hot summers bake the ground to a crisp, but wildflowers carpet the hillsides in early spring. A number of rocky crags, such as Flag Hill and Indian Joe Cave Rocks, offer dramatic vistas as well as nesting sites for birds of prey.

Wildlife abounds in the park. The riparian (streamside) forests, particularly the sycamores with their hollow limbs and trunks, support cavity-nesting wildlife, such as woodpeckers, screech owls, wood ducks, and gray squirrels. The acorn-rich oak forests support scrub jays, wild turkeys, ground and gray squirrels, and black-tailed deer. Yellow-billed magpies nest at the tops of the oaks.

The fun: This is a very popular park in spring and summer, as families come from nearby communities to picnic, hike, and play in Alameda Creek. To escape the crowds, consider a relatively easy overnight backpack trip to one of the area's four backpack campsites. The hike is about 4 miles in each direction, with about a 1,700 foot climb over the length of the trail, to the campsites, which overlook the green rolling hills. Pit toilets and piped water are available at the campsites, but the park recommends that you boil or filter the water before drinking.

Reserve your campsite early. Reservations for the following season open the first Monday in November for Alameda/Contra Costa County residents, first Monday in February for everyone else. Call (510) 636–1684. Arrive early in the day to get a jump on the day-use visitors. There are a number of trail routes to consider. Try Camp Ohlone Road through Little Yosemite and up Backpack Road on your way out, and return on McCorkle Trail or branch off at Cerro Este Road to Cave Rocks Road and back down Indian Joe Creek Trail. Pick up a trail map at the entrance station.

Take your time, stop often, and enjoy the wildlife and flowers along the trail. Save room in your pack for your binoculars and bird and flower guides. Free-ranging cattle can be intimidating, but the camping area is fenced to keep out the cows—and the cow pies.

Special tips: Rattlesnakes and poison oak are common in the park. Both can be avoided by staying on the trails and watching for their presence.

Food and lodging: The Livermore area offers a variety of accommodations and restaurants. Contact the Tri-Valley Conference and Visitors Bureau at (888) 874–9253 or www.trivalleycvb.com.

Next best: The ranchlands of the East Bay area are rapidly being absorbed by growing suburbs. To explore some of the most remote backcountry of Alameda and Santa Clara Counties, take a 70-mile driving loop starting on Mines Road in Livermore south to San Antonio Valley Road and west over Mt. Hamilton to San Jose. Historic Lick Observatory at the 4,200-foot summit of Mt. Hamilton is open for tours daily (www.ucolick.org).

For more information:
Sunol Regional Wilderness
East Bay Regional Park District
(925) 862–2600
www.ebparks.org/parks/sunol.htm

Spring Flowers and Fairy Falls

Lupines, poppies, and wild onions carpet the hillsides during spring. A 100-foot waterfall runs year-round, with a wonderful swimming hole downstream. If you like watching wildlife, there's everything from river otters and deer to wood ducks and elusive black rails.

Site: Spenceville Wildlife Management and Recreation Area, about 30 miles (one hour) northeast of Lincoln (near Sacramento).
Recommended time: April/May for wildflowers; year-round for falls.
Minimum time commitment: Four hours.

What to bring: Binoculars, mosquito repellent, sunscreen, drinking water (there are no facilities at this undeveloped area), hiking boots, and a hat.
Hours: Normally open sunrise to sunset, seven days a week.
Admission fee: None.

Directions: From the town of Lincoln, go north on California Highway 65 to Wheatland. Turn right onto Spenceville Road. Travel about 6 miles until the road Ts. Turn right onto Camp Far West Road. Pass the entrance to Camp Far West and cross the bridge. Almost immediately, turn right onto Blackford Road. Go about 1 mile; the pavement ends. Continue on the dirt road about 5 miles. At the T, turn right and travel about 2 miles to the end of the road and park near the old cement bridge.

From Marysville, drive about 21 miles east on California Highway 20. At the BEALE AIR FORCE BASE sign, turn south onto Smartville Road. After 0.9 mile, take the left fork and continue on Smartville Road about 3.8 miles to Waldo Road. Continue along Waldo Road for 1.8 miles to the Waldo Bridge, which was built in 1901 to serve the now extinct towns of Waldo and Spenceville. After crossing the bridge, continue to the left along Spenceville Road for 2.3 miles. Park near the old cement bridge.

The background: The 11,213-acre Spenceville Wildlife Management and Recreation Area, managed by the California Department of Fish and Game, is a sleeper! Located northeast of Camp Far West and east of Beale Air Force Base, it is just a quick trip from urban Sacramento. Whether you like wildflowers, bird-watching, hiking, horseback riding, fishing, or hunt-

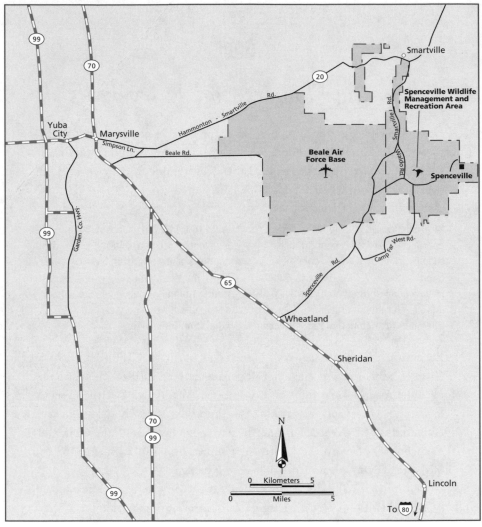

ing, this natural area offers it all—and a respite from the big crowds attracted to better known sites.

The rolling, blue oak woodland is interspersed with gray pine and laced with creeks and lush riparian areas that teem with wildlife. It boasts wildflower displays that rival many better known areas, but you will need to do some walking to enjoy them. Call the wildlife area office to check on the peak blooming period, as it varies by several weeks if the weather is unseasonably hot or cold.

Wood ducks inhabit riparian corridors, making their nests in tree cavities or artificial nesting boxes. WILLIAM E. GRENFELL

The trails to the falls are normally open; portions of the wildlife area are closed during hunting season, and you may see turkey hunters March to May. While the 2.5-mile trip to the falls and back can be done in a few hours, bring a picnic lunch, a fishing rod (the ponds have largemouth bass and sunfish), a lawn chair or two, and stay awhile!

The fun: The drive in on well-graded dirt roads forces you to leave your "city pace" behind. Travel slowly and you may seer deer in the grasslands, spring turkeys feeding in the open, and red-tailed hawks cruising above your vehicle. The road dead-ends near two bridges that cross Dry Creek. Park and take the cement bridge on your left (to the north). At the far side of the bridge, you'll see the remains of the old copper mine, a once-toxic site that is now being restored to natural habitat. Turn right (east) at the end of the bridge onto the Old Spenceville Road Trail.

The road begins to rise almost immediately. The pastoral hills before you were once the site of a bustling 1880s mining town that housed sixty-seven families. No visible evidence of the town remains today.

If you come in late March or early April, the grasslands will be lightly carpeted with spring wildflowers, such as California poppies, blue-headed gillia, wild onion, and valley lupine. You will be treated to colorful displays throughout your trip to the falls; more than seventy-five wildflower species occur here.

Spenceville Wildlife Management and Recreation Area was an old stage stop. History buffs may recognize the narrow ruts that occasionally run parallel to the service road. This is the old Emigrant Trail, and rescuers once passed through here to search for the missing Donner Party. If you enjoy wildlife, pause often and you'll be rewarded. Waterfowl inhabit the creeks and ponds. Songbirds find perches along the creek. More than 175 species of birds occur here.

After about 1 mile, take the trail marked FALLS; turn right at the locked gate, and follow the old road. You will eventually come to Dry Creek. Enjoy the sandy beaches and look for the grinding holes in flat rocks made by the Maidu people. A short climb will take you to Fairy Falls.

Over 100 feet high, the falls run all year, making the area a popular escape during the hot summer months. There is no safe access to Dry Creek at the falls, so don't try! Return to the beaches, or try the swimming hole downstream, near an old campsite that is visible from the road.

Remember, the wildlife area is not staffed, nor are there any facilities. There are signs pointing to the falls, but most trails are not named. All organized groups/events must obtain a free use permit at the office. Be sure to visit the Friends of Spenceville Web site at www.gv.net/~rsthomas/. You can download an excellent map and get very detailed trail information, a list of wildflowers, and much more.

Food and lodging: Food and gas are available in Sheridan. Closest lodging is in Marysville or Roseville. Contact Lincoln Chamber of Commerce at (916) 645–2035 or www.lincolnchamber.com.

Special tips: There are very few trail markers. Rattlesnakes and poison oak are also bountiful; both can be avoided by remaining on the trail. Visitors are asked to respect area closures and to reclose any gates they pass through: Cattle are carefully placed in specific areas to help rejuvenate the grasslands by controlling star thistle and medusa head, both invasive, nonnative plants. Call ahead: Hunting occurs during deer and upland bird seasons.

Next best: Table Mountain (near Oroville) boasts excellent wildflower displays. Camp Far West offers picnicking, boating, and horseback riding trails. Sacramento National Wildlife Refuge (see Weekend 1) and Gray Lodge Wildlife Area are also within an hour's drive.

For more information:
Spenceville Wildlife Management and Recreation Area Office
(not located on-site)
945 Oro Dam Boulevard
West Oroville, CA 95965
(530) 538–2236
www.dfg.ca.gov

Godwits and Marshes of Humboldt Bay

Humboldt Bay, the largest estuary north of San Francisco Bay, is the winter home of thousands of marbled godwits and a great wildlife festival that shares their name.

Site: Humboldt Bay is located about six hours north of San Francisco on U.S. Highway 101. The city of Eureka is perched on its shores. The Godwit Days Festival is headquartered in Arcata on the north end of Humboldt Bay.

Recommended time: The wildlife festival occurs on the third weekend in April prior to the northern spring shorebird migration. From late fall through spring, shorebirds and waterfowl cover the mudflats and shallow waters of Humboldt Bay. Winter rains subside in April, making it an ideal month for bird-watching and outdoor recreation in the Humboldt Bay area.

Minimum time commitment: Two days to take in a number of field trips and workshops associated with the festival.

What to bring: Rain gear, warm clothes, waterproof boots, day pack, binoculars, and your favorite bird guide.

Hours: The festival begins on Friday afternoon and continues through Sunday afternoon. A variety of post-festival activities continue through Wednesday.

Admission fee: $40 basic registration. Some field trips and workshops require additional fees.

Directions: Festival headquarters is located at the Arcata Community Center. From Eureka, travel north on US 101 to the Samoa Boulevard East exit. Take the first left at Union Street and continue 1 block to the community center located on the left.

The background: The pastures, mudflats, and shallow waters of the Humboldt Bay support large concentrations of shorebirds, waterfowl, and birds of prey during winter. Most migrate north to arctic breeding grounds in spring. More than twenty-five varieties of shorebirds feed on the tidal mudflats surrounding the bay. They range in size from the sparrow-size western sandpiper to the duck-size long-billed curlew. Each species uses unique feeding behaviors to capture different types of clams, worms, and crustaceans living in the mud.

Mudflats and estuaries are the most productive habitats in the world. Beyond supporting the large populations of shorebirds seen on the exposed mudflats, the murky waters of the bay serve as an important nursery for coastal fish populations. Extensive eelgrass beds, the largest beds south of the Puget Sound in Washington, provide food and cover for the animals living in the bay. Eelgrass is sensitive to water pollution, and the extensive beds of Humboldt Bay reflect the health of the bay's habitats.

Humboldt Bay is one of the few natural ports on the north coast. Settlers first arrived to the area starting in the 1850s, but the communities of Eureka and Arcata boomed in the 1870s as the rich bottomlands were diked and drained for farming and the coastal redwoods were cut and milled along the shores of the bay. Coastal schooners transported lumber and farm products to San Francisco to support the demands of the growing city. Fort Humboldt, built on a bluff overlooking the port, reflects the dark side of early settlement, when local settlers and soldiers attacked and imprisoned Wiyot Indian families who had lived for generations along the edge of the bay. Today the communities of Eureka and Arcata offer a blending of historic preservation and modern growth along scenic Humboldt Bay.

The fun: Start your trip by visiting the Web site for the Godwit Days Festival (www.godwitdays.com). The event organizers have cleverly put together weekend packages from the wide selection of field trips and workshops available throughout the weekend. Customize your own itinerary, or choose a package if you are a beginning birder, want to try a variety of outdoor recreational options, or want to focus on a specific type of habitat or wildlife. The organizers have thought of everything here, offering guided birding trips on the return from the festival as you drive south on US 101 or east across California Highway 299 to Redding and south on Interstate 5.

A couple of must-do visits include a stop at the Arcata wastewater facility, a hike through the Lanphere Dunes, and a paddle along Humboldt Bay.

The Arcata wastewater facility, located in the Arcata bottoms off Samoa Boulevard, is world renowned for its low-tech solution to wastewater treatment—moving partially treated sewage through a series of holding ponds where naturally occurring bacteria and organisms break down the waste before the cleaned water is discharged into the bay. The rich soup of organisms living in the ponds, in turn, attracts hundreds of species of birds and hoards of birders. A visitor center, nature trails, and volunteer docents are available.

AMAZING DUNES

Carried to land by the sea and sculpted by the wind and waves, undulating hills of sand protect many California beach uplands from the brunt of Pacific storms. Barrier dunes, some standing more than 80 feet tall, are part of the dynamic world of the seashore.

Those closest to the water and exposed to the wind, called the fore-dunes, may be spotted with sparse grasses. The phalanx of more-protected dunes behind the foredunes may be laced with vegetation, even seasonal wildflowers. Dune vegetation usually grows in low, dome-shaped clumps, presenting a low profile to the wind. This vegetation helps stabilize the dunes, which, in turn, protect the more vulnerable dune scrub communities growing behind them.

The defiant dunes and their vegetation are assaulted by a range of conditions, from wind and abrasive salt spray to high ground temperatures. Dune plants cope with the dry, salty environment by storing water in their succulent stems. They often have tiny hairs that help reflect heat and sunlight and capture dew from summer fog. Some plants are able to withstand gale force winds because they are firmly anchored to the sand by substantial underground rootlike stems called rhizomes.

Unfortunately, most dune systems are in decline. Nearby rivers are often dammed or diverted and the sand needed to replenish the fore-dunes no longer washes onto the shore. The dunes that remain are vitally important to coastal ecosystems. These sparsely vegetated areas between the land and sea provide a haven for many wildlife species while protecting coastal uplands and forests from serious erosion.

The Lanphere Dunes Unit of the Humboldt Bay National Wildlife Refuge, located near the town of Samoa off Samoa Boulevard, protects unique sand dune habitats that occur between the bay and ocean. Only accessible by guided tours, the dunes are a magical place of fog-shrouded pine and spruce forests, boggy meadows, and mats of wildflowers.

The Eureka waterfront provides the setting for a kayak trip out to view the egret rookeries on Indian Island in Humboldt Bay. The guided paddle trip is great for beginners and provides a nice blending of boat and building viewing in the harbor and wildlife viewing around the island. Egrets nest in colonies on the tops of trees. Most of the young will have fledged by April, but some birds should still be in the nests.

Special tips: Plan for rain. Mosquitoes can be a nuisance in some locations.

Food and lodging: Arcata and Eureka offer a wide selection of accommodations and restaurants. Contact the Arcata Chamber of Commerce at (707) 822–3619 or www.arcata.com/chamber.

Next best: Visit Old Town Eureka to get a taste of the Victorian storefronts and huge mansions built in the oldest part of town. The town square in Arcata is the center of the college town dominated by Humboldt State University. The Saturday morning farmers' market on the square is an interesting place to people-watch as students, local families, and free-spirited individuals converge for great produce, music, and socializing. If you're in the mood for big trees, travel north into redwood country (see Weekend 33).

For more information:
Godwit Days Wildlife Festival and Local Trip Planning
Arcata MainStreet
(800) 908–9464
www.godwitdays.com

Friends of the Dunes
(707) 444–1397
www.friendsofthedunes.org

Humboldt Bay National Wildlife Refuge
(707) 733–5406
http://pacific.fws.gov/humboldtbay

Grandfather Oaks and a Free-flowing River

Driving along the tour route, hiking a trail, or paddling down a quiet stream, it is easy to imagine Old California at the Cosumnes River Preserve, where Miwok Indians once camped under century-old valley oaks, grasslands teemed with herds of pronghorn and tule elk, and sandhill cranes performed courtship dances on secluded seasonal marshes.

Site: Cosumnes River Preserve, located 3 miles north of Galt.

Recommended time: Spring, though it is excellent any time of year.

Minimum time commitment: Four to eight hours.

What to bring: Comfortable walking shoes, layered clothing, mosquito repellent (summer months), drinking water and food, binoculars, and nature guides.

Hours: Visitor center, Lost Slough Boardwalk Trail and Willow Slough Trail usually open daily, daylight hours. Visitor center open most weekends 9:00 A.M. to 5:00 P.M.; hours during July and August are 8:00 A.M. until noon. Driving tour is on public roads; viewing is best during daylight hours.

Admission fee: None.

Directions: From Sacramento or Stockton, take Interstate 5 South to the Twin Cities Road exit. Turn east onto Twin Cities Road. Turn south (right) onto Franklin Boulevard. Go 1.3 miles to reach the Willow Slough trailhead, located on the left. To reach the visitor center and Lost Slough Boardwalk Trail, continue 0.2 mile south on Franklin Boulevard. (The Franklin Boulevard Bridge over the Mokelumne River is currently under construction and expected to be completed by the end of 2004. When the road is reopened, visitors from the south will be able to exit I–5 at Walnut Grove–Thornton Road, turn right, and make an immediate left onto Thornton Road, which becomes Franklin Boulevard at the County Line.)

The background: From its source on the western flank of the Sierra Nevada Range, the Cosumnes River descends to the Central Valley floor, the last free-flowing western Sierra river to course down ancient stream channels unrestricted by dams. It winds 60 miles, joining the Mokelumne

River at the Cosumnes River Preserve, and then continues to flow into the Sacramento–San Joaquin Delta.

Its banks are cloaked with a Central Valley jungle of alders, willows, and cottonwoods, bordered by blackberries and wild rose and joined by lianas of wild grape. The riparian corridor and grasslands are dotted with some of the state's finest and oldest valley oaks, a species found only in California. Forest branches and shrubs offer a respite and shelter for many species of birds year-round, from western bluebirds to Bewick's wrens. In spring, migratory songbird numbers soar and tree cavities shelter woodpeckers and wood ducks.

Winter rain spills the river across its banks, creating broad seasonal wetlands that are a beacon for waterfowl and wading birds. Greater sandhill cranes feed in rice fields near and within the preserve, returning to roost in the shallow wetlands at night. Grasslands stretch as far as you can see, dotted by vernal pools and blue oaks.

Only a fraction of the Central Valley native habitats remain, and some of the best are showcased at Cosumnes River Preserve. The preserve includes 37,000 acres protected by a partnership led by The Nature Conservancy, with ten federal, state, county, and private organizations. It offers many examples of restoration and management in action and opportunities for you to participate.

The fun: This stunning preserve combines tranquil scenery, bountiful wildlife, and lots of ways to explore—all located a half hour's drive from Sacramento. Two self-guided nature trails allow you to explore wetland and upland habitats at a leisurely stroll. Start your trip at the visitor center, and then orient yourself with a 1-mile walk on the Lost Slough Boardwalk Trail, which explores life within a wetland. The Lost Slough Boardwalk is level and wheelchair-accessible. The Willow Slough Trail, located about 100 yards north of the boardwalk trail, is a 3-mile loop that penetrates the marshes and the riparian jungle. Both of these trails are open during daylight hours. Each month the visitor center also publicizes guided walks, paddling trips, bird counts, photography tours, and restoration days.

These two trails offer a peek of the preserve. The driving tour allows you to see a greater variety of preserve habitats from the comfort of your vehicle, all from public roads. The driving route passes seasonal and permanent wetlands that teem with waterfowl during the winter months, as the preserve is an important resting area and stopover for Pacific Flyway migrants. It passes rice fields that attract foraging sandhill cranes from

YUCK, IT'S A TICK!

The warmer spring weather entices all of us to get outdoors. Spring also is the prime season for ticks. There are a number of different species of ticks found in California; though they may differ slightly in size or color, their habits are much the same. Ticks feed on warm-blooded "prey"—everything from rabbits and squirrels as subadults to livestock, deer, and humans when mature.

When it comes to humans, these match head–sized parasites climb to the tops of grass stems and low shrubs and wait for the chance to grab a passing leg. High-topped boots and long pants help deter the ticks, but they can find their way up a pant leg or crawl outside your clothes in search of a soft spot to burrow into your skin. A barbed mouth holds the tick in place while it drinks; it can stay attached for weeks.

To avoid ticks, stay on the trail and out of the brush. Consider tucking your pants legs into the tops of your socks or boots. Insect repellent may help. Carefully examine yourself and your partner at the end of each hike. You can often feel the little critters climbing up your leg or across your neck, so be observant and grab them before they bite. It is amazing how quickly you will drop your drawers in a crowd when you a feel a tick heading towards your tender spots! The scalp and areas around the waistbands and legbands of undergarments are favorite locations for ticks to burrow and should be checked when you get back to your accommodations. Don't forget your pets. If you aren't using a topical form of tick and flea control, you must inspect pets after each outing.

Most ticks do not carry Lyme disease, but the disease has now been diagnosed in many California locations. Once attached, ticks should be pulled straight out by grasping the tick with tweezers as close to the head as possible. If the barbed head remains attached, use a needle to remove it. Always apply antibiotic cream or alcohol to the area, and watch for a secondary infection. Visit your physician if you notice any persistent redness around the bite or if you experience achy joints or flulike symptoms. For more information check with your pet's veterinarian, or search the Internet for "Lyme disease."

While you're hiking or traveling on the driving tour route, you might catch a glimpse of coyotes, deer, and other mammals that are common at this river preserve.
WILLIAM E. GRENFELL

October through February and offers several views of the Valensin Ranch, a unit of the preserve, where Swainson's hawks, considered rare at most places, are a common sight. Even packs of coyotes have been spotted hunting for ground squirrels during the early morning and evening. You can check the Web site or contact the preserve for the tour route.

Whether it's a cool spring or hot summer day, the most intimate way to experience the preserve is on a guided canoe or kayak tour. A naturalist leads you down tree-lined waterways and flavors the trip with animal sightings and stories. You can take your own self-guided canoe or kayak trip throughout the year; the put-in and take-out are at the visitor center. The preserve occasionally offers guided paddling trips; check the Web site for information. Guided or on your own, you must provide your own canoe or kayak, which can be rented from Sacramento outfitters.

Special tips: Trails, bridges, and roads can flood during winter.

Food and lodging: Galt, Lodi, and Walnut Grove have restaurants; lodging in Galt and Lodi. Sacramento is only 20 miles to the north. For information contact the Sacramento Convention and Visitors Bureau, 1303 J Street, Suite 600, Sacramento, CA 95814; (916) 264–7777 or www.sacramentocvb.org.

Next best: If you visit during fall, you can see greater sandhill cranes at Woodbridge Ecological Reserve, located just south in Lodi. Call (916) 359–2900 for directions. Stone Lakes National Wildlife Refuge, at the preserve's northern border, is generally open the second and fourth Saturdays of each month, depending on weather. Call (916) 775–4420 before visiting the refuge. Yolo Bypass Wildlife Area is located in Davis. You are also near the gateway to many historic, foothill mining towns, and wineries near Jackson that have special charm, good restaurants, and shopping.

For more information:
Cosumnes River Preserve
13501 Franklin Road
Galt, CA 95632
(916) 684–2816 (also has recorded information)
www.cosumnes.org

Houseboating on Shasta Lake

Watch a star-spangled sky, catch a big one, read a book, and barbecue a dinner—all from the deck of a houseboat on picturesque Shasta Lake, where more than 365 miles of shoreline await exploration.

Site: Shasta Lake, about 10 miles north of Redding, with many access points.

Recommended time: Year-round. Peak houseboat rental season is mid-May through Labor Day. Houseboats can be rented at lower rates during other times of year. The lowest rates are usually January through late May.

Minimum time commitment: Minimum houseboat rental is three days; some companies allow two-day rentals in the off-season.

What to bring: Houseboats are equipped in a variety of quality ranges. Most include staterooms with beds; a kitchen/galley with stove, refrigerator, cookware, and utensils; and living space and usually a propane grill. You will need to bring your own pillows, sheets, and blankets or sleeping bags; bath and kitchen towels; food; and personal items (clothing, toiletries, binoculars, cameras, games, etc). Houseboat rental companies will provide a list of what each boat includes and what you will need to furnish.

Admission fee: There is no access fee to enjoy national forestlands within the Shasta-Trinity National Forest, although there is a fee to park in some private areas. There is a $6.00 use fee at all USDA Forest Service boat ramps to launch fishing boats and personal watercraft. Private marinas may charge up to $20 unless you are a houseboat customer. There are ten private campgrounds as well as public campgrounds, including thirteen developed, five shoreline, four boat-in, and six group camping facilities. All charge an overnight fee; reservations are often required and are always a good idea. Forest Service campsites can be reserved at www.reserveusa.com.

Houseboat costs: Houseboat rental costs vary with the season, size/model of boat, and length of rental. For example, a basic houseboat for eight to twelve people rented for three nights may cost $800 during January through late May, while a luxury houseboat may cost $2,200. In contrast, during the peak summer season the same basic houseboat may run $1,275, while the luxury model may cost as much as $6,000. Houseboats can be rented for as many as twelve to eighteen people and for three, four, or seven days. More money buys you greater comfort and more amenities, such as a

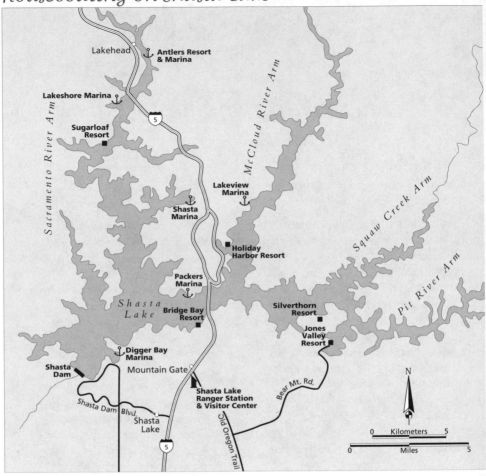

hot tub, satellite TV, multimedia sound systems, sunken kitchens with professional quality appliances/cookware, and luxury bathrooms. In addition to the rental, you will need to factor in the cost of purchasing gasoline during your travels.

Marina information: Eleven marinas on Shasta Lake offer many services, such as lodging, mooring, houseboat rentals, boat rentals, fuel, cabins, food, campsites, hookups, and groceries. You may access these commercial marinas through the USDA Forest Service, Shasta Lake Business Owners Association, or Shasta-Cascade Wonderland Association Web site.

Directions: The map shows the locations of the eleven marinas that rent houseboats and other recreational boats. If you are interested in visiting Shasta Lake to camp, hike, fish, or use a personal watercraft, consider orienting yourself at the Shasta Lake Ranger Station and Visitor Center, located on Interstate 5 at Mountain Gate, 8 miles north of Redding. The USDA Forest Service Web site includes information about public access points.

The background: The snow-clad peaks of Mounts Shasta and Lassen, wild volcanic formations, secluded islands, and lush, forested shorelines are just some of the scenery that can be savored from Shasta Lake. Even though it covers almost 30,000 acres, this vast, beautiful reservoir may still be one California's secrets.

Shasta, Trinity, and Lewiston Lakes, managed by the Forest Service, and Whiskeytown Lake, managed by the National Park Service, are part of the Whiskeytown-Shasta-Trinity National Recreation Area (NRA)—one of just eighteen NRAs in the nation. Shasta lake was formed when Shasta Dam was constructed (1938 to 1945), which backed up the waters of the Sacramento, McCloud, and Pit Rivers and Squaw Creek. The dam has the nation's highest center spillway, which is three times higher than Niagara Falls, and is the second largest concrete structure in the nation. The newly formed lake submerged many old towns, ranches, and portions of the Oregon Trail and the Central Pacific Railroad line.

The lake and much of the surrounding land are part of the Shasta Trinity National Forest, managed by the Forest Service. It is a recreation wonderland, offering boating, waterskiing and wakeboarding, swimming, fishing, camping, picnicking, hiking, wildlife viewing, mountain biking, and hunting. The National Forest provides twelve trails to explore, ranging from a 0.5-mile hike to Potem Falls to an 8-mile trek on foot, bicycle, or horse along the Clikapudi Trail.

The wildlife viewing can be superb; so is the fishing. Shasta Lake is a renowned trophy bass lake; anglers also come for the three- to ten-pound rainbow trout, salmon, sturgeon, catfish, crappie, and bluegill.

But first, it is a true boater's paradise and, many believe, one of the nation's top houseboating lakes. The four arms of the lake offer more than 365 miles of shoreline, secluded islands, caverns, and waterfalls to explore. The best way to take in all of this grandeur is on a houseboat.

The fun: Don't let their size or a lack of houseboating experience deter you. Houseboat rental companies provide easy precruise training and orientation to novices and experienced boaters alike. Once you've taken the controls, you are in for a lot of fun. You can enjoy some of northern California's best scenery right from the deck of your floating home.

The Sacramento Arm is the most developed and also the busiest. A visitor information center at the dam includes photographs and information about the dam construction. The west shore is faced with basaltic lava from Mt. Shasta, and tree cover is sparse. Near the town of Delta, formerly called Antlers after a local hotel festooned with deer antlers, the lava is shaped in tall columns. On a hot summer day, you can motor to Indian Creek for a hike up to a lush seasonal waterfall or to Riverview's sandy beach.

A trip on the McCloud Arm begins with a view of the ocean—that is, ancient ocean sediments riddled with fossilized corals, clams, snails, and other marine creatures that formed into gray limestone mountains called the Gray Rocks. Centuries of water running over the formation have opened two caverns. During summer, a ferry makes a trip every half hour between 9:00 A.M. and 4:00 P.M. to the Shasta Caverns, revealing a world of wild geologic formations. Two miles south of the McCloud Bridge, you can also explore the Samwel Cave, once frequented by Wintu Indians. According to local lore, it is also called the Cave of the Lost Maiden because an Indian maiden fleeing from raiding Shasta Indians disappeared in the cave, never to be seen again. A permit and key deposit are required to enter Samwel Cave and are available through the Shasta Lake Visitor Information Center. Reservations are recommended.

If you want remote, rugged beauty, the Squaw Arm of the lake is your destination. It is extremely popular with houseboaters, who are drawn to excellent wildlife viewing. Ospreys, an occasional bald eagle, river otters, elk, and even bears may be seen, along with many smaller creatures. The ruins of the Bully Hill Mine draw boaters, who come to explore the copper mines, imagine the old mining town now submerged beneath Shasta's waters, or to feast on wild grapes, plums, and figs during summer.

The dramatic Pit River Arm is the longest at 30 miles, offering dazzling views of Mt. Shasta and Mt. Lassen. It includes the largest inland marina on the West Coast at Bridge Bay—and some of the most rugged and natural areas. The bass fishing is outstanding, perhaps the best on the lake. The arm includes eleven of the twenty-two bald eagle nesting territories on the lake. You can explore dozens of undulating coves and inlets, catch the spray from 70-foot-tall Potem Falls, and watch bald eagles and ospreys show their fishing prowess.

Special tips: If you've never rented a houseboat, take advantage of the wealth of information available on the Internet. Many sites include excellent information about the features to consider, rental contracts, and more. Book in advance; if you can be flexible, look for specials during slower weeks of the season.

Food and lodging: If you want to enjoy Shasta, but not on a houseboat, there are numerous campgrounds, motels, and other lodging available on or near the lake and in Redding, Shasta Lake, and other communities. Contact the Shasta Cascade Wonderland Association at (800) 474–2782 or www.shastacascade.com or the Greater Redding Chamber of Commerce at (530) 223–4433 or www.reddingchamber.com.

Next best: If you love the water, add Whiskeytown, Trinity, and Lewiston Lakes to your "to visit" list. If you're looking for a few diversions in town, visit the Turtle Bay Museum or the Schreder Planetarium, both in Redding.

For more information:
USDA Forest Service
Shasta Lake Ranger Station
14225 Holiday Road
Redding, CA 96003
(530) 275–1587
www.fs.fed.us/r5/shastatrinity

Shasta Lake Business Owners Association
www.shastalake.org

Sierra Giants and Spring Blossoms

The largest trees in the world, the Sierra redwoods almost demand quiet and respect in two groves found in Calaveras Big Trees State Park. In spring the white-flowering Pacific dogwoods growing beneath the redwoods offer a spectacular contrast to the red-barked giants.

Site: Calaveras Big Trees State Park in Calaveras County.

Recommended time: Each season offers a unique backdrop for the giant sequoias. In summer, warm days and crowded trails are the rule. Fall brings the first rains and the colorful fall foliage, pinks for dogwoods and yellow for the bigleaf maples. In winter, occasional snowstorms blanket the trees and trail with snow and provide for cross-country skiing and snowshoeing. Spring is dominated by the bright green leaves and large white blossoms of the Pacific dogwood and the rushing waters of the Stanislaus River.

Minimum time commitment: Two hours to hike the popular North Grove Trail and stop at the visitor center; six hours to hike and explore the park. A weekend to take in the next best attractions.

What to bring: Comfortable hiking boots (tennis shoes are fine for on-trail walking), mosquito repellent, water, a trail lunch, layered clothing, binoculars, camera and plenty of film, and nature guides.

Hours: Daily, from sunrise to sunset.

Admission fee: Day-use fee, $4.00 per vehicle.

Directions: From Angels Camp at the junction of California Highways 49 (the Gold Rush Highway) and 4, travel east on CA 4 about 25 miles to the park. From Arnold, travel 4 miles east to the park.

The background: The Calaveras big trees have been a popular tourist destination since the giant sequoias were first discovered here in 1852 by August T. Dowd, who was hunting in the area. The trees and the North Grove quickly gained international fame. Considered more a natural oddity than a unique plant to be protected for future generations, one of the largest trees was cut simply to watch it fall. Ironically, the tree fell when the work crew was out to lunch. A dance pavilion was later built on top of the huge stump. The grove's popularity led to a push to create the state park in 1931 to protect the North Grove. The park was later expanded to its current 6,500 acres to encompass and protect the South Grove.

Sierra redwoods, or giant sequoias, are only found in a few groves along the western slope of the Sierra Nevada. ROBERT W. GARRISON

The Sierra redwood, or giant sequoia, is the largest living thing on the planet. While the coast redwood gets the honors as the tallest tree in the world, the Sierra redwood's massive trunk makes it the largest in bulk. Some of the biggest trees top 30 feet in diameter at their base and 15 feet in diameter 150 feet from the ground. Even at such a great age, estimated between 1,800 and 2,700 years old for the largest trees, the giant sequoias continue to add about 40 cubic feet of new wood each year, equivalent to a tree 50 feet high and 12 inches in diameter. If these statistics don't impress you, try standing next to one of these giants!

The remaining groves of giant sequoias are all found on the western slope of the Sierra Nevada, generally in flat areas with year-round streams. They share the forest community with white firs, sugar pines, ponderosa pines, incense cedars, black oaks, bigleaf maples and Pacific dogwoods. In spring, the brilliant white blossoms of the Pacific dogwood offer dramatic contrast to the rich reds of the fibrous sequoia bark.

The fun: Start your visit with a quick walk through the North Grove. This is the most popular and easily accessible grove in the park, though be forewarned—it can be crowded. Pick up a self-guiding brochure at the start of the 1-mile loop trail to learn about the early history of the park. The potentially crowded trail and evidence of the early exploitation of the trees provides a great contrast to the real gem of the park, the South Grove.

The South Grove is located on the south rim of the Stanislaus River Canyon on Big Trees Creek. The grove itself is protected as a natural preserve and remains in its primeval condition. The 5-mile trail passes an area logged in the early 1950s, which led to a statewide initiative to purchase and protect the South Grove from additional logging in 1954. Once in the preserve, a loop trail passes through a portion of the lower grove. A spur trail takes you to the Agassiz Tree, the largest tree in the park. Within the preserve, you are allowed to hike off-trail and visit some of the trees not on the trail route.

Don't be in a hurry. Bring a lunch and spend the afternoon exploring the trees and wildlife of the South Grove.

Special tips: Mosquito repellent is a must this time of year.

Food and lodging: Camping is available within the park (reservations recommended). Arnold and Dorrington offer a variety of accommodations and food services. For information contact the Calaveras County Visitors Bureau at (800) 225–3764 or www.visitcalaveras.org. A full-service supermarket is available in Arnold for picnic supplies.

California's Floral Legacy

Within its borders, California contains the continent's second tallest mountain peak (14,495-foot Mt. Whitney) and lowest point (-282 feet in Death Valley). More than 1,000 miles of coastline and three separate mountain ranges combine to form one of the most complex and beautiful landscapes in the world. The state's Mediterranean climate, comprising cool, wet winters and dry, hot summers, is further influenced by the state's north-south orientation, with Crescent City receiving 75 inches of rain and San Diego only 10 inches. This juxtaposition of climate, topography, and geology has resulted in the most diverse and unique botanical riches found in North America.

More than 6,000 varieties of native plants grow within California, about a quarter of all of the plant species found north of the Mexican border. About 40 percent of the plants grow nowhere else in the world. Some of the most famous include the coast redwood, giant sequoia, and Monterey pine. Less famous perhaps, but equally stunning, are the small annuals and perennials that carpet the state in colorful mosaics in spring.

Consider for a moment what makes California the fifth largest economy in the world, the most populated state in the country, and the state with the greatest number of native plants. The common thread that binds these is California's rich natural landscape. Balancing the needs of people and nature will be our biggest challenge in the years to come, as our human population continues to grow and our flowered wildlands are replaced by houses.

Next best: Head down to the gold rush towns of Angels Camp, Murphys, and San Andreas to add a little wine tasting, shopping, and spelunking into your weekend. A number of excellent wineries have tasting rooms around the communities of Angels Camp and Murphys. If you like to shop and eat, Murphys has a number of small boutique-type shops and cafes on the pedestrian-friendly historic main street. Three limestone caverns—Mercer, Moaning, and California Caverns—offer guided tours in the towns of Murphys, Angels Camp, and San Andreas, respectively. Tours range from standard walks to high-adventure trips. Links are available at www.visitcalaveras.org.

For more information:
Calaveras Big Trees State Park
(209) 795–2334
www.parks.ca.gov

California State Park Camping Reservations
(800) 444–7275
www.parks.ca.gov

Tidepools and Surfers Side by Side

Some of the year's lowest tides occur in spring, exposing a hidden world to those willing to get nose-to-nose with a variety of fish, crabs, urchins, anemones, and sea stars. Nearby, the world's best surfers tackle huge waves at Mavericks.

Site: Fitzgerald Marine Reserve, 10 miles south of Daly City at Moss Beach and 7 miles north of Half Moon Bay.
Recommended time: Late spring and early summer provide the lowest tides during daylight hours for exploring tide-pools.
Minimum time commitment: Four hours.
What to bring: Old rubber-soled shoes and heavy jeans to wear in the water, warm shirt and jacket, towel, change of clothes, hot beverages, and snacks. *Pacific Intertidal Life* by Ron Russo and Pam Olhausen and *The Natural History of Fitzgerald Marine Reserve* are great pocket guides. Both guides are sold on-site. Bring binoculars for watching surfers.
Hours: Sunrise to sunset.
Admission fee: None.

Directions: From San Francisco, take California Highway 1 south to Moss Beach. Turn west onto California Avenue, and drive to parking area.

The background: California boasts more than 1,100 miles of coastline and, with it, some of the world's richest tidal life. Cold, nutrient-rich waters and rocky shorelines provide the perfect habitat for hundreds of species of plants and animals. At first glance, the wave-swept rocks may seem devoid of life, but the rocky pools exposed only at the lowest tides bear a rich assortment of plants and animals plastered together so thickly that only a small portion of the rocks are visible.

The trick to successful tidepooling is to select the best location and times to venture into the surf zone. Fitzgerald Marine Reserve is one of the best and most accessible locations to view tidal life. Established in 1969, the reserve protects an expansive, shallow rock shelf, stretching from the Montara Light Station to Pillar Point Harbor. You must time your visit to coincide with the lowest tides, when the rock shelf is exposed. There are two high tides and two low tides per day, and their intensity and timing are based on the gravitational pull from the sun and moon. When the sun and moon are aligned on the same side of the earth, extreme high and low tides result. Use the tide table Web site (http://tbone.biol.sc.edu/tide/) to access the annual tide tables for Año Nuevo Island, the nearest location to the reserve identified in the tide charts. Look for low tides (+1.5 or lower) in the low tide columns, and check the date and time of day that they occur. Plan to arrive at least two hours before the lowest tide.

The fun: Imagine the challenge of surviving surging waves, scouring sand, and the drying sun at low tide. If you're a sea creature, while you're trying to keep from getting bashed about in the surf, you must hunt for food, hide from enemies, and reproduce. Some species, like barnacles and anemones, permanently attach themselves to the rocks and wait for the waves to carry them food. Snails and sea stars clamp down on the rocks during low tides and heavy surf but move about in search of food at high tide. Soft-bodied nudibranchs (sea slugs) and fish tend to be the most active hunters and retreat to protected coves and deep water during storms and low tides. Part of the fun of exploring tidepools is being able to watch from just inches away and guess why the animals look and act as they do.

Tidepool viewing is not for the faint of heart. But with a willingness to get wet (yes, you will get wet), some commonsense safety measures, and a spirit of adventure, you will be rewarded with hours of viewing pleasure. The best viewing occurs in the lowest exposed tidepools. Pass up the animals exposed to the air and the pools closest to shore. Search for the deep pools, where animals will be feeding. Without entering the pools, gently push aside floating kelp to look beneath, but leave the animals alone. Quietly watch the pools for movements to discover crabs and fish that hide from view when they are disturbed. Brightly colored nudibranchs often hide in the kelp fronds. The reserve also supports a year-round harbor seal rookery—watch for groups of seals resting on the outlying rocks.

Never pick up the animals, and carefully place each footstep to avoid stepping on sea life. Collecting is not allowed in the preserve and shouldn't be done at any location.

Special tips: Safety first! Wear long pants and old shoes that have good tread to protect your feet and legs from cuts and scrapes. Walk with extreme caution on the slippery rocks, and walk between rocks (don't rock hop). Pay attention: Stay clear of areas swept by waves, never let the incoming tide cut off your route back to shore, and always face the incoming waves.

Food and lodging: Numerous accommodations and restaurants are available in the Half Moon Bay Area. Contact the Half Moon Bay Coast-side Chamber of Commerce and Visitors Bureau at (650) 726–8380 or www.halfmoonbaychamber.org.

Next best: Take a walk out to the end of Pillar Point from the Pillar Point Harbor in Princeton to see the surfing world's mecca—Mavericks. This is a shallow reef located about a half mile offshore that funnels swells coming off the Pacific into huge waves. Sporting some of the world's largest waves, regularly topping 25 feet, Mavericks attracts the best surfers from all parts of the globe. Bring your binoculars to enjoy the action. About 10 miles south is Half Moon Bay, where you can watch harbor seals during spring at Cowell Ranch Beach and life in a wetland at Pescadero Marsh Natural Reserve. Monterey Bay is just miles beyond.

For more information:
Fitzgerald Marine Reserve
San Mateo County Department of Parks and Recreation
(650) 728–3584

WEEKEND *23*

May

Nature's Geologic Staircase

Step back into time on a staircase, where each step takes you back 100,000 years. The wildlife and plants along the Mendocino coast live in a stratified world, starting at the coastal bluffs and climbing to the ancient White Plains of Mendocino. Dramatic scenery, clean air, spring wildflowers and, in May, uncrowded trails and sunny weather make this a must-do annual pilgrimage.

Site: Jug Handle State Reserve, about 5 miles south of Fort Bragg.

Recommended time: Travel in mid- to late May before Memorial Day weekend to avoid the summer crowds while catching the start of the wildflower season. This is the height of the breeding season for summer and resident bird species. Spring and fall generally offer the best weather—sunny, calm days in between winter rains and summer fog.

Minimum time commitment: Four hours

round-trip for the hike. This trip deserves a long weekend due to the three- to four-hour one-way drive times from Sacramento or the Bay Area (excluding viewing stops along the way).

What to bring: Good quality hiking boots or walking shoes, a hat, water, binoculars, and flower and bird guides; a lightweight rain parka for wind and rain.

Hours: Sunrise to sunset, seven days a week.

Admission fee: None.

Directions: Jug Handle State Reserve's Ecological Staircase is located 5 miles south of Fort Bragg on the west side of California Highway 1. Watch for the park sign and follow the signs to the Ecological Staircase trailhead. Pick up a self-guided trail brochure at the start of the trail.

The background: Think of the Mendocino coast as a series of giant sandstone steps, carved by the ocean waves and then lifted from the sea as the Pacific Plate slides under the mainland a few miles offshore. Five distinct steps or terraces can be seen along this portion of the coast. Each step is approximately 100,000 years older than the one below, very young in terms of geologic time. High annual rainfall has leached the nutrients from the sandy soils in the upper terraces, creating a unique set of growing conditions and habitats on each terrace.

The grassy headlands form the youngest terrace. Thin layers of topsoil primarily support grasses and wildflowers. Watch for California poppies, sea

You can see five distinct terraces, each 100,000 years older than the next, at the Ecological Staircase within scenic Jug Handle State Reserve. ROBERT W. GARRISON

thrift, baby blue-eyes, and yarrow growing amidst the primarily nonnative grasses. The burrows of moles, pocket gophers, and ground squirrels abound in the grasslands. Be on the lookout for the rarely seen but fairly common long-tailed weasel in areas of extensive burrows. On the bluffs overlooking the ocean, watch for black oystercatchers and three species of cormorants on the outermost rocks and groups of harbor seals sunning on the rocks near the water's edge.

The second terrace has rich, well-developed soils that support redwood and spruce-fir forests. Rhododendrons and azaleas grow in the filtered sunlight along the margins of the forest. In the dense shade, look for blooming evergreen and red huckleberries and redwood sorrel, a clover-shaped groundcover with pink flowers. Ospreys nest in the tops of forest snags. Chestnut-backed chickadees, Wilson's warblers, bushtits, winter wrens, pygmy nuthatches, and Steller's jays are common in the surrounding forest. Watch for black-tailed deer in the margins between forest and meadow.

The third through fifth terraces are home to the rare pygmy forest. In these upper terraces, rainwater leaching through sandy soils rich in iron formed an impenetrable hardpan about 18 inches below the surface that holds groundwater throughout the year. In some areas, bogs form around year-round pools. While other areas may appear dry, the presence of stunted pygmy cypress, less than a few feet high but hundreds of years old, indicates water close to the surface. Watch for California quail and wrentits, as well as other forest birds. Common garter snakes can be found in the shallow ponds and on the forest floor.

The fun: Jug Handle State Reserve is the best starting point for a weekend of wildlife viewing along the Mendocino coast. The Ecological Staircase is a 5.4-mile loop trail that takes you through all the distinct habitats found in the area. This "primer" hike will familiarize you with the plants and animals of the area in preparation for additional hikes and viewing.

If the weather is warm, start your hike early. Wildlife is generally more active in early morning and late afternoon, so you will double your pleasure by staying cool and seeing more wildlife. Carry a snack to enjoy in the pygmy forest before returning to your car.

After your hike, stop in Mendocino for some delicious baked goods and a favorite beverage. Decide what steps of the staircase interested you the most, and then review the Next best section to decide which of the many parks in the area to visit for the remainder of your trip.

Special tips: Carry a California wildflower book on your hike and journeys. Winter rains and spring blooms can be unpredictable, but if you hit the right weekend, the diversity of wildflowers, particularly along the coastal bluffs, can be spectacular.

Food and lodging: A wide variety of bed-and-breakfasts, country inns, motels, vacation rentals, and campgrounds are available along the Mendocino coast. This area is a popular weekend destination, so make your reservations ahead of time. Restaurant selections abound in the towns of Mendocino and Fort Bragg, but smaller communities offer fine and casual dining as well. Visit the following Web sites for a listing of some of the accommodations and restaurants in the area. Contact the Fort Bragg Mendocino Coast Chamber of Commerce at (707) 961–6300 or www.mendocinocoast2.com.

Next best: There are numerous parks, trails, and recreational opportunities along the Mendocino coast. Mendocino Headlands State Park offers some of the best coastal vistas from grassy headlands adjoining the town of Mendocino. Russian Gulch and Van Damme State Parks offer streamside trails in the second-growth redwood forests. These are good areas to look for salamanders and forest birds, such as the varied thrush and winter wren. Canoe and kayak concessions along the Big River just south of Mendocino provide access to newly acquired state parklands within the watershed. Kingfishers and ospreys are common along the river, and if you're lucky you may spot river otters. North of Fort Bragg, MacKerricher State Park protects unique sand dune habitats, inglenook fens (small freshwater springs amid the dunes), rocky headlands, and tidepools.

For more information:
Jug Handle State Reserve
(707) 937–5804
www.parks.ca.gov

Everything's Possible on the Bizz Johnson Trail

Ride a bicycle or horse, hike, or cross-country ski along the rugged Susan River Canyon on a former railroad line, complete with bridge trestles, tunnels, many favorite swimming holes, and outstanding scenery.

Site: Bizz Johnson Trail, beginning in Susanville, located north of Reno (one hour, forty-five minutes).
Recommended time: Any time of year.
Minimum time commitment: A half day to enjoy a few miles of the trail.
What to bring: Clothing suitable for the season for day trips, drinking water or a method of treating springwater found along the trail, food, maps, flashlight or headlamp, nature guides, and personal items needed for overnight stays.
Hours: Trail is open twenty-four hours, seven days a week. The Depot Trailhead Visitor Center and Museum is open 9:00 A.M. to 5:00 P.M. daily. Check on hours at the Westwood Museum.
Admission fee: None.

Directions: From the Sacramento area, take U.S. Highway 395 north from Reno 86 miles (one hour, forty-five minutes) to Susanville. From Red Bluff and Redding, take California Highway 36 east approximately 103 miles (two and a half hours) to Susanville. To reach Westwood, travel west on CA 36 for 25 miles.

The background: Can you imagine old steam trains traveling the Fernley to Lassen Branch Line laden with logs, chugging along a forest canyon dotted with logging camps? This was the scene a century ago, when trains regularly ran this route that includes an incredibly scenic portion of the Susan River Canyon. The railroad line waned with the closing of the Westwood lumber companies in the mid-1950s. After Southern Pacific abandoned the line in 1978, the Bureau of Land Management (BLM) and local interests worked with Congressman Harold "Bizz" Johnson to acquire the right-of-way for recreational purposes. It became one of just two BLM projects funded by Congress in 1980 and is one of the highlights of the national Rails-to-Trails system. BLM then worked with the USDA Forest Service to purchase privately owned parcels within the trail corridor.

Hike, bike, or ride your horse from Susanville, Westwood, or points in between on the Bizz Johnson Trail. CALIFORNIA DEPT. OF TRANSPORTATION

This unusual trail includes twelve bridges—one that extends 270 feet and stands 70 feet above the river—two unlighted tunnels blasted through a mountain of rock, and hours' worth of incredible vistas. It winds through a semiarid, picturesque canyon and high-desert habitat, then traverses grassy oak woodlands before ascending into deep forests of cedar and pine. The opportunity to learn about natural history is remarkable. In the space of 25.4 miles as the trail climbs from Susanville to Mason Station, it moves through three distinct bioregions: the Great Basin, Sierra Nevada, and Cascade Range. An additional 4.5 miles of trail then follows rural roads into the town of Westwood.

Between the beginning and ending trailheads at Susanville and Westwood, there are five additional trail access points. Hikers and bicyclists who plan to enjoy the entire trail can leave their vehicle at the Susanville or

Westwood trailheads and get a shuttle ride back on Monday through Friday. Contact Lassen Rural Bus (530) 252–7433 for a schedule and costs. At other times you can arrange for transportation by calling Mt. Lassen Cab and Shuttle Service at (530) 257–5277. Those who want to start at one of the access points in between need to arrange their own transportation if they don't wish to backtrack to their vehicle.

The fun: Your first challenge is to decide how and when to experience the trail. You can hike, bicycle, ride horses and, during winter, cross-country ski and even snowmobile at the extreme western end of the trail. It's a good idea to visit the Susanville Depot Trailhead Visitor Center and Museum or the Westwood Museum at the trailheads, where you can steep yourself in railroad history and pick up a guide and other materials to help plan your outing. You can also pick up a guide at the BLM office in Susanville or any Lassen National Forest office.

Hikers will find the 18-mile section contouring the Susan River between Westwood Junction and Susanville both scenic and an easy hike, with a maximum 3 percent grade. While you can backpack along the trail, it is also possible to plan day hikes from several of the access points.

The trail is a bicyclist's dream, providing a good surface for riding and a very easy ride if you begin in Westwood, by the giant redwood Paul Bunyan statue marking the trailhead. From here it climbs only 500 feet in the 12 miles to Westwood Junction, and then drops 1,300 feet in the remaining 18 miles to Susanville. Die-hard bikers can run the route backward for a great workout. You can bring your own bicycle or rent one in Susanville. Wide tires and multigeared bikes are recommended, but single-speed bicycles will also work. Be careful when crossing the planking on decked bridges. All visitors should come prepared with flashlights or headlamps to pass through the two unlighted tunnels; one is 800 feet long and the second is 450 feet. Those who want to forego the tunnel experience can follow a riverside trail.

Equestrians will be able to cross all twelve bridges and use the tunnels, though alternative trails are available. There is good parking for horse trailers at Hobo Camp.

During winter, cross-country skiers can traverse the 18.5-mile segment located west of CA 36 and the Devils Corral area. This shady stretch from the 4,760 to 5,500 feet elevation offers fairly reliable snow conditions. Another 9-mile stretch between Goumaz and CA 36 combines snowed-in

Make Your Bicycle Trip a Safe One

Veterans of mountain bike riding know that off-road and remote-area riding are highly different from easy day rides on paved bicycle trails and roads. Many of the weekend getaways desribed in this guide can be enjoyed from a bicycle. You don't need to own one—rental businesses are often located within or near the sites. If you haven't ridden a bicycle for a while, or haven't biked on unpaved surfaces, here are a few tips to make your trip fun and safe:

- Ask the rental agent to select the right bicycle for your purposes, depending on whether you'll be riding on paved trails or gravel or dirt surfaces.
- Ask the rental agent to fit you with the right size bicycle for each member of your group. Be sure the seat is adjusted so that each person can sit and pedal comfortably.
- Before you leave the rental agent, ask to see how the shifting mechanism works, and be sure the agent double-checks the condition of the tires, gears, brakes, tire pump, and any supplies that might be provided. A water bottle holder on the frame is also very handy. In popular areas, bikes can be rented several times a day, so don't assume that a busy rental center will always have time to check each bike.
- If you will be doing any riding in remote areas or taking an overnight trip, ask if you can rent panniers, tools, a spare tire, duct tape, or other supplies to use in an emergency. You should bring a flashlight for use in tunnels and get a bike lock if you anticipate being away from your bike for a while. If you don't want to rent these items, for day rides a fanny pack should hold what you need.
- Check the trail conditions and weather before you leave, and bring suitable clothing.
- If you are pedaling into a remote area, let someone know where you'll be, where your vehicle is parked, and when you plan to return.
- On the trail, if you want to stop to rest or make reparis, pull completely off the trail. Be courteous to other users, and always yield to equestrians. Most will appreciate it if you stop while they pass—not everyone will be on a bomb proof horse!
- Be sure to bring plenty of water for each person, snacks as needed, binoculars, and a lighweight camera if you want to capture some memories.

road and trail skiing. If you plan to ski, check on these and other alternatives and local weather conditions before leaving.

However you see the trail, you'll enjoy incredible scenery and may see lots of wildlife. Kingfishers and other birds are common along the river. You may see beavers and muskrats. Open areas may provide views of hunting birds of prey. Campers may see raccoons, opossums, or even black bears. There are numerous scenic picnic spots. Those who want tables and a barbecue grill will find them at Hobo Camp.

Special tips: To make this a pleasant experience for all, exercise trail courtesy. Walkers and bicyclists should always yield to horseback riders. Call out to let them know you are near so that you don't startle them or their horses. Bicyclists should stop when horses are passing.

Food and lodging: There are plenty of restaurants and motels in Susanville. Primitive camping is allowed along the trail on BLM and USDA Forest Service Land. There is an undeveloped drive-in campground area at Goumaz. Many areas have camping restrictions, so check before you set up camp. Contact the Lassen County Chamber of Commerce at 84 North Lassen Street, Susanville, at (530) 257–4323 or www.pe.net/~rksnow /cacountysusanvillecha.htm.

Next best: If you can't make it in June, consider a fall trip. The autumn colors are stunning, and Susanville hosts the Rails-to-Trails Festival during October. Hikers, wildlife viewers, and anglers should tie in a trip to nearby Eagle Lake, named for its wintering bald eagles. The lake is known for its rainbow trout fishing.

For more information:
Susanville Depot Trailhead Visitor Center and Museum
601 Richmond Road
Susanville, CA 96130
(530) 257–3252

Westwood Museum
311 Ash Street
Westwood, CA 96137
(530) 256–2233

Bureau of Land Management, Eagle Lake Office
2950 Riverside
Susanville, CA 96130

(530) 257–0456
www.ca.blm.gov/eaglelake/bizztrail.html
www.ca.blm.gov/caso/wf-bizzwild.html

USDA Forest Service, Lassen National Forest
2550 Riverside Drive
Susanville, CA 96130
(530) 257–2151
www.fs.fed.us/r5/lassen/recreation/trails/

Tufa Towers and Nesting Birds

Paddle a kayak among oddly shaped tufa mounds, listen to the cacophony of nesting gulls in June, and savor the lake scenery and night sky at one of the oldest lakes in the Western Hemisphere.

Site: Mono Lake Tufa State Reserve and Mono Basin National Forest Scenic Area, east of Lee Vining (two to three hours from Reno).

Recommended time: April to October for nesting and migrating birds. Any time of year for resident wildlife and outstanding scenery and natural history.

Minimum time commitment: Two to three hours. You can easily spend a day or more at the lake.

What to bring: Binoculars, nature guides, day pack, hat, sunscreen, food and beverages for a picnic.

Hours: USDA Forest Service Visitor Center open daily 9:00 A.M. to 4:30 P.M. in summer. Check with the Forest Service for winter hours.

Admission fee: None except $3.00 entry fee per person at South Tufa (age eighteen and under, Golden Eagle, Age, and Access card holders admitted free of charge).

Directions: From Sacramento, take Interstate 80 to Reno and then take U.S. Highway 395 south. Or take U.S. Highway 50 east to California Highway 89 east, then on to US 395 south. Mono Basin Scenic Area Visitor Center is 0.5 mile north of Lee Vining on US 395. To reach the South Tufa Area, follow signs and travel 5 miles south of Lee Vining on US 395 and then 5 miles east on State Road 120 to the dirt road leading to the parking area.

The background: In almost the same breath, Mono Lake has been compared to a dramatic moonscape and among the most hauntingly beautiful places on earth. One of the oldest inland lakes in the Western Hemisphere lies in a basin bordered by weathered hills, volcanic craters and domes, snow-draped Sierra Nevada peaks, and the rolling sagebrush of the Great Basin desert. Many a traveler has been deceptively tantalized by the deep azure water of this more than million-year-old lake, only to find that it is more than twice as salty as the ocean and extremely alkaline. Although its

Spires of rugged tufa, glassy water, and towering Sierra Nevada peaks are everyday scenery at Mono Lake. Mono Lake Committee

water might kill a thirsty person, this vast inland sea teams with life and a rich history. People have come from around the world to float in its buoyant water, view the fantastic shapes of its calcium carbonate "tufa" (pronounced *too-fah*) formations, photograph some of the largest populations of shorebirds in North America, or simply to enjoy serenity in the shadow of 13,000-foot Sierra Nevada peaks.

It is a natural history treasure that was nearly lost. In 1941 the Los Angeles Department of Water and Power began to divert water from the lake for its growing population 350 miles distant, lowering the lake level by about a foot and a half each year. By 1981 the water level had dropped 46 vertical feet and its saline concentration had nearly doubled. The unique Mono Lake ecosystem was nearly destroyed. The once-abundant gull population plummeted as predators suddenly had access to the islands. The remaining migratory bird population could have been decimated if the lake had dropped a few more feet, causing overly saline conditions for the shrimp upon which they fed.

No one knew better the value of Mono Lake than the local citizens, who had grown up by its shores. They formed the Mono Lake Committee, which eventually aroused broad support and lobbied to have the lake protected. It was first protected as a state reserve in 1981 and three years later as part of the Mono Basin National Forest Scenic Area. Through their perseverance, in 1994 the State Water Board ruled that the lake elevation must be increased by 17 feet, a task that will still take another fifteen to twenty years to achieve.

The fun: Part of the fun is getting there! US 395 winds past beautiful forested peaks and follows the tree-lined West Walker River (known for its trophy trout) before reaching Mono Lake. Begin your visit at the visitor center, where excellent exhibits and a twenty-minute film will orient you to the lake, its access points, and its fascinating history.

If you like discovering on your own, take the 1-mile self-guided nature trail at South Tufa to see the wildly shaped towers and knobs of the tufa grove. You can view the north shore tufa and marsh from a viewing platform at the end of the state reserve boardwalk below the Mono Lake County Park. These calcium-carbonate structures formed from the reaction of calcium-rich springwater mixing with the carbonate-rich lake water. You can clearly see them from shore or seasonally paddle amidst the fantastic forms in a canoe or kayak.

If you visit the lake between July and September, consider taking one of the ranger- or docent-led guided tours offered daily. Weekly bird walks are also offered at Mono Lake County Park mid-May through mid-September. Visitors during the rest of the year should time their visit to include a weekend to take guided tours then offered by the state reserve, Forest Service, or Mono Lake Committee. Check with the visitor center or the Lee Vining Chamber of Commerce for their schedules.

Boating is allowed year-round on the lake, though access to the islands is restricted between April 1 and August 1 to avoid disturbing one of the nation's greatest concentrations of nesting birds. The best place to launch your canoe or kayak is Navy Beach. Caldera Kayaks (760–935–4942) rents kayaks from Navy Beach by prior reservations. The Mono Lake Committee offers guided natural history canoe tours on the lake, also from Navy Beach, with reservations from late June through mid September. Winter visitors can enjoy cross-country ski tours in the basin.

During spring through fall, one of the main attractions is the wildlife. In addition to coyotes and other creatures of the land, this basin once thought to be a dead sea hosts millions of birds. It attracts more than 300 species, including 100 species that nest. While you may think that the ubiquitous California gulls sighted along the Pacific Coast breed on its beaches, between 45,000 and 65,000 of them, representing up to 25 percent of the world's population, navigate to Mono Lake's secluded islands to nest in May. By June, birds are hatching and the fledglings can be seen later that month and during July, feeding on some of the trillions of alkali flies and brine shrimp growing within the lake.

By midsummer they share the feast with 150,000 red-necked and Wilson's phalaropes. The Wilson's phalaropes fatten up here for their three-day nonstop fall flight to South America. Included in the mix are many other shorebirds, from American avocets to dowitchers.

If you save your visit until fall, you won't be disappointed. Legions of mallards, ruddy ducks, teal, and other waterfowl bob in the buoyant water. Sometimes there are more than 1.5 million eared grebes. Some have been known to gain so much weight from dining on shrimp that they actually have to lose weight before they migrate! This international avian treasure is celebrated at the annual Mono Basin Bird Chautaqua, a late-June bird festival sponsored by the community and many partners. (See www.birdschautaqua.org.)

Food and lodging: Accommodations and food are available at Lee Vining, Mammoth Lake, June Lake, and Bridgeport. Camping in the national forest at Lundy Canyon, Lee Vining Canyon, and June Lake Loop. Private campgrounds in the area. Contact Lee Vining Chamber of Commerce at (760) 647–6629 or www.monolake.org/chamber/.

Special tips: Many old-timers swear by the water. Swimmers will find it surprisingly buoyant. Avoid getting it in your eyes or cuts, though—it will sting! Winter travelers can check on road conditions at (800) 427–7623 or www.dot.ca.gov/hq/roadinfo.

Next best: Plan on spending several days to explore this area. In addition to the lake, the basin is full of adventures, from its volcanic craters to trails into Lundy Canyon and Rush Creek. Lee Vining is the eastern gateway to Yosemite, just 13 miles to the west. And a trip to the historic mining town of Bodie is a must. As you walk its deserted streets, it's hard to believe that instead of abandoned buildings and tumbleweeds, in the 1880s this now-forsaken area once bristled with gold miners, shopkeepers, gunfighters, and robbers.

For more information:

Mono Lake Tufa State Reserve
(760) 647–6331
www.parks.ca.gov

USDA Forest Service
Mono Basin Scenic Area Visitor Center
(760) 647–3044
www.fs.fed.us/r5/inyo/vc/mono

Mono Lake Committee Information Center
Corner of Highway 395 and Third Street
P.O. Box 29
Lee Vining, CA 93541
(760) 647–6595
Voice mail: (760) 647–6386
www.monolake.org

WEEKEND 26
June

Riding the River

Hear the roar of white water and feel the bite of spray as your raft plunges through foamy rapids. Savor beautiful scenery and a day on the water on California's most popular river.

Site: South Fork American River in parts of Placer and Sacramento Counties.

Recommended time: April 1 (very fast water) to October.

Minimum time commitment: Full day or more.

What to bring: Sunscreen, sunglasses, snacks, shoes, and sandals. If you rent a raft, be sure a personal flotation device (PFD) is provided for each passenger. You can bring beverages (no glass containers), small ice chests, and food; you can also pay to have these provided. Please do not bring pets. For guided trips, the outfitter will provide a list; most should supply waterproof cases for cameras, and PFDs must be provided.

Hours: Daytime.

Admission fee: Fees vary widely. The lower end of the fee range is for midweek trips. Prices listed are per person. Guided half-day trips, which may include a shuttle, snack, and beverages, can run $65 to $100. A full-day trip, including shuttle and meals, may range from $80 to $150. Two-day trips may range from $200 to $250. Even novices can rent equipment to use on the calmer Lower American River. Depending on the number of occupants they hold, raft fees can range from $35 (four-person raft) to $100 or more (twelve persons). Most companies have rental packages that cover the cost of raft rental, shuttle, and even lunch.

Directions: About forty rafting companies offer guided trips on the South Fork American River. There are even a few rafting companies in urban areas bordering the river. You can find rafting companies listed in the Yellow Pages of Sacramento-area phone books. The Internet is also rich with rafting information. Do a search, starting with "South Fork American River."

The background: How do people cope with Sacramento's hot summer weather and enjoy some recreation? Simple. They get out on the water. California's state capital is located on a major reservoir, Folsom Lake, and two historic waterways, the Sacramento and American Rivers. While the Sacramento draws anglers, touring boats, water-skiers and personal watercraft, the rugged and wild American River is the domain for rafters, kayakers, and

Beat the summer heat on a guided raft trip on the scenic South Fork of the American River. ROBERT W. GARRISON

experienced canoeists. You can enjoy inner tubes on the quieter, lower stretches of the river.

Whether you like a wild ride down steep river canyons or a gentle float, the American River has something for everyone. The South Fork American River is the most commercially rafted river in California, maybe the entire West.

It includes huge boulders and gorges, rapids and waterfalls, and quiet water bordered by lush riparian scenery. It passes massive quarries, old sawmills, Chinese cemeteries, ranches, old and current mining operations, and more. In a gentle sweep, the river flows through Coloma, the site where James Marshall discovered a gold nugget that changed the history of this nation. It is wildly beautiful scenery, replete with spring wildflowers in April and May and the chance to see wildlife, from great blue herons and golden eagles to raccoons, squirrels, and other species.

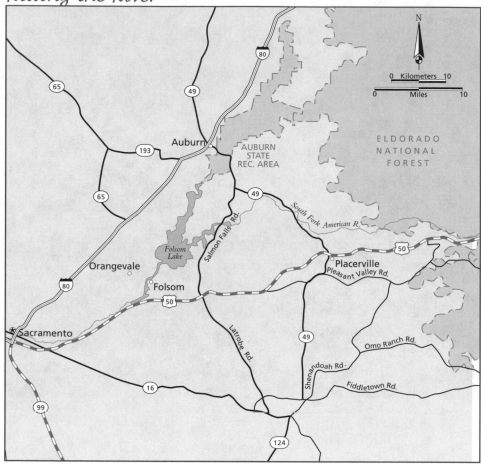

Rivers are rated by boating difficulty in relation to the skills needed to navigate them, from Class I to Class V. Class I water is basically smooth; Class III water could have high waves and very swift currents and rapids. The South Fork water varies from Class I to Class III. The Middle and North Forks are far more challenging.

The fun: The American River is divided by Folsom Lake into two types of rafting experiences. The Lower American below Folsom and Nimbus Dams offers Class I water and is perfect for a self-guided raft trip. The river and steep canyons above Folsom Lake make for an exciting ride but should not be attempted without a guide.

If you're the type that likes a little white-knuckled fun, then names of rapids like the Meatgrinder, Troublemaker, Satan's Cesspool, and Hospital

Bar ought to get your adrenaline going. Most guided raft trips allow you to choose just how much of the heart-pounding excitement you'd like. For example, there are a number of half-day trips in portions of the Chili Bar section of the river. A popular day trip is the 14-mile trip from Coloma to Folsom Lake, which includes beautiful scenery, a rockbound canyon, and lots of white water. There are shorter and longer day trips, as well as two day trips that involve a campout with great food, a hot shower, and lots of rafting stories. All the trips include plenty of white water and memories for a lifetime.

A novice can rent a raft or inner tubes and enjoy a three- to four-hour ride on the Lower American River. You and your raft are shuttled to a point above the San Juan Rapids. Put in, enjoy the scenery and moderately wild white-water ride, and then relax and float to Goethe (pronounced *gay-te*) Park, where shuttles will return you to your vehicle. On a busy summer weekend, you will be sharing the river with a flotilla of rafts. Wildlife takes on a new meaning as friendly water fights spontaneously break out between rafts. Wear your bathing suit and plan to get wet and have fun.

For a guided trip, you must make advance reservations. River flows can fluctuate, so check before you go to be sure river flows are adequate. Most companies have alternative river trips to offer.

Special tips: There are many raft companies. Ask about their safety record and the level of river and safety training their guides have received. Be sure you understand how rough (or not) the trip will be before you make reservations so that you are not disappointed.

Food and lodging: Sacramento and environs have numerous motels, hotels, inns, and restaurants. Contact the Sacramento Convention and Visitors Bureau at (916) 264–7777 or www.sacramentocvb.org or the Placer County Visitors Council at (530) 887–2111 or www.visitplacer.com.

Next best: Want something more tame? Rent a canoe and paddle in the quieter lower reaches of the river below Goethe Park. Consider a riverboat ride on the Sacramento River out of Old Sacramento. Or rent a houseboat for a few days and tour the delta. Anxious for more white water? There are numerous other white-water rivers in Northern California.

For more information: Learn about rafting on the American River at www.american-rivers.com. Do an Internet search under "rafting the American River" to find some of the forty companies offering trips or raft rentals. Check the Yellow Pages of the Sacramento and Folsom phone books for rafting company listings.

Pitcher Plants and Train Whistles on the Feather River

Travel the Feather River National Scenic Byway to Butterfly Valley, a unique and seldom-visited Sierra bog complete with butterflies, orchids, and five insect-capturing plants, including the rare California pitcher plant.

Site: Butterfly Valley Botanical Area, located 9 miles northwest of Quincy.
Recommended time: Peak blooming season is May through July.
Minimum time commitment: Three to four hours to explore the fen and search for the rare plants and plentiful butterflies.

What to bring: Rubber boots or old running shoes to get wet, insect repellent, sun hat, flower guide, butterfly/insect guide, water and snacks.
Hours: Open daily, twenty-four hours.
Admission fee: None.

Directions: From Oroville, travel northeast on California Highway 70 through the Feather River Canyon to the Mt. Hough (pronounced *Huff*) Ranger District Office about 3 miles beyond the town of Keddie and 3.5 miles before Quincy. Return north 0.3 mile to Blackhawk Road on left. Set trip odometer at zero and follow mileages in "Fun" section below.

The background: All that remains of the gold rush town of Butterfly Valley is its name. As the gold played out and the miners moved to richer diggings, ranchers and loggers slowly moved into the valley. Botanists first recognized the significance of the area in the 1870s. The area was last logged about 1950, and the Butterfly Valley Botanical Area was established by the Plumas National Forest in 1976 to protect the "outstanding abundance and diversity of plant life present."

The 500-acre area supports more than 500 species of plants, which include twelve species of orchids and twenty-four members of the lily family. The centerpiece of the area is a unique and rare mountain fen habitat, where the California pitcher plant and four other insect-capturing plants grow. The wet soils and low levels of nitrogen found in the fens benefit plants that can find alternative sources of nitrogen. Insectivorous plants use decomposing bugs as a ready source of nutrients.

The California pitcher plant, *Darlingtonia californica,* only grows in isolated fens along the southern Oregon and northern California coasts, and in the Cascade and Sierra Nevada Ranges. Also called the cobra lily because of its distinctive leaf shape, the pitcher plant captures insects in its hollow, hooded leaves. A waxy throat and downturned spikes force the hapless insect into a vat of liquid at the base of the leaves.

The other four insectivorous plants use different strategies to capture their prey. Two types of sundews capture insects on their sticky leaves, where digestion takes place. Two types of bladderworts float on the surface of ponds and capture aquatic insects by sucking them into hollow leaves with specialized trapdoors.

The fun: If you arrive on a weekday, stop at the Mt. Hough Ranger District Office to pick up a brochure and list of the plants found in Butterfly Valley. They also sell a variety of flower guides. The office is open 8:00 A.M. to 4:30 P.M. Monday through Friday. Continue on to Blackhawk Road, as identified in the directions above. Make sure you set your trip odometer at the beginning of the road and stay on the main road as you travel west.

1.4 miles—Begin gravel Forest Road 25N12. Stay on this road.

3.9 miles—Immediately after passing the BUTTERFLY BOTANICAL AREA sign, Fern Glen is on your left. This is a good place to look at ferns and search for orchids.

5.3 miles—Turn right onto Bog Road (Forest Road 25N47).

5.4 miles—Beargrass Glade. Follow the old logging road to the west about 300 yards to a small trickle of water. Follow the ravine back to the road and look for several types of lilies, including the white-flowering bear grass.

6.0 miles—Darlingtonia Bog. Pitcher plants line both sides of the road. Put on your water shoes and walk southeast through the Sweetwater Marsh; look for the small reddish sundews often hidden underneath other vegetation. Continue 200 yards to Pond Reservoir, where the tiny floating bladderworts grow.

Take the time to soak in the subtle beauty of this unique area. Get on your hands and knees and watch the dramatic interplay between plant and insect. Search out the delicate lilies and orchids. Enjoy the sounds of birds in the surrounding forest and the whistle of the trains rolling through the canyon.

Special tips: This is a very fragile and wet environment. Tread lightly, and stay on firm ground where possible. Collecting is not allowed. There are no restrooms or other amenities in the botanical area.

Food and lodging: Quincy and communities to the east offer a variety of accommodations and restaurants. For more information contact the Plumas County Visitors Bureau at (530) 283–6345 or www.plumascounty.org.

Next best: East on CA 70, Plumas Eureka State Park surrounds the historic mining town of Johnsville, interpreting the mining history of the area and offering camping and miles of hiking trails. Try fishing, golfing, or horseback riding in Blairsden and Graeagle. Visit the Portola Railroad Museum, where you can climb on and explore a variety of engines and rolling stock that reflect the rich railroading history of the Western Pacific's and now Union Pacific's Feather River Line.

For more information:
Mt. Hough Ranger District Office
Plumas National Forest
(530) 283–0555
www.fs.fed.us/r5/plumas/

Rain Shadows, Rare Cranes, and Steam Trains

With rugged Mt. Shasta as a backdrop, the broad Shasta Valley stretches across an arid landscape pocked with debris from an ancient landslide. The Little Shasta River meanders through the valley, providing water for family farms, ranches—and a remote state wildlife area that teems with wildlife.

Site: Shasta Valley Wildlife Area, located near Montague, east of Yreka.
Recommended time: California Highway 3 through Montague remains open year-round, but the secondary roads to and through the wildlife area may be impassable after winter snowstorms. Wildlife viewing is good year-round, but the greater sandhill cranes arrive in spring to nest and depart in fall. The Blue Goose Steam Train operates on weekends from late May through late October and Wednesday through Sunday in summer. Seasonal closures from October through January during hunting season.

Minimum time commitment: A full day to include a visit to the wildlife area and a steam train ride.
What to bring: Binoculars, walking shoes, water and food, bird guide, insect repellent.
Hours: Open daily, one hour before sunrise to one hour after sunset. Steam train excursions depart at 11:00 A.M. from Yreka.
Admission fee: No fees at wildlife area. Steam train fares are $14.00 for adults, $11.00 for seniors, and $7.00 for children ages three to twelve.

Directions: The Blue Goose Steam Train leaves from the Yreka train depot. From Interstate 5 take the central Yreka exit; travel east and make an immediate right turn onto Foothill Drive to the depot. To reach the wildlife area, from I–5 in Yreka take the California Highway 3 exit and travel east 8 miles to Montague. In town, take Ball Mountain/Little Shasta Road east 1.5 miles to entrance sign; turn right and continue 0.5 mile to area headquarters.

The background: Gold was discovered in Yreka in 1851, and the town quickly grew around the diggings and serviced the mines in the mountains to the west. As the mines played out in the 1880s, Yreka became an important stop along the stage and shipping route that would later become I–5.

Farmers and ranchers moved into the valley, and in 1889 the Yreka–Western Railroad was built to connect Yreka with the Southern Pacific's West Coast line to the east. The town of Montague was built at the junction of the two railroads.

Mt. Shasta dominates the landscape surrounding the Shasta Valley. Many cinder cone–like mounds are the remains of a huge landslide that blanketed the area 360,000 years ago during the formation of Mt. Shasta. To the west, the massive Klamath Mountains create a rain shadow and prevent most of the rain from reaching the valley, which averages only 12 inches of precipitation each year. The dry juniper uplands stand in stark contrast to the lush corridor of bulrushes, cattails, and willows bordering the Little Shasta River where it winds through the valley. Farmers and ranchers tap the river water to irrigate crops and fields, which support people and foraging wildlife alike. A number of small reservoirs located in the wildlife area ensure a year-round water supply, attracting wildlife species that might not otherwise occur in this arid region.

The scenic and isolated valley is a magnet to seasonal and resident wildlife. The diverse mixture of habitats support nearly 300 species of animals throughout the year. Every spring and fall, the guttural calls of greater sandhill cranes echo across the valley as these huge wading birds make their dramatic return to nest. Flocks of glossy yellow-headed blackbirds call from the tules during summer, golden eagles soar over head from spring through fall, and you might catch a prickly porcupine napping in a juniper tree any time of year. The sense of peace and isolation is ever present in this area that's far removed from California's urban centers.

The fun: Yreka, Montague, and Shasta Valley Wildlife Area make a great weekend getaway to a part of the state that most people zoom by on their race north or south on I–5. Think about making a special weekend trip to explore the area, or add on a visit during your next trip to this region of the state.

Sometime during your stay, make the time to explore the historic downtown district of Yreka, view the million-dollar gold display at the county courthouse, and ride the Blue Goose Steam Train through the Shasta Valley. The three-and-a-half hour trip leaves at 11:00 A.M. from the Yreka station. A one-hour stop at Montague provides enough time to eat lunch and take a self-guided walking tour of the town before returning to Yreka at 2:30 P. M.

Shasta Valley Wildlife Area is best explored early in the morning or late in the afternoon, when the wildlife is most active. The rolling hills and open terrain allow you to look for and view wildlife over a broad area. A well-maintained network of gravel roads traverses the 4,600-acre area. In addition to the signature species previously mentioned, the area is known for its rich diversity of mammals. Watch for coyotes, badgers, and long-tail weasels in the grasslands; deer and porcupines in the juniper woodlands; and raccoons, beavers, and river otters in the river bottoms. Pick up a bird checklist at headquarters to keep track of some of the 245 species that frequent the area throughout the year.

Special tips: Seasonal hunting occurs October 1 through January 31, and the area is closed to viewing on hunt days. Check on seasonal closings in advance of your visit during this time of year.

Food and lodging: Yreka offers a variety of accommodations and restaurants. Contact the Siskiyou County Visitors Bureau at (530) 926–3850 or www.visitsiskiyou.org.

Next best: Take along your bikes and drive west on California Highway 3 to the historic Scotts Valley and the towns of Fort Jones, Etna, and Callahan. The relatively flat paved roads through the valley have little traffic and parallel the Scott River. Enjoy the Victorian architecture in the towns, and stop at the Etna Brewery for a cold one. The Marble Mountain Wilderness, east of Scotts Road, offers hiking and camping.

For more information:
Shasta Valley Wildlife Area
(530) 459–3926
www.dfg.ca.gov/lands/newsites/wa/region1/shastavalley.html

Blue Goose Steam Train Excursion
(800) 973–5277
www.yrekawesternrr.com

Glacial Lakes and Colorful Bouquets at Carson Pass

Spring comes late to the crest of the Sierra, where plants must squeeze in a season of growth within a few months before the first frost. During summer, wildflowers carpet the slopes, ablaze with color in a stunning alpine setting.

Site: Carson Pass is the highest point on California Highway 88, about 65 miles east of Jackson.

Recommended time: Wildflowers are generally at their peak in mid-July, but the actual blooming season depends on when the snow melts and current weather conditions. Call ahead to check on the flower and trail conditions.

Minimum time commitment: Four hours.

What to bring: Good hiking boots, sunscreen and sun hat, day pack, water, lunch, warm sweatshirt, windbreaker, and rain coat for changeable weather, insect repellent, flower guide, binoculars, and camera.

Hours: Trail open twenty-four hours. Visitor center open 8:00 A.M. to 4:00 P.M. on weekdays and 9:00 A.M. to 5:00 P.M. on weekends during summer.

Admission fee: $3.00 per car.

Directions: From Jackson, travel east approximately 65 miles to the Carson Pass summit parking area. From South Lake Tahoe, travel south on California Highway 89 over Luther Pass to the Hope Valley Junction. Turn right (west) onto CA 88 and travel approximately 7 miles to the parking area.

The background: John C. Fremont led an overland expedition to California in 1843–44. His party, which included Kit Carson, camped below the pass near Grover Hot Springs in February 1844 and attempted to cross the Sierra to Sacramento. The crossing failed and the party turned back, but the pass was named after Kit Carson, one of the first Americans to reach the summit.

The pass rises to a respectable 8,600-foot elevation—not the highest mountain pass but one of the most accessible. The top of Carson Pass, like much of the High Sierra, was carved by glaciers. Frog and Winnemucca Lakes rest in depressions left behind as the glaciers melted. As the glaciers advanced then receded, they scraped and scoured the mountain, leaving

Stunning wildflowers and scenery at Carson Pass are great rewards for this high-elevation hike. ROBERT W. GARRISON

behind the gravelly ridges called moraines that now surround the lakes. These ridges provide the perfect habitat for seasonal and perennial wildflowers. The south- and west-facing slopes are the first to melt in spring. The gravelly soil retains just enough moisture through the growing season to support the flowers but not enough for the lodgepole pines and red firs to dominate the slopes. The gravelly soil also insulates the perennial rootstock during long winters.

Flowers with such fanciful names as butterweed and elephant heads join the ranks of lupine, larkspur, and paintbrush to cover the hillsides with bright reds, purples, pinks, yellows, and whites. At their peak, the flowers are breathtaking. Hummingbirds and various nectar-feeding insects converge on the blooms for a drink.

In the hollows and on deeper soils, high-elevation pines and firs stand broken and wind sculpted from the severe winter winds and storms. This is the habitat of the Clark's nutcracker, a member of the jay family that collects and stores the nuts of the limber and white-bark pines in caches they bury in the ground and later retrieve throughout the winter. Listen for their loud calls, and look for their distinctive gray, white, and black coloring.

The fun: For a high-elevation hike, this is one of the easiest and most accessible. The trail starts at the parking area and small visitor center at 8,600 feet and at its highest point, reaches an elevation of 9,050 feet over a 2.1-mile distance. For flatlanders, the elevation can cause a shortness of breath; for that reason alone, this is considered a hike of moderate difficulty.

Depending on your ability and the time available, you can hike all the way to Winnemucca Lake and back, a 4.2-mile route, or stop at Frog Lake, a 1.8-mile loop. Frog Lake overlooks Red Lake Peak, Red Lake, and Hope Valley to the north. The views are spectacular. From the trail to Winnemucca Lake, the views west over Caples Lake are equally breathtaking. Flowers will be blooming on both routes.

Take your lunch and spend some time with your flower guide matching flowers to names. Watch for the red elephant heads; you'll never guess how the individual flowers are shaped! This is a great hike to bring along your camera. It's nearly impossible to take a bad shot amid this botanical and scenic splendor.

Special tips: Take and drink plenty of water, and rest often. The high elevation can affect anyone arriving from a low elevation. The "thin air" is just that. It takes more breaths to get the same amount of oxygen, which can cause an increased heart rate, shortness of breath, and dizziness. The thin air also exposes you to more of the sun's damaging rays, so use a hat and sunscreen.

Food and lodging: Excellent rustic lodges are available at Caples Lake, Silver Lake, Hope Valley, and Kirkwood. These and other regional accommodations and restaurant listings can be found at the Alpine County Chamber of Commerce at (530) 694–2475 or www.alpinecounty.com.

Next best: This area of the Sierra Nevada has some awesome country lodges. Check out the Alpine County Chamber of Commerce Web site for links to some of these small inns, and make a weekend out of it. If you like to fish, lake and stream trout fishing are available, and there are miles of hiking trails throughout the region. If you need a soak after your hike and are staying near Hope Valley, ease your pains at Grover Hot Springs (see September).

For more information:
Eldorado National Forest
Carson Pass Management Area
(530) 622–5061
www.fs.fed.us/r5/eldorado/moke/cpma.html

July

Biking and Kayaking into the Past

Escape the congested roadways and hectic cities of the Bay Area for a day of biking, walking, and kayaking on and around Angel Island State Park. A twenty-minute ferry ride transports you to a place where bikes outnumber cars, historic buildings reflect important stories of our past, and every vista takes your breath away.

Site: Angel Island, located near Tiburon in San Francisco Bay.

Recommended time: Angel Island is accessible by private boat year round; ferry services are limited to weekends from fall through spring. Summer offers the most consistent and reliable weather with morning fog and afternoon clearing. Almost any time of year will work, but reschedule your trip if winter rains are in the forecast.

Minimum time commitment: Six hours, including ferry transfers.

What to bring: Bicycle and helmet (or rent on the island), bike lock, day pack, water bottle, lunch, layered clothing including a windbreaker, a change of clothes if kayaking.

Hours: Listed ferry schedules are for weekends during summer. These times may change; confirm times before you leave home.

From Fisherman's Wharf in San Francisco, the Blue and Gold Ferry departs at 9:45 A.M., 11:30 A.M., and 2:00 P.M. and returns from Angel Island at 10:20 A.M., 12:50 P.M., 3:00 P.M., and 4:40 P.M. Call (415) 773-1188 or check www.blueand goldfleet.com.

From Tiburon, the ferry departs hourly 10:00 A.M. to 5:00 P.M. and returns at twenty minutes past the hour between 10:20 A.M. and 5:20 P.M. Call (415) 435-2131 or check www.angelisland/ ferry.com.

Admission fee: Day-use fees are included in the ferry fares. Round-trip fares from San Francisco are $12.00 for adults, $6.50 for children six to twelve, and no charge under age five. Bikes are $1.00. Round-trip fares from Tiburon are $8.00 for adults, $6.00 for children five to eleven, and no charge under age four. Bikes are $1.00.

Directions: Tiburon Ferry Terminal: From U.S. Highway 101 in Marin County, take the Mill Valley/Tiburon exit and follow Tiburon Boulevard 4 miles into downtown Tiburon. Turn right onto Main Street. The ferry is located on the left at 21 Main Street. Paid parking is available nearby. Fisherman's Wharf Ferry Terminal: In San Francisco follow the tourism signs to Fisherman's Wharf. The Blue and Gold Ferry terminal is located at Pier 41 next to Pier 39 on the Embarcadero. Paid parking is available in the Pier 39 lot.

The background: Angel Island State Park is a place of scenic beauty and natural diversity, but the layers of human history reflected in the old buildings and building sites provide the context for your visit.

The island's human history began with its seasonal use by the coastal Miwoks, who traveled the bay on canoes built from tule reeds. In 1775 Spanish Lt. Juan Manuel de Ayala anchored off the island to explore and produce the first map of San Francisco Bay. He named the island Isla de Los Angeles (Spanish for Island of the Angels).

Prior to the Civil War, the United States military recognized the strategic importance of Angel Island in protecting San Francisco Bay and built the first artillery batteries facing the Golden Gate. For more than a century, as technology and military needs changed, various forts or garrisons were built on new sections of the island, leaving the old buildings and gun and missile emplacements relatively intact. At its busiest at the end of World War II in 1945, the island's Fort McDowell discharged more than 23,600 soldiers in a single month.

A quarantine station was built in Ayala Cove in the late 1800s to fumigate incoming ships and quarantine sick individuals. Only a few of these buildings survive. In 1910 at nearby China Cove, a controversial immigration station was opened by the Immigration Service to control the flow of Chinese into the country based on the Chinese Exclusion Act of 1882. More than 175,000 individuals, primarily Chinese, were detained in spartan barracks for weeks and months at a time, awaiting word of their fate. Carved poems on the walls reflect the anguish and suffering that occurred there. The station was closed in 1940 and turned over to the military for housing prisoners of war during World War II.

Today the park protects and interprets the human history of the island but also provides outstanding recreational facilities and interpretive programs.

The fun: Throw your bike on the rack and head for Angel Island. Eight miles of roadways are available for biking, including the paved Perimeter Road that takes you to most areas of the park. There are some steep sections, but overall the road is well suited for young riders. The lack of traffic and the spectacular vistas overlooking the entire Bay Area make the bike ride a joy. Stop and explore the various buildings, watch for island wildlife, and enjoy the native and exotic plants. If you don't have a bike, or don't want to take it with you, you can rent one on the island for $10/hour or $30/day. You can also walk the entire island in a day.

Ten primitive campsites are available if you've always wanted to over-look the San Francisco skyline at night from your sleeping bag or be able to kayak to a campsite right on the bay. The campsites are popular, so reserve your spot early. Plan on carrying your gear 2 miles to most of the sites. One site is fully accessible. Campsites can be reserved by calling Reserve America at (800) 444–7275.

For water lovers, make reservations for a two-and-a-half-hour guided kayak trip. The trips are offered every Sunday at 10:30 A.M. and 1:30 P.M. The $75 trips begin and end from the beach at Ayala Cove, to the right of the ferry landing. Routes vary by day and season to protect paddlers from westerly winds. If you have your own boat, day-use boat slips are available in Ayala Cove on a first-come, first-served basis for $4.00/day. Overnight mooring buoys run $7.00 to $10.00 per night, depending on the season.

Special tips: Poison oak is common. Stay on the trails and roadways to avoid contact. Helmets are mandatory for riders seventeen and younger but are recommended for all riders. Ride on the bay side of the roads; inexperienced riders should walk their bikes up and down steep sections of trail.

Food and lodging: Tiburon and San Francisco have almost unlimited selections. Contact the Marin County Convention and Visitors Bureau at (415) 499–5000 or www.visitmarin.org or the San Francisco Convention and Visitors Bureau at (415) 391–2000 or www.sfvisitor.org.

Next best: Check the descriptions for Ring Mountain, Viansa Winery Wet-lands, Golden Gate National Recreation Area, and Bolinas Lagoon for other North Bay Area options. The Bay Area Discovery Museum at Fort Baker near Sausalito is a great family experience. Try a bike ride in Golden Gate Park.

For more information:
Angel Island State Park
(415) 435–1915
www.parks.ca.gov
www.angelisland.org (cooperating association Web site)

Sea Trek Sea Kayaking
(415) 332–8494
www.seatrekkayak.com

WEEKEND 31
July

From Skyline Redwoods to the Pacific Ocean

Hike across sun-drenched ridgetops and down cool, fern-lined canyons shaded by old-growth redwoods so tall they seem to jab the sky. Stay in a cozy tent cabin, feel the spirit of these rough-barked giants, and bank some mem ories in the oldest park in the State Park System.

Site: Big Basin Redwoods State Park, about 25 miles (forty-five minutes) north of Santa Cruz.
Recommended time: Spring through fall; heavy winter rain.
Minimum time commitment: One-half day (enough time only for a short walk and picnic).

What to bring: For day use, sturdy hiking shoes (waterproof in spring and winter), binoculars, nature guides, day pack, hat, sunscreen, insect repellent, food and water.
Hours: Day use 6:00 a.m to 10:00 P.M. Visitor center hours vary; call in advance.
Admission fee: $5.00 per vehicle or annual park pass.

Directions: From Santa Cruz take California Highway 9 north. Turn west onto California Highway 236 and travel 9 miles into park. The stretch on CA 236 has many curves. From Saratoga take CA 9 south and turn west onto CA 236. Travel 9 miles to park. The entire route from Saratoga has many curves.

The background: By 1900, magnificent groves of coastal redwoods had already fallen to the saw along the state's northern coast. A large continuous stand of these giants remained just south of San Francisco, snuggled in the rain-soaked canyons of the Santa Cruz Mountains. When Andrew P. Hill and others anxious to save this virgin forest camped at Slippery Rock, the idea of conservation was in its infancy. Because of their shared vision, the Sempervirens Club was born, named after the coastal redwood, and 3,800 acres of old-growth forest were deeded to the state in 1902, becoming California's first state park.

From towering redwoods in lush, fern-lined canyons to the drier chaparral-covered slopes, from sunny ridges to the foggy beach, Big Basin

REDWOODS—THE TALLEST TREES

You don't need to know anything about coastal redwoods to be awed by their majesty. Coastal visitors instinctively feel the imposing grandeur of these venerable giants—and a taste of timelessness while standing within a hushed grove where the sunlight seldom reaches the forest floor.

Coast redwoods are considered the tallest trees in the world and are among the very oldest. The top of a grandfather tree can be 240 feet tall, while its base may span 15 feet. The oldest trees have lived for more than 2,000 years.

Because the wood is both beautiful and very resistant to fungus diseases and insects, redwood was coveted as a choice building material; the virgin forests were heavily logged. Almost a century ago, there were so few old-growth stands that the Save-the-Redwoods League was formed in 1918 to preserve some of the remaining coastal redwood groves. These trees are now protected at Redwood National Park and several other parks, such as Humboldt Redwoods, managed by the state.

Like its heartwood, redwood bark contains high levels of tannin that help to insulate it from periodic fires that rage through the forest. Although its cone is barely an inch long, it may include up to two dozen seeds, helping to improve the odds that some will germinate. New trees may also sprout from an existing tree's roots.

Coast redwoods have specifically adapted to the coastal environment, growing even taller than their inland cousin, the giant sequoia. They tend to grow in a narrow coastal band stretching from southern Oregon to central California, where the temperature is mild and moisture is provided by fog and heavy winter rainfall.

It is not enough just to leave the old patriarchs standing. By itself, the soil at their feet contains few nutrients. It is enriched by fallen trees, decaying plants, and other forest life that is constantly dying and decomposing. In order for redwoods to survive, the entire ecosystem of which they are a part must remain intact.

The intrinsic value of redwoods is reason enough for saving them. But their cones, shady boughs, and fallen comrades also provide cover or food for an incredible array of wildlife—from Roosevelt elk, raccoons, porcupines, and forest birds to rare species, such as ringtails, spotted owls, and marbled murrelets. Their shaded groves are also a source of spiritual renewal—a legacy to be savored, and saved, for generations of humans to come.

is a jewel of the state park system, boasting an incredible diversity of environments—and ways to enjoy them. Its shady groves and remote trails preserve a feeling of wildness and isolation, even though the park is located less than an hour's drive from millions of Bay Area residents.

You can see gushing waterfalls and discover wild violets and mushrooms growing in the shadow of grandfather trees, some 2,000 years old. Park wildlife is very diverse. Several hundred bird species can be observed throughout the year, from common Steller's jays to the rare marbled murrelet, an imperiled bird that lives at sea and comes ashore only to nest in old-growth forests. Raccoons and squirrels are common campground visitors, and you may glimpse coyotes and bobcats ghosting through the forest. Many smaller creatures abound, including large numbers of less charismatic but fascinating banana slugs, which inhabit the undergrowth beneath the redwoods. The last sighting of a live grizzly in the area was at Big Basin—in 1876.

The shorter walks and most accessible campgrounds can be crowded during summer. Fall is beautiful, and there are fewer people after Labor Day.

The fun: The park boasts more than 80 miles of trails for hiking. In a landscape of stunning scenery, it offers walks for people of all abilities, from short rambles to overnight treks on trails that connect Big Basin to other area parks. A park trail guide and map is available for $2.00 and is highly recommended to help you make selections.

The popular Redwood Trail is a short, wheelchair- and stroller-accessible 0.5-mile walk amid a grove of virgin redwoods, where you can feel the spirit of these venerable trees. For the more adventurous, there are several five- and six-hour walks. The well-trod paths of the Berry Falls Loop contour Berry and Waddell Creeks, traveling through the heart of the old redwoods and past a series of waterfalls on Berry Creek.

If you want a few days of backcountry variety and a very rigorous walk, the 32-mile (one-way) Skyline-to-Sea Trail is considered by some to be the best overnight hike in the Bay Area. The hike begins at Castle Rock State Park near Saratoga, traverses redwood-covered slopes, crosses through Big Basin, and ends at Waddell Beach, located within the park and adjacent to a freshwater marsh at the Theodore J. Hoover Natural Preserve. There are walk-in trail camps along the way for en-route camping, but don't get too comfortable: The park requires that you stay at a different camp each night. You *must* make reservations in advance to use these camps. Be sure you check on camp rules and be prepared to carry your own water; only a few camps having potable water.

Horses are allowed on some trails, and bicyclists may use paved or dirt roads only. Those who like to keep their creature comforts close at hand can camp in established campgrounds, rent a rustic park cabin complete with a wood-burning stove, or enjoy a local lodge or motel. You can find maps for sale, trail tips, and other information about Big Basin at the park Web site, listed under For more information, at www.bigbasin.org, or at the Mountain Parks Foundation at www.mountainparks.org. Or just stop by the visitor center or park headquarters when you arrive.

Special tips: Roads to the park have many tight curves, particularly CA 9. There are myriad camping requirements you must check in advance, from where to purchase firewood to rules regarding pets. This is an extremely popular park. If you wish to camp, make reservations well in advance.

Food and lodging: Food and lodging are available between Saratoga and Santa Cruz. There are numerous small mountain communities with local inns and charm. To reserve a campsite at any of the Santa Cruz Mountains state parks, call Parknet at (800) 444–7275. Camping is $16 per night per vehicle. An additional small fee will be charged to book the reservation. Tent cabins rent for about $49 per night, depending on the season. Call (800) 874–8368 for reservations. To reserve an en-route camp for the Skyline-to-the-Sea Trail, call (831) 338–8861 between 10:00 A.M. and 5:00 P.M. For more information contact the Santa Cruz Chamber of Commerce at (831) 423–1111 or www.santacruzchamber.org or the Saratoga Chamber of Commerce at (408) 867–0753 or www.saratogachamber.org.

Next best: You can easily spend the entire weekend at Big Basin. But if you're looking to explore the area, the Santa Cruz Mountains include Henry Cowell Redwoods and Castle Rock State Parks and smaller local parks in Boulder Creek and Ben Lomond. Consider a fun train ride on the Roaring Camp and Big Trees Narrow Gauge Railroad in Felton, the steepest of North America's narrow-gauge railroads, famous for white-knuckle turns and breathtaking views.

For more information:
Big Basin Redwoods State Park
21600 Big Basin Way
Boulder Creek, CA 95006-9064
(831) 338–8860
www.parks.ca.gov

A Wildlife Smorgasbord on Monterey Bay

The fins of leopard and smoothhound sharks cut through the shallow ribbons of water in Elkhorn Slough as shorebirds feed nearby. In the main channel, dozens of sea otters groom and feed while harbor seals bask on the muddy banks.

Site: Elkhorn Slough National Estuarine Research Reserve, located inland from Moss Landing, north of Monterey.
Recommended time: Summer for sharks and nesting herons and egrets. Fall to spring for shorebirds and waterfowl. Year-round for otters, harbor seals, birds of prey, and beautiful scenery.
Minimum time commitment: Four hours.

What to bring: Binoculars, bird guide, walking shoes, water shoes (if kayaking), warm, layered clothing, polarized sunglasses, sun hat, water and lunch.
Hours: Reserve trails and visitor center open 9:00 A.M. to 5:00 P.M. Wednesday through Sunday. Docent-led tours 10:00 A.M. and 1:00 P.M. Saturday and Sunday.
Admission fee: $2.50 per person; various charges for boat tours in Moss Landing.

Directions: Elkhorn Slough Visitor Center: From California Highway 1 in Moss Landing, turn east at the power plant on Dolan Road. Continue 3.5 miles to Elkhorn Road. Turn left and continue 2.2 miles to reserve, on left.

Moss Landing Wildlife Area: From the junction of Dolan Road and CA 1, travel north on CA 1 about 0.5 mile and turn right onto an inconspicuous dirt road immediately past the bridge crossing the mouth of Elkhorn Slough. Follow signs around private buildings to parking area and boardwalk.

The background: Tucked on the edge of Monterey Bay, Elkhorn Slough winds inland almost 7 miles through some of the richest and rarest habitats in California. More than 2,500 acres of tidal salt marshes and freshwater marshes are protected within the watershed. Coastal oak woodlands, grasslands, and rare coastal maritime chaparral are found in the uplands. This mosaic of water, mudflats, and sandy hillsides was created as an ancient river cut through the sandy plain, creating the slough and adjoining Monterey

Shorebirds gather in the hundreds along the sloughs to rest and feed. CALIFORNIA DEPT. OF FISH AND GAME

Bay Submarine Canyon before the San Andreas Fault cut off its flow to the east. Today only seasonal creeks drain into the slough but the daily tidal flow from Monterey Bay brings fresh nutrients to the microscopic plants and animals that, in turn, feed hundreds of species of wildlife.

Elkhorn Slough is one of twenty-six National Estuarine Research Reserves and has been designated a Globally Important Bird Area. Supporting seven threatened and endangered species, including the southern sea otter, brown pelican, snowy plover, and peregrine falcon, the slough is the most significant wildlife habitat on Monterey Bay and the second largest tidal marsh in the state after San Francisco Bay. More than 250 bird species have been seen in the reserve, 116 species at one spot on one fall day. This remarkable number reflects the diversity of habitats and rich food supplies found around the slough (more than 500 species of invertebrates at last count).

Near the slough's mouth at Moss Landing lies the Monterey Bay Submarine Canyon, which plummets 2 miles into the inky darkness over its 60-mile length. In spring, nutrient-rich currents rise from the depths of the canyon and wash into the slough, creating a food chain that starts with the growth of minute algae and ends with the top predators. Many species of marine fish and invertebrates enter the relative safety of the estuary to breed and lay their eggs. In summer, leopard and smoothhound sharks, some more than 4 feet long, can be seen in the shallow side sloughs preparing to give live birth to their pups. Harbor seals and southern sea otters also enter the estuary to rest and feed on the marine life. The seals spend hours basking on the mudflats, but the sea otters rarely leave the water.

In the past few years the sea otter population along the central California coast has declined more than 10 percent. Parasites and heart disease were found in some of the animals that died, but other environmental conditions may also be a factor. Remain at least 100 feet from the otters and other marine mammals to prevent further stress.

The fun: Rated as one of the top bird-watching destinations in the county, and one of the only places to watch dozens of sea otters in one place, Elkhorn Slough is a wildlife viewer's paradise. The visitor center contains excellent exhibits on the slough and should be the first stop on your visit. Pick up an area map and bird list, and check with the well-informed and friendly docents about current wildlife sightings to help plan your day. A great selection of regional field guides is available for sale. Tours of the reserve are offered at 10:00 A.M. and 1:00 P.M. on Saturday and Sunday.

From the visitor center, hike the 5 miles of trails to view the sharks, shorebirds, ducks, and upland species. Wear a visored hat and polarized sunglasses to cut the glare when looking for sharks in the murky water and watch for their dorsal fins as they enter shallow water. In spring, egrets and herons nest in the trees along the trail. Visit Moss Landing Wildlife Area at the mouth of the slough for seabirds, loons, grebes, pelicans, gulls, terns, and snowy plovers. Scan the mud banks on the opposite shore for harbor seals and the open water for otters.

A guided boat trip is a great way to see the wildlife and learn about the natural history from a trained guide. Try a kayak trip if you want a mild to moderate workout and don't mind getting a bit wet. Kayak Connection, located at 2370 CA 1 on the west side of the highway opposite the entrance to Moss Landing Wildlife Area, offers a variety of trips. Monterey Bay Kayaks is next door and offers similar trips. Prices range from $25 for a two-hour sunset paddle to $65 for a five- to six-hour tour. For reservations call Kayak Connections at (831) 724–5692 (www.kayakconnection.com) or Monterey Bay Kayaks at (831) 373–0119 (www.montereybaykayaks.com). Elkhorn Slough Safari offers two-hour pontoon boat wildlife tours at various times throughout the week. Current rates are $26 for adults, $19 for children ages three to fourteen, $24 for seniors.

Special tips: Poison oak (see page 160) is plentiful year-round, and the ticks (see page 86) are thick in spring and summer. Stay on the trails and away from the brush to avoid both.

Food and lodging: Phil's Fish Market & Eatery, a Moss Landing local favorite, is one of many restaurants in town. For accommodations, Marina, 10 miles south on CA 1, is your best bet. Contact the Monterey County Conference and Visitors Bureau at (888) 221–1010 or www.montereyinfo.org.

Next best: Visit the local produce stands for fresh artichokes, strawberries, brussels sprouts on the stalk, and other local delicacies. Many state beaches line Monterey Bay from Santa Cruz to Monterey and offer miles of beach-combing, bird-watching, and beach play. Check out the sportfishing action at the Moss Landing marina, or shop at the many antiques shops in town. The Monterey Bay Aquarium is always an option in Pacific Grove.

For more information:
Elkhorn Slough National Estuarine Research Reserve
(831) 728–2822
www.elkhornslough.org/esnerr.htm

WEEKEND 33
August

North Coast Getaway with Lots of Options

The wave-battered coast, its quiet beaches, and the weathered redwoods of the north coast will help you leave home chores and work behind. Unwind with great hiking, postcard sunsets, and incredible views of whales, elk, and other wildlife.

Site: Redwood National and State Parks, largely located in the 40-mile stretch between Orick and Crescent City, are about 180 miles from Redding and 320 miles from San Francisco.

Recommended time: Mid-May to mid-June for rhododendrons, azaleas, wildflowers. November to December and March to April for migrating gray whales. Year-round for birding, tidepooling (at low tide), and beautiful scenery.

Minimum time commitment: Four hours to a full day.

What to bring: Binoculars, appropriate shoes (walking and beach shoes), layered clothing suitable for changing weather conditions, sun hat, maps and trail guide, nature guides, water, and a picnic, if you'd like.

Hours: Parks are open year-round, twenty-four hours. Crescent City Information Center and Thomas H. Kuchel Visitor Center open 9:00 A.M. to 5:00 P.M. daily. Hiouchi Information Center open mid-June to mid-September 9:00 A.M. to 5:00 P.M. Check state parks for visitor center hours.

Admission fee: None for national park. State parks charge $4.00 per vehicle, but the fee is good for the day at all state parks.

Directions: From Redding take California Highway 299 west, and then turn north onto U.S. Highway 101 at Arcata. Coastal travelers may take US 101 north. Park access points begin in Orick, Prairie Creek Redwoods, and Del Norte Coast Redwoods State Parks are located on US 101 between Orick and Crescent City. Jedediah Smith State Park is located east of Crescent City on U.S. Highway 199.

The background: As you drive among the giant redwoods and pass sleepy communities between Eureka and Crescent City, it's hard to imagine that half a century ago the area was jammed with loggers and logging equipment, though the scars of their clear-cuts are evident today. At one time,

Visitors to the redwood parks on US 101 often see Roosevelt elk grazing near the road at Prairie Creek Redwoods State Park. ROBERT W. GARRISON

some of the world's finest redwood was cut from these old-growth forests. In the 1850s ancient redwoods covered two million acres. Today less than a hundred thousand acres remain. These coastal groves, with some of the tallest and oldest trees in the world, are testimony to the vision of early preservationists who fought to protect an international treasure and a vanishing resource.

The effort to save the coast redwoods spurred the creation of the Save-the-Redwoods League in 1918. This nonprofit organization leveraged donations and grants to purchase more than 100,000 acres of redwood forest between 1920 and 1960, largely along the north coast. In the 1920s and 1930s, state parks were established at Del Norte Coast Redwoods, Prairie Creek Redwoods, and Jedediah Smith. Redwood National Park was established in 1968 and expanded in 1978. The state and federal governments joined forces in 1994 to comanage the four parks, which encompass 106,000 acres. Within this landscape, the parks protect 45 percent of the remaining old-growth redwood forest in California.

For most, these majestic trees are simply awesome, touching something eternal within each of us. Redwoods have existed for twenty million years, adapting to many microclimates within the cool coastal environment. They flourish near the ocean, on steep slopes and ridges, flanking rivers and creeks, and inland, shading a range of trees and plants from bigleaf maple to lush ferns, from showy groves of rhododendrons and azaleas to delicate wildflowers. With them you'll find an incredible variety of wildlife, from Roosevelt elk to songbirds.

The fun: You think you'd like to take a scenic drive, but maybe you'd enjoy a hike. You're pretty sure you want to camp, but a motel might be nice. You want to bring your fishing rod and kayak, but you heard there were several bluffs where the whale watching was great. You might want to see a traditional dance by the Tolowa or Yurok tribe, but you're sure you want to walk barefoot on the beach and see a dazzling sunset. If you aren't sure what you'd like to do, this north coast getaway is for you—you can do all these things, and more, at these interconnected redwood parks.

To savor and plan your trip in advance, visit the national park Web site at www.nps.gov/redw and go to the trip planner. In one-stop shopping you can find information about scenic drives, hiking trails, fishing, bicycling, events and activities, camping and lodging, and much more. When you arrive you can stop at the Redwood Information Center at Orick, the main information center in Crescent City, or the Hiouchi Information Center on CA 199 or visit any of the parks along the way to pick up the jointly published *Redwood National Park Trail Guide,* maps, and brochures to help you make selections.

You will be stunned by the choices you have and wish for more hours in the day. During May and June, flower lovers visit the parks' many rhododendron and azalea groves, such as the Lady Bird Johnson Grove outside of Orick. During winter and spring, whale watchers gather at the Thomas H. Kuchel Visitor Center, Crescent Beach Overlook, Wilson Creek, the High Bluff Overlook, and Gold Bluffs Beach to see gray whales spouting off the coast. Those who fancy seabirds and tidepools can get their fill at Enderts Beach and the Lagoon Creek—Yurok Loop. Hikers will find more than 200 miles of trails. Any time of year there's apt to be a traffic bottleneck near the entrance of Prairie Creek Redwoods State Park or the Elk Meadow Day Use Area north of Orick, where Roosevelt elk often graze in the fields adjacent to the road.

Whether you end up watching wildlife, picnicking in a redwood grove, or joining a ranger for a guided walk, you will be filled with the immensity of the trees. The light of day falls softly through these old giants, creating a world of light and shadow beneath their canopies. There is a comforting silence within their presence as they touch the spirit and leave behind a deep feeling of peace.

Special tips: Campers should be aware of black bears. Trails can be slippery when wet, and some trails and bridges may not be passable during the rainy season. Be cautious when driving—people often slow down or stop to look at wildlife.

Food and lodging: There are numerous motels, lodges, restaurants, and stores between Eureka and Crescent City and many opportunities to camp in the parks. Overnight camping fees range from $12 (off-season) to $15 (May through September 15), plus a $4.00 day-use fee per vehicle. You can make reservations for some sites by calling (800) 444–7275. For more information contact the Crescent City/Del Norte Chamber of Commerce at (800) 343–8300 or www.northerncalifornia.net. Contact the Arcata Chamber of Commerce at (707) 822–3619 or www.arcata.com/chamber.

Next best: Even a weekend stay will barely allow you to scratch the surface of these four parks. If you have enough time, Lake Earl Wildlife Area and State Park, the Six Rivers National Forest, and numerous other state parks are all within an hour's drive. The Aleutian Canada Goose Festival is held in Crescent City (see Weekend 12).

For more information:
Redwood National and State Parks★
1111 Second Street
Crescent City, CA 95531
(707) 464–6101, ext. 5201
www.nps.gov/redw/index.htm

★Information for all parks can be picked up here.

From Boiling Mudpots to Icy Lakes

Here's your chance to visit the land of extremes! Lassen Volcanic National Park's rugged lava flows, serrated craters, and geothermal mudpots—with names like Bumpass Hell, Devil's Kitchen, and Boiling Springs Lake—are a sharp contrast to the park's sparkling lakes, dense forests, and wildflower-strewn meadows.

Site: Lassen Volcanic National Park, located 47 miles (one hour) from Red Bluff.
Recommended time: Portions open year-round; best time July through late September.
Minimum time commitment: Allow at least one hour to drive the auto tour and several hours to make a few brief stops.
What to bring: Camera, binoculars, food, water, layered clothing, day pack, sun hat.

Food services and gifts are also available at the Lassen Chalet by the southwest entrance and the camper store near the north entrance.
Hours: Park headquarters open 8:00 A.M. to 4:30 P.M. Monday through Friday; closed on holidays. The Loomis Museum is open daily 9:00 A.M. to 5:00 P.M. late June through late September.
Admission fee: $5.00 per individual or $10.00 per vehicle; good for seven days.

Directions: Take California Highway 36 east from Red Bluff or California Highway 44 east from Redding to tour the main park road.

The background: Almost a century ago, Lassen Peak was little more than a silent giant. That all changed in May 1914, when a huge eruption began a seven-year cycle of volcanic activity that transformed the peak into an active volcano. The earth shook and the sky blazed red in 1915. Molten lava melted the mountain snowpack, causing catastrophic mud flows. Not long after, a great hot blast leveled forests that cloaked Lassen's flanks. Lassen Peak is thought to be the world's largest plug dome volcano and was declared a national park in 1916.

If you've never seen the results of volcanism, your trip to Lassen will be as educational as it is recreational. Today the east side of the 106,000-acre park is a mile-high lava plateau dotted with cinder cones and boiling springs and is considered a wilderness area. The southwest part of the park

Lassen Peak provides a stunning backdrop for the meandering stream and dense forest bordering Kings Creek Meadow. NATIONAL PARK SERVICE

includes volcanoes, craggy pinnacles, and a scattering of boiling springs, steaming fumaroles, and bubbling mudpots. The area's dense forests, alpine meadows, and crystal-clear lakes offer beautiful scenery and prime recreation areas—and are strong testimony to the restorative powers of Mother Nature. Following the eruption of Mount St. Helens in 1980, many volcanists sought guidance from Lassen as a living study in the evolution of recovery.

You can live among this incredible scenery by staying in one of the park's eight campgrounds or renting a rustic cabin at Drakesbad Guest Ranch near the town of Chester. Plan to stay for a few days, if you can. The park offers many activities you can enjoy throughout the year, from nature walks to canoeing (you must bring your own canoe), from stargazing in summer to guided snowshoe hikes during winter. The park is only about 50 miles from Redding, but it is a world apart.

The fun: Whether you enter via Redding or Red Bluff, you can get a great overview by purchasing a road guide at the entrance station and starting off with the auto tour on the main road through the park. You'll get a drive-by taste of the volcanic scenery and pass signs to places with names that will pique your curiosity, like Emerald Lake, Sulphur Works, Bumpass Hell, and the Devastated Area.

Most visitors plan an extended stop at Bumpass Hell, the park's largest geothermal area. A 3-mile, three-hour round-trip hike will take you past a landscape that could be out of Dante's *Inferno,* complete with boiling lakes, steam vents, and mudpots. Summer visitors can see wildflowers in mountain meadows and surrounding the lakes. A visit to King Creek Falls is a must.

The park's 150 miles of hiking trails offer incredible scenery and a respite from crowds. Horse lovers can bring their mounts to corrals at Summit, Butte, and Juniper Lakes, but call first to reserve a spot (530–335–7029). Campers will find a bevy of day and nighttime programs for children and adults, from talks about the park's early pioneers to its wildlife. Free wilderness permits are available to those who want to experience the park's backcountry.

While the volcanic scenery is an obvious attraction, the wildlife won't disappoint you. You might see squirrels, Steller's jays, and Clark's nutcrackers in the campgrounds and mule deer in the meadows. Canada geese and other waterfowl inhabit the park's numerous lakes. Songbirds and birds of prey are abundant.

If you have only a weekend to see this 106,000-acre park, do some advance research so that you can pack lots of fun into it! The National Park Service's newsletter, *Peak Experiences,* includes helpful information about various attractions, the distance of each hike, and what you'll see.

Special tips: Snow can cover most of the park from late-October through mid-June. Make reservations for rustic cabins at Drakesbad Guest Ranch well in advance.

Food and lodging: Camping in the park. Cabins and rooms at Drakesbad, but make reservations well in advance. Motels, lodges, and resorts in Red Bluff, Redding, Chester, Mineral, Mill Creek, Hat Creek, Old Station, and Shingletown.

Next best: Enjoy fishing, boating, and hiking at Lake Almanor. If you have extra time, visit the Wild Horse Sanctuary near Shingletown, located outside the park. The nonprofit organization provides a home to wild horses that the federal government cannot care for and also adopts horses out to willing individuals. About 200 wild horses and burros roam the fenced 5,000-acre sanctuary. You can see the horses on Wednesday and Saturday from 10:00 A.M. to 4:00 P.M. You can also take two- or three-day trail rides. For more information call (530) 335–2241 or visit www.wildhorsesanctuary.com.

For more information:

Lassen Volcanic National Park

P.O. Box 100

Mineral, CA 96063-0100

(530) 595–4444

www.nps.gov/lavo

Serenity and Solitude in California's Alps

Rugged snowcapped peaks, meadows strewn with wildflowers, bubbling creeks, and sapphire lakes are often yours alone to enjoy. Leave your watch at home, and let the sun, moon, and your whims be your timepiece.

Site: Trinity Alps Wilderness, north and west of Weaverville (many access points).

Recommended time: The weather is most reliable from the middle of June through the end of October. Snow can block back-country access early in the season; some of the highest or well-shaded areas may retain snowpack well into summer.

Minimum time commitment: One day.

What to bring: Sturdy hiking shoes, day pack and safety items, flashlight, matches, hat, layered clothing, binoculars, mammal and wildflower guides, maps, insect repellent (lower meadows/ponds, early in summer), water and food. Even for day use, summer temperatures can drop into the 20s overnight and zoom up to the 90s during the day. If you plan to back-pack, provision well in advance or in Weaverville. There are a few small stores along California Highway 3 between Weaverville and Callahan for last-minute supplies.

Hours: Daily, twenty-four hours.

Admission fee: None. The area within the Trinity Alps is a designated wilderness area. You must obtain a permit for overnight camping, as well as a campfire permit. They are available at several USDA Forest Service ranger stations. There is a group size limit of ten persons in the Trinity Alps. Contact the Weaverville Ranger Station well in advance if your group is larger.

Directions: From Redding, drive west on California Highway 299 about 45 miles (allow ninety minutes for this winding road with hairpin turns). In Weaverville, stop at the Weaverville Ranger Station to orient yourself, select a destination (if you haven't in advance), pick up maps, and learn about regulations. There are numerous backcountry accesses off CA 299 west of Weaverville and CA 3 north of Weaverville.

The background: Snowcapped granite peaks; steep, forested canyons; emerald and sapphire lakes; meandering rivers and creeks—you don't have to go to Switzerland to experience the grandeur of the Alps. You can enjoy them in Northern California's own backyard, the Trinity Alps. Bordered by

Lakes in the Trinity Alps are known for their serenity and isolation. JEANNE L. CLARK

the Klamath Mountains and defined by the Trinity and Salmon Rivers, this backcountry haven spans more than a half million acres. It is perhaps one of California's largest designated Wilderness Areas, a place where you can find solitude by a quiet pond, catch trout for breakfast in a creek, and still step on remote paths where few have hiked before you. Summer wildflower displays can be subtle or dazzling; wildlife abounds.

The area includes more than 700 miles of trails and almost one hundred lakes at elevations ranging from 2,000 to 9,000 feet, offering dozens of possibilities for day hikes or backpacking trips. Most trails are marked, though not all, so it is a good idea to have a topographical map and compass. There are several established campgrounds for those who wish to have a few comforts and establish a base camp for daily outings. A scattering of small communities strung along CA 299 and CA 3 offer a few small lodges, motels, or cabin rentals. These accommodations can be booked in the popular summer

THE PERSEID METEOR SHOWER

Light pollution from our cities and towns has taken away a birthright that reaches back to our earliest ancestors. The stars, planets, and moon guided our travel, directed when we planted our crops, and provided a reassuring sameness in the constellations that progressed through the night sky. Most of us have lost the ability to step out of our houses and see all but the brightest stars in the sky. The faint ghostly cloud of the Milky Way that stretches across the night sky is lost to most, as is the annual return of the Perseid meteor shower in August.

When is the last time you laid your sleeping bag on the ground and just gazed up at the heavens, drifting off to sleep in awe of the billions of stars overhead? August is the perfect month to head out to dark-sky country for some stargazing. Warm weather and clear skies make for great viewing, but you must get away from the cities to get the best views. On about August 12 or 13, the Perseid meteor shower makes its annual appearance in the late-night skies. The dates change each year, so check the Internet for this year's predictions. Some years are better than others, in part due to the light from the moon, which can interfere with viewing. No matter the date, the best times to view the shower are from 2:00 A.M. to dawn. The "shooting stars" appear to originate from the constellation Perseus, hence their name.

The shower is formed from dust particles left behind by the Swift-Tuttle Comet, which hurtles through the solar system once every 130 years. The earth passes through the dust trail every August as it orbits the sun. The tiny dust grains, no bigger than a grain of sand, get caught in the earth's atmosphere and burn up in a fiery streak as they blaze across the sky at about 132,000 miles per hour. Up to one hundred meteors per hour can be seen on the best nights, but dozens are the norm. And don't worry—they all burn up long before hitting the earth.

months, so it's a good idea to call in advance for reservations. However, campers and backpackers can usually arrive without reservations and enjoy a wilderness experience without feeling crowded.

There are numerous backcountry regulations, even for day use. Follow commonsense safety rules, make sure you have adequate supplies, and always let someone know where you'll be trekking if you plan to go alone.

If you're hankering for some true solitude and distance from others, ask for suggestions about which of the more popular areas to avoid. The heavily forested area to the west, often called the "Green Trinities," may be just the ticket.

Don't forget your fishing gear. The Trinity River, Coffee Creek, and smaller streams produce outstanding rainbow trout—just perfect for a camping breakfast. Many fly fisherman like to keep these lovely, uncrowded creeks their special secret.

The fun: Some old-timers who have hiked the Alps for fifty years swear they are still discovering new finds. A first trip will only allow you to scratch the surface, and you will have many areas to consider. If you'd like an easy day of just 7.6 miles round-trip, consider visiting Tangle Blue Lake, accessed off CA 3 (Forest Road 39N20). You'll hardly feel the elevation gain of 1,100 feet as you follow an old logging road, cross a bridge spanning Tangle Blue Creek, and then parallel the creek with its rushing water and clear, deep pools as it ascends a rugged canyon. The path splits about a mile from the lake; bear left and enjoy the fresh scent of incense cedars. Once you pass the weathered remains of an old cabin, the final stretch is an easy walk past tiny willow- and fern-lined creeks. The picturesque twelve-acre lake is flanked by towering granite, but you can easily walk around the entire lake. Enjoy fishing, a picnic, and may even a nap. Other popular short day hikes to consider are Boulder Lakes, Adams Lake, and Stoddard Lake.

Backpackers will find their choices almost limitless. If you like the process of dreaming and preplanning, pick up the Falcon guide *Hiking California's Trinity Alps Wilderness.* This excellent resource provides lively descriptions of more than fifty hikes, ranging from day hikes to some spanning five days, depending on your speed and the side trips you make. If you need a tease, consider Caribou Lakes. This 19-mile round-trip could be made in a single overnight, but you'll want to stay longer when you see the stunning scenery. Water is limited, so make sure you bring at least two quarts. A moderate but sometimes steep hike through deep forest and meadows will lead to a first glimpse of Thompson Peak and the Caribou Basin. Rest or camp near a meadow or at Snowslide, dally awhile at scenic Lower or Upper Caribou Lake, and then prepare yourself for the alpine scenery of Caribou. Steep granite slopes, hidden meadows, and shores lined with wildflowers all flank the largest and one of the most beautiful of the Trinity Alps lakes, set beneath a canopy of cerulean blue or star-spangled skies.

The Alps are a horseback rider's dream—but not for novices! You should be an experienced equestrian, have a seasoned horse, and be sure your stock is conditioned to the higher elevation. An easy break-in ride is to Stoddard Lake. Check with the ranger station to find out which trailheads offer ample room for horse trailers and what may be in store on some of the trails; several include creek crossings, slick granite, and bridges.

Special tips: Whether you take day hikes or overnighters, familiarize yourself with zero-impact hiking and camping to help preserve this wilderness. Black bears and mountain lions are not uncommon; learn how to avoid encounters and what to do if you have one. Campers should hang food properly or use a bear canister. Bury human waste 200 feet away from water sources and at least 6 to 8 inches deep. Pack out your garbage. Be very cautious with stream crossings, especially in spring when the water is running high. Come prepared. You can check the USDA Forest Service Web site for current trail conditions. Purchase a Trinity Alps Wilderness map.

Food and lodging: There are numerous Forest Service campgrounds, and most are seldom crowded. There are private campgrounds, grocery stores, a few restaurants, cabins, and some lodging in communities west and north of Weaverville. Contact the Trinity Chamber of Commerce, located in Weaverville, at (800) 487–4648, (530) 623–6101, or www.trinitycounty.com.

Next best: The Alps are a long way from most urban areas, so unless you are nearly local, you'll need to spend the weekend. If you have several days, take a drive to Trinity Lake, which borders CA 3, a popular fishing and boating lake. And be sure to visit the historic town of Weaverville, with its Chinese Joss House, local shops, and small town charm.

For more information:
USDA Forest Service, Weaverville Ranger Station
210 Main Street
Weaverville, CA 96093
(530) 623–2121
www.fs.fed.us/r5/shastatrinity/recreation/

Wildlife and Wild Seas at the Point of the Sea Wolves

This rocky promontory south of Carmel-by-the-Sea is to nature enthusiasts what Pebble Beach is to golfers or the Monterey Bay Aquarium is to museum lovers. Pockets of white sand beaches, unusual geology, bountiful wildlife, wind-sculpted trees, and centuries of human habitation combine into a 456–acre gem of a park.

Site: Point Lobos State Reserve, located south of Carmel on California Highway 1.
Recommended time: Any time of year to enjoy the scenic vistas, geology, and resident wildlife. Winter and spring for migrating gray whales and monarch butterflies. Spring and summer for wildflowers and nesting herons. Summer for tidepools and diving.

Minimum time commitment: Five hours to hike the 6-mile perimeter trails.
What to bring: Walking shoes, layers of clothing for changeable weather, binoculars, day pack, your favorite bird guide, water and lunch.
Hours: 9:00 A.M. to 7:00 P.M. summer; 9:00 A.M. to 5:00 P.M. winter.
Admission fee: $5.00 per vehicle.

Directions: From CA 1 in Carmel, travel south 3 miles to reserve entrance on the right.

The background: The barking calls of California sea lions echo through the reserve from offshore rocks that Spanish explorers named Punta de los Lobos Marinos, Point of the Sea Wolves. This poetic and descriptive name captures the natural beauty and historic significance of this remarkable point of land.

Point Lobos is a landscape of contrasts. The wave-battered headlands and pounding surf reflect the ruggedness of this coastline, yet the same forces created the quiet sandy coves and protected deep inlets that harbor a multitude of sea life. Two contrasting types of rock make up the majority of the reserve, and their interplay has resulted in the fanciful landscapes that make the area so appealing. The narrow inlets and white sand beaches are formed from Santa Lucia granite, a course-grained rock that is very wave resistant but tends to weather along parallel joints in the rock. The broader

From sea life–encrusted tidepools to pine- and oak-studded uplands, Point Lobos packs in a huge range of diversity, including outstanding opportunities to view sea otters, harbor seals, seabirds, and more. CALIFORNIA DEPT. OF FISH AND GAME

coves and unusual cliffs are formed from a colorful sedimentary rock created from a hodgepodge of rounded pebbles, rocks, and boulders called the Carmelo Formation.

Away from the cliffs and coves, grassy meadows give way to wind-sculpted thickets of wild lilac, sticky monkey-flower, and poison oak. Open forests of Monterey pine and coastal live oak grow in the uplands. Only two naturally occurring groves of Monterey cypress remain in the world—at Cypress Point and here, at Point Lobos, the reason the reserve was created in 1933. The cypress cling to the rocky cliff faces, and their contorted branches and gnarled trunks are testimony to their rugged existence.

Point Lobos supports a diverse variety of wildlife. California sea lions, harbor seals, and sea otters are common in the coves; gulls, cormorants, American black oystercatchers, and brown pelicans roost on the off-shore islands; great blue and black-crowned night herons nest in the treetops; and deer, squirrels, and brush rabbits live in the forest. And that's just above the water! An additional 750-acre underwater preserve was created in 1960, the first in the nation. As a result, the area contains some of the richest marine life found on the California coast.

The fun: Point Lobos State Reserve packs a lot of diversity into a very small reserve. Limited parking quickly fills on weekends, so arrive early. The 6-mile perimeter hike takes you to all the main parts of the reserve if you have the time. There are many trail options if you must limit your selection to just a few loops. Each trail is different from the next, so take a few minutes to read the reserve brochure and map to plan your day. The information station at the parking area near Sea Lion Point is staffed on most weekends by well-informed docents.

Whalers and Bluefish Coves are open to limited diving and snorkeling. If you dive, this is *the* place to do it. Divers must reserve a spot two months in advance for weekends. Check the Web site for more details. If you don't dive, the Whaler's Cove parking area is a fun place to watch divers getting ready to go in or returning from a dive. Stop at the whaler's cabin to learn about the human history of the area, and hike over to Bluefish Cove to see the nesting herons.

The Cypress Grove Trail winds through the Monterey cypress grove and is well worth the time. Nearby, the newly constructed Sand Hill Trail is fully accessible and offers nice views of the sea lion rocks. To the south, the Bird Island Trail overlooks many offshore rocks filled with seabirds. The trail also passes China Cove, a white sand beach with azure water surrounded by tall granite cliffs. Weston Beach showcases the fantastic shapes and colors of the Carmelo rock formations.

Special tips: Poison oak (see page 160) is everywhere. Stay on the trail and familiarize yourself with its appearance so that you can avoid it. Ticks are common in spring and summer.

Food and lodging: Carmel and Monterey have almost unlimited options for accommodations and food. Contact the Monterey County Conference and Visitors Bureau at (888) 221–1010 or www.montereyinfo.org. Camping spots are more difficult to find. Andrew Molera State Park, 21 miles south on CA 1, has primitive campsites.

Next best: If you are traveling south to camp, or even if you are staying in Carmel, drive 19 miles south on CA 1 to Point Sur and take a guided tour

POISON OAK

"Leaflets three, let it be" is a handy rhyme to keep in mind any time you are hiking in northern California below the 5,000-foot elevation. Poison oak grows in an easily identified three-leaflet pattern. The glossy, rounded leaves will range from green in spring and summer to bright red in fall. In winter the bare twigs may display white berries and tiny leaves awaiting spring growth. The plant can range from a small shrub to a large vine encircling a tree.

Poison oak contains oils that cause severe rashes in about half the population. Sensitivity to the oils can change over time, so just because you don't react today doesn't mean you won't react tomorrow. Use caution when hiking in poison oak country. Know what the plant looks like in all seasons, and stay clear. The oils can be transferred from the glossy leaves, bare stems, fallen dried leaves, or from the smoke of burning leaves. The most common way to be exposed to the oils is by touching your shoes after a hike or petting a dog that has been traveling with you. Another member of the family can also be exposed to the plant simply by picking up affected clothes or shoes.

If you accidentally touch poison oak, try to rinse the area with cold water or rubbing alcohol within five minutes of exposure. The oil is readily absorbed into the skin, so a delayed wash or shower will not stop the rash from forming, but it will help keep the oils from being spread to other parts of the body. Always shower with cool water to keep the pores of your skin closed as you wash the oils away. The rash generally shows up within six hours of exposure and quickly forms very itchy, watery blisters. Contrary to popular belief, the serum from the blisters does not cause the rash to spread, but remaining oils on the skin are easily spread from the hands to other parts of the body. The rash generally lasts about a week, but reexposure can occur from shoes and clothing. Get in the habit of scrubbing off your boots at the end of the trip and placing your clothes directly into the washing machine on your way to the shower. If a rash does occur, a product called Tecnu, available at most pharmacies, helps reduce the rash and itching and can also be applied to offer protection before you take a walk in the woods.

Endangered southern sea otters can usually be seen in the offshore kelp beds sleeping, eating, or grooming. WILLIAM E. GRENFELL

of the Point Sur Lighthouse. The fascinating three-hour tour is offered at 10:00 A.M. and 2:00 P.M. on Saturday and 10:00 A.M. on Sunday. Whale watching is great from the lighthouse January through May, so bring your binoculars.

For more information:
Point Lobos State Reserve
(831) 624–4909
www.pt-lobos.parks.state.us

Point Sur State Historic Park
(831) 625–4419
www.pointsur.org

Giving Thanks to the Acorn

Towering oaks and golden meadows surround an ancient limestone slab containing more than 1,100 acorn grinding holes produced by untold generations of women over thousands of years. The Big Time celebration gives thanks to the fall acorn harvest through song, dance, games, and food.

Site: Indian Grinding Rock State Historic Park near Pine Grove, located 11 miles east of Jackson.

Recommended time: The Big Time celebration generally occurs the last weekend in September. The park is open year-round. Visit in fall for fall colors and the harvest celebration. Winters can be cold and wet, with occasional snow. Spring brings wildflowers and green meadows; summers, hot days.

Minimum time commitment: Four hours for Big Time.

What to bring: Comfortable walking shoes, sun hat, day pack, binoculars.

Hours: The Regional Indian Museum is open midweek 11:00 A.M. to 3:00 P.M. and on weekends 10:00 A.M. to 4:00 P.M. The Big Time celebration occurs from 10:00 A.M. to 5:00 P.M. Saturday and Sunday. The park is open sunrise to sunset. Parking is limited during Big Time, so arrive early.

Admission fee: $3.00 day-use fee per vehicle. Camping fees are $12 per night in the twenty-three-site campground. The campground is closed during Big Time.

Directions: From Jackson, drive east on California Highway 88, 11 miles to Pine Grove–Volcano Road. Turn left (north) and drive 1.5 miles to the park.

The background: Indian Grinding Rock State Historic Park was created in 1968 to protect the largest collection of bedrock mortars in North America. At last count, 1,185 acorn grinding holes cover the limestone slab, called *chaw'se,* by the Northern Miwok people, whose ancestors once lived in this valley. Here in the Sierra foothills, a mild climate, year–round water, extensive woodlands of black oak, and a huge slab of limestone provided the perfect setting for a large village site that was occupied for thousands of years. The depth and number of mortar holes, along with more than 300 images carved on the surface of the rock, can only hint at the age and importance of this site.

California black oaks grow along the western slopes of the Sierra Nevada and produce acorns prized by the mountain tribal groups. Rich in protein and flavor, the acorns provided the foundation for daily meals. In fall, extended family groups would harvest acorns from family trees and store the nuts in elevated granaries for use throughout the year. The bitter acorns required extensive processing before the meal could be cooked as bread, porridge, or soup. The women of the village would first husk the acorns then pound them to meal in the bedrock mortars using a pounding stone. The meal was then collected and rinsed numerous times to wash away the bitter tannins.

The demise of this village site was quick and inevitable. By 1849 miners flooded the foothills in search of gold and within a few months destroyed the Indian way of life. Violence and disease took many lives, and those who survived were driven from their homelands.

By 1968, when the park was created, the Miwok and other Sierra Nevada tribes had returned to reclaim their heritage. Ceremonial and social life traditionally revolved around the village roundhouse, and in 1974 the Chaw'se Roundhouse was completed and dedicated. Today the roundhouse is used by the Indian community for private ceremonies and is opened once a year to the public during Big Time, the traditional fall harvest festival. The Chaw'se Regional Indian Museum tells the story of the ten Sierra Nevada tribal groups through an excellent collection of artifacts and exhibits.

The fun: From the wooden platform overlooking the chaw'se, the sounds of drumbeats and chanting echo from the roundhouse. Wood smoke that first cleanses the dancers drifts from the smoke hole to fill the air with the smell of fall. In the distance, spirited games of dice pit the skills of one family team against another.

For two days a year, you have the opportunity to observe and participate in Big Time. The event both honors the past and celebrates the present. The highlight of the event is watching traditional dances in the roundhouse. The spiritual setting, rhythmic drumming, and energetic dancing combine to make it an unforgettable experience. After the dances, appease your appetite by trying venison and acorn soup or Indian fry bread and tacos. After a snack, head over to the Indian dice games. Two types of dice are used—one made from black walnut shells split in half, the others made from split sticks. Two teams, usually family groups, compete in these high-stakes games as each team bets on how many of the dice will face up

CALIFORNIA'S FIRST PEOPLE

California has been a crossroads of cultures since the first people arrived here more than 10,000 years ago. Throughout the centuries, many different groups traveled from the north and east and settled here. By the time Spain claimed Alta California in 1542, 300,000 to a million American Indians lived in the state, the most densely populated region north of Mexico. More than 150 tribal groups, each speaking a different dialect, lived side by side. While extensive trade routes moved goods throughout the state, most individuals remained within 20 miles of their homes throughout their lives. The rich diversity of plant and animal foods and the temperate climate allowed tribes and extended families to settle in one place and thus develop dialects that were not understood by neighboring groups.

As European and American exploration and settlement began in California, American Indian culture soon collapsed as disease and violence spread throughout the land. The tribes of the south coast were the first to be affected as the Spanish built twenty-one missions along the coast, starting in San Diego in 1769. In 1812 the Russians established Fort Ross on the Sonoma coast, and by the 1820s American explorers arrived overland from the east. The final blow came when the gold rush brought a new wave of immigrants from around the world in search of fortune. By the 1870s fewer than 20,000 California Indians survived.

Today little physical evidence remains of the original cultures that thrived throughout the state. Bedrock mortars, rock paintings and carvings, and a scattering of stone tools can only hint at the rich, early life of the California Indians. For the families and individuals that survived, the spiritual essence of California Indians continues to be passed on from generation to generation. Several of the natural areas featured in this guide include remnants of this great cultural history.

or down when thrown. There are many subtleties in this game, and it's fun to watch the action.

Visit the Chaw'se Regional Indian Museum to learn more about the lives of the Sierra Nevada tribes, both past and present. Take a hike on the 1-mile loop trail that traverses the ridge surrounding the meadow, or take the 0.5-mile self-guided nature trail to learn about the some of the plants used by the Miwok. Watch for acorn woodpeckers, California quail, and scrub jays. On such a busy weekend, the wildlife may be long gone, but the park is usually filled with wildlife that rely on the acorns as well.

Special tips: Poison oak is common in the park. Yellowjackets can be bothersome around the food booths and picnic area. Western rattlesnakes warm themselves on the limestone on summer evenings.

Food and lodging: The park has twenty-three campsites that are available on a first-come, first-served basis. Pine Grove and Volcano offer limited lodging and restaurants. Jackson has a more diverse selection. Contact the Amador County Chamber of Commerce and Visitors Bureau at (209) 223–0350 or www.amadorcountychamber.com.

Next best: There are a number of locations to visit to learn more about Sierra Nevada Indians. Wassama Roundhouse State Historic Park, located 7 miles north of Oakhurst in the town of Ahwahnee, features a partially restored Yokut village with a roundhouse, sweat lodge, burial ground, and grinding rocks. Yosemite Valley has an excellent museum and rebuilt village site. The California State Indian Museum on the grounds of Sutter's Fort in Sacramento offers exhibits, artifacts, and programs on all the state's tribal groups. Nearby, visit Volcano, Jackson, Sutter Creek, and the many other gold rush towns in the area.

For more information:
Indian Grinding Rock State Historic Park
(209) 296–7488
www.parks.ca.gov

Tarantulas and Moonlight Walks at an Ancient Volcano

See the setting sun burnish the volcanic cliffs and spires in rich, warm hues; explore the dark, cool world of a cave; or watch determined tarantulas search for a mate at one of California's most unusual natural settings.

Site: Pinnacles National Monument, located 25 miles south of Hollister or 12 miles east of Soledad (both about thirty minutes).

Recommended time: March to April for wildflowers, September through October for tarantulas, and fall through spring for hiking. Summer can be very hot.

Minimum time commitment: Six hours.

What to bring: Sturdy hiking shoes, change of shoes in winter due to wet stream crossings, sun or rain hat, layered clothing and rain gear in winter, plenty of water (carry it with you), snacks or picnic, day pack, binoculars, flashlights for caves, nature guides.

Hours: Open daily; hours vary with the season but are usually 7:30 A.M. to 6:30 or 8:30 P.M.

Admission fee: $5.00 for seven-day vehicle permit; $2.00 for walk-ins, bicycles, and motorcycles.

Directions: Two entrances. For the west entrance, take U.S. Highway 101 south from the Monterey Peninsula or north from Kings City. From Soledad, travel 12 miles east on California Highway 146 to the Chaparral entrance. For the east entrance, from Hollister take California Highway 25 south of the city of Hollister for 30 miles. Turn west on CA 146 into the park (about forty-five minutes).

The background: Have you ever had the itch to visit a place that was really different? If you want to see spectacular geological formations and unusual wildlife, Pinnacles National Monument may be the place for you. Millions of years ago east of Salinas, an ancient volcano rumbled and spewed, earthquakes split and moved the tortured terrain, and erosion further carved or smoothed its features. The result was a wild landscape sculpted with spires and steep canyons, marked with caves, and traversed by talus passages. Today the Pinnacles are a place of incredible diversity, where delicate spring wildflowers may bloom a stone's throw from rugged volcanic towers, where male tarantulas crossing a road to seek a mate can stop traffic in the fall, and where guided night walks explore the flights of bats beneath the dazzling canopy of the stars.

In 1891 the Pinnacles became the special passion of a local homesteader, Schuyler Hain, who explored their caves, led tours, and urged the area's preservation. His advocacy reached the ears of President Theodore Roosevelt, who established the area as a national monument in 1908. Its original 2,500 acres have been expanded nearly tenfold, and much of the area is further protected as wilderness.

The rugged landscape is divided into east and west districts, and there are trails but no roads linking the two sides of the monument. The steep, rough volcanic formations are a rock climber's haven, and many technical climbers migrate here to test their skills. There are 30 miles of trails, from easy 2-mile loops to long, strenuous hikes for those who like to keep their feet on the ground. The area is open for day use only. The monument has no campgrounds, although there is a private campground adjacent to it.

The fun: After leaving the productive Hollister area and its oak woodlands, arriving at Pinnacles National Monument may feel a little like landing on the moon. The smooth slopes are dotted with manzanita, buckbrush, and toyon. Riparian (streamside) vegetation defines several seasonal creeks, but the predominant scenery is volcanic formations. This unusual park brims with experiences found at few other natural areas. Before you hike, stop at the Bear Gulch Visitor Center if you approach from the east or the Chaparral Ranger Station if you arrive from the west to get a good overview of the park, learn about trail and cave conditions and closures, or hear the latest about earthquake faults.

Roads are limited, so the best way to explore the monument is on foot. As you walk you will undoubtedly see rock climbers, hanging by slim fingerholds on the near-vertical cliffs. Every hike offers special rewards—from the High Peaks Trail with its spectacular views of the monument to the Bear Gulch and Pinnacles Trails, which lead to the cool, spelunker's world of the Balconies Cave. The Condor Gulch Trail was named for California condors, now endangered, that once nested in the park. Although absent for almost thirty years, California condors have begun their triumphant return. Today you can once again see these huge dark birds with long white patches on the underside of their wings flying lazy patterns in the sky, often among smaller turkey vultures.

Bats—Creatures of the Night

They fly silently during our sleeping hours and have undeserved reputations both as the vampires of the mammal world and major carriers of rabies. The fact is that the occurrence of rabies in bats is no greater than it is for other wild animals. And only three of the world's 1,000 species of bats are vampires. Vampire bats live in South America, where they usually feed on birds and small mammals. By contrast, California's twenty-three species of bats have much more tame appetites—eating insects, moths, spiders, beetles, and similar species or dining on nectar while pollinating plants.

Biases aside, bats are really remarkable creatures. Throughout the world they range in size from barely an ounce (Thailand's bumblebee bat) to over two pounds (an Indonesian fruit bat). California bats come in many sizes; the dainty western pipistrelle has a wingspan of about 5 inches, while the western mastiff bat has a 22-inch wingspan. Bats have a long lifespan; the world's longest-lived, a little brown bat, survived for thirty-four years. They also reproduce slowly, and most females have just one pup each year.

Bats are nocturnal, usually seeking warm, hidden roosting areas to pass the day. They may hide in caves, cracks, and cavelike spaces in cliffs,

The Pinnacles' wildflower show competes with some of the best in the region. March to April, the grasslands bordering CA 25 are awash in color, and the displays continue within the park, their delicate, colorful blooms a sharp contrast to the volcanic formations surrounding them. The fall season is no less full of surprises, as roads and trails may be crossed by a moving river of hairy, eight-legged travelers. In September and October the normally nocturnal male tarantulas are on the move, investigating burrows to find a mate. If you're lucky you may see a little fellow stand on his legs to intimidate such prey as an insect, lizard, or small rodent and then use his fangs to insert a digestive enzyme that prepares the prey for eating. People aren't on their prey list, though some who get too close have been bitten—normally an experience similar to a bad bee sting.

The setting sun is not a signal to leave the park but rather to watch as rocks are bronzed with rich color that gradually fades into darkness. The evening belongs to the park's night creatures, including fourteen species of

rocky outcrops, and trees. They also find human-made caves and crevices in mines, tunnels, and buildings and under bridges. Some bat species are solitary, roosting in the foliage of trees and bushes. Others are social, gathering in large colonies to roost upside down in tightly packed clusters that allow them to share body heat. At a few California bridges and highway structures, bats gather in the tens of thousands. Their dramatic departures at sunset are nothing short of a natural spectacle.

As the skies darken, these amazing navigators fly out to hunt for a meal. They are able to avoid colliding with objects and locate their prey by echolocation, emitting ultrasonic shouts inaudible to the human ear that bounce off objects and echo back to the bats' ears, creating a three-dimensional image of the environment. Their "radar" is so accurate that in the midst of their swift aerial maneuvers, bats can chase down and catch their insect prey in midair.

Bats are also environmentally friendly. A colony of 1,000 bats can eat up to ten pounds of insects in one night, including many agricultural pests. Many farmers put up bat houses to encourage local bats to hunt over their orchards and crops. According to some sources, a single bat can eat 500 mosquitoes an hour. West Nile virus, a disease associated with mosquitoes, has been detected in California, so communities fortunate enough to support bats already have nature's own free pest control force in residence.

bats that live in its caves, cliffs, and trees. Consider timing your visit to take a guided night walk, where you can learn about the bats' fascinating life history, hear their squeaks as they use echolocation to hunt, and enjoy a lesson in astronomy as you gaze at a velvet night sky studded with stars. If you're not a creature of the night, there is plenty of wildlife to see during the day, from songbirds and hawks to mule deer and feral pigs.

Special tips: In addition to sharp volcanic rocks, there is poison oak (see page 160) and stinging nettle. The arid country also supports rattlesnakes. Parking lots can fill early in the day during spring. Tarantulas (and other wildlife) have the right-of-way, so be prepared to stop.

Food and lodging: Soledad, Hollister, and King City have restaurants and lodging. The privately owned Pinnacles Campground is next to the east entrance and can be reached at (831) 389–4462. A bed-and-breakfast is located near the west entrance (Inn at the Pinnacles; 831–678–2400).

Contact the San Benito Chamber of Commerce at (831) 637–5315 or www.sbccc.org.

Next best: Lake San Antonio (see Weekend 6) is southwest of the park. Salinas offers the National Steinbeck Center, a complex honoring John Steinbeck with theaters, archives, exhibits, and more. The Monterey Peninsula just to the northwest offers a wealth of things to do (see Weekend 32 and Weekend 36).

For more information:
Pinnacles National Monument
5000 Highway 146
Paicines, CA 95043
(831) 389–4485
www.nps.gov/pinn/index.htm

Bay Vistas and Hawks That Ride the Wind

Soaring and gliding on powerful wings, thousands of birds of prey pass over the highest point in the Marin Headlands each fall, a spectacular sight in an incredible setting. After you watch their aerial acrobatics, visit the lagoon, walk to the lighthouse, or stop at the marine mammal rehabilitation center.

Site: Hawk Hill, Golden Gate National Recreation Area, located in the Marin Headlands near Sausalito.
Recommended time: September through November for hawks. Best viewing usually occurs between 10:00 A.M. and 2:00 P.M. The Marin Headlands are open year-round, with good wildlife viewing all year. Waterfowl and shorebird viewing is best October through April.
Minimum time commitment: Four hours.

What to bring: Comfortable walking shoes, binoculars, layered clothing, sun hat, sunscreen, hawk guide, water, and picnic or snack.
Hours: Marin Headlands is open daily, twenty-four hours. Overnight parking allowed only when camping. Marin Headlands Visitor Center is open 9:30 A.M. to 4:30 P.M. daily except Thanksgiving and Christmas; (415) 331-1540.
Admission fee: None.

Directions: From San Francisco, take U.S. Highway 101 across the Golden Gate Bridge. Take the Alexander exit (second exit after the bridge). Travelers driving southbound on US 101 should go through the Waldo tunnel and take the Sausalito exit. From this point, follow the signs to the visitor center. If you want to go directly to Hawk Hill, remain on the road that passes under US 101, which becomes Conzelman Road. Drive almost 2 miles to the turning circle and parking lot. Follow the signs to the Hawk Hill trailhead. (If you miss the turn, Conzelman becomes a one way road, ending at Rodeo Lagoon.)

The background: Every fall birds of prey such as Cooper's hawks, ospreys, and golden eagles leave Canada and Alaska for milder climates to the south. They ride prevailing winds and soar on thermal currents along the Pacific coastline, always staying within sight of land. When they reach the Marin Headlands, each fall more than 20,000 may pass within sight of

Bay Vistas and Hawks That Ride the Wind

San Francisco Bay

Horseshoe Bay

East Rd.

Murray Cir.

Alexander Ave.

Lime Point Lighthouse

Golden Gate Bridge

101

To San Francisco

Waldo Tunnel

Coastal Trail

SCA Trail

Coastal Trail

Kirby Cove

McCullough Rd.

Bunker Rd.

Conzelman Rd.

Trail

Coastal Trail

Rodeo Valley Trail

Rodeo Valley Cutoff

Hawk Hill

One-way traffic from here

Point Diablo

Bobcat Trail

Miwok Trail

Wolf Ridge Trail

Miwok Trail

Bunker Rd.

Marin Headlands Visitor Center

Conzelman Rd.

Rodeo Lagoon

Lagoon Trail

Bonita Cove

Point Bonita Lighthouse

N

Kilometer

Mile

the highest point in the headlands before continuing their journey across the bay.

This gathering point, called Hawk Hill, is located within the Golden Gate National Recreation Area, one of the largest urban national parks in the world. Spanning San Francisco, San Mateo, and Marin Counties, the entire recreation area encompasses 75,000 acres and 28 miles of coastline. The area includes numerous sites, including Alcatraz, Fort Funston, Fort Mason, and Muir Woods National Monument. This sweeping landscape protects 1,250 historic structures, more than two dozen threatened and endangered species, and several imperiled habitats that are dwindling in the crowded Bay Area.

The Marin Headlands are dotted with abandoned structures from World War II, from buildings and fortifications to gun batteries. Hawk Hill is one such seacoast fortification, the last battery built, but never armed, in the headlands. Soldiers that once climbed the steep hill to the site have given way to birders drawn by the opportunity to see the largest migration of birds of prey in the Pacific.

The fun: After climbing the short but steep trail up to the lookout, you'll see the weathered remains of a seacoast fortification. If the weather is clear, the broken slabs of concrete and lookout boxes of Hill 129, Hawk Hill's original name, won't distract you for long. The panoramic views from the highest point in the Marin Headlands are nothing short of stunning. Ahead there are sweeping vistas of water, the Golden Gate Bridge, the towers of the San Francisco skyline, and, beyond, Alcatraz and the East Bay. Mt. Tamalpais lies behind you, and Rodeo Lagoon is to the west.

Only after you've taken in the view will you notice people's excited voices and begin to see birds of prey, also called raptors, flying by at rate that can reach a hundred or more birds every hour during the peak season, if the weather is clear. Overhead they swoop by in ones, twos, and groups—sometimes catching a ride on thermal currents to continue their journey across the bay and at other times gathering in a churning mass near the ridges.

If you're a novice and you listen to the chatter, you'll pick up a lot of tips in a short period of time: Accipiters, like Cooper's hawks, use their short wings and long tails to advantage to maneuver in tight spaces. The golden eagle and other broad-winged hawks usually hunt from a tree or other perch, using speed to grab prey on the run. Buteos, like the common red-tailed hawk, use their wingspan of 6 feet or more to take advantage of stronger breezes, soaring effortlessly on the wind.

The largest migration of birds of prey in the Pacific, which includes the red-tailed hawk, passes over Hawk Hill each fall. WILLIAM E. GRENFELL

In addition to many experienced birders, volunteers from the Golden Gate Raptor Observatory are frequently on hand to share their knowledge and give you tips about how to differentiate between the species. The observatory hosts a fun, interactive Web site where you can see a live camera view of Hawk Hill, test your skills at identifying birds of prey, learn when the peak viewing periods are, get answers to questions, and much more. Visit it at www.ggro.org/camap.html.

Don't forget your camera. Shutterbugs will find great subject matter here, and you can easily spend a day or more at the headlands. Make time to stop at the visitor center, especially if you're inspired to buy a new guide about birds of prey. Stop in at the California Marine Mammal Center and learn about their work to rehabilitate sick, injured, and orphaned seals, sea lions, and other marine mammals. You'll find tranquility and great bird life at Rodeo Beach and Lagoon, with its incredible western views. If you're a history buff, a visit to Barracks 1059 is a must. This restored mobilization barracks looks exactly as it did when it was in use during World War II, the Korean War, and the 1960s. You can also hike a half-mile trail that travels through a tunnel (open year-round Saturday, Sunday, and Monday from 12:30 to 3:30 P.M.) to the Point Bonita Lighthouse. The Coast Guard still operates the beacon in this wild and windswept landscape.

Special tips: On foggy days it's not only hard to see the birds but it's also hard for them to see well enough fly. Oh, and don't be surprised if you see also a bride; Hawk Hill is a popular site for small outdoor weddings!

Food and lodging: Available in all price ranges in San Francisco, Sausalito, Mill Valley, and beyond. There are two hike-in and two walk-in (a short distance from parked vehicles) campgrounds at the Marin Headlands. Reservations are required; call (415) 331–1540. There are numerous other campsites at nearby Marin state parks, such as China Camp, Sam Taylor, and Mt. Tamalpais. Contact the Marin County Conference and Visitors Bureau at (415) 499–5000 or www.visitmarin.org.

Next best: When you're at the visitor center, pick up information about the many other sites within the Golden Gate Recreation Area in Marin and San Francisco. Check the descriptions for Ring Mountain (Weekend 14), Bolinas Lagoon (Weekend 8), and Angel Island (Weekend 30). Stop by Pier 39's K Dock in San Francisco to see California sea lions snoozing a stone's throw from shoppers.

For more information:
Golden Gate National Recreation Area
Fort Mason, Building 201
San Francisco, CA 94123-0022
(415) 561–4700
www.nps.gov/goga/index.htm

WEEKEND *40*
October

Enjoy a Tahoe Creek with No Wet Feet

With glittering Lake Tahoe in the distance, follow a boardwalk through a quiet marsh to an underground chamber, where huge windows take you into the world of spawning salmon in October and creek life throughout the year.

Site: Taylor Creek Stream Profile Chamber.
Recommended time: Fall for kokanee salmon, winter for bald eagles, summer for wildflowers and nesting birds.
Minimum time commitment: Two hours.
What to bring: Comfortable walking shoes, binoculars, day pack, water and snacks, sun hat, sunscreen.
Hours: At visitor center, weekends Memorial Day through the second week of June

from 8:00 A.M. to 4:30 P.M.; daily mid-June through September from 8:00 A.M. to 5:30 P.M. Closed in winter. At Stream Profile Chamber, daily Memorial Day through second week of June from 8:00 A.M. to 4:00 P.M. Summer months daily from 8:00 A.M. to 5:00 P.M. Closed in winter. October daily from 8:00 A.M. to 4:00 P.M.
Admission fee: None.

Directions: From South Lake Tahoe, drive north on California Highway 89 for 3 miles; turn right into visitor center.

The background: The crown jewel of California's lakes is a glittering sapphire set in a rough ring of forest-clad granite peaks. Scoured from glaciers millions of years ago, today Lake Tahoe's crystal clear water remains legendary. So is its size. The Washoe Indians who camped by its shores receive credit for naming this famous lake. At least one version suggests that "tahoe" aptly means "big lake." Even the Washoe might have been surprised that this high-mountain lake, at 1,645 feet deep, is the third deepest in North America. It holds so much water that it could cover the entire state with a depth of 14 inches!

Together, the water and incredible scenery make a powerful draw. From summer water recreation to winter snow sports, from spring wildflower hikes to fall color adventures, you can enjoy nature here year-round and in myriad ways. One of the most unusual fall events is the return of the kokanee salmon to Taylor Creek. Kokanee are landlocked sockeye salmon that were planted in the lake by biologists in the 1950s. They spend their adult life in the lake. Like other salmon, each fish has a strong urge to return to the stream of its birth to spawn, a feat achieved by keen sense of smell and ability to recognize the unique chemistry of its home stream water. By the time it is three years old, the male's silvery blue color changes to a brilliant red and green and it develops a toothy, hooked jaw. Females are generally smaller and less red. Thousands return to Taylor Creek to spawn before dying.

The USDA Forest Service has made it easy to watch the salmon, or to enjoy observing creek life throughout the rest of the year, at their Stream Profile Chamber located on Taylor Creek. A subterranean glassed-in area allows you to see what creek life is like from below the water level. The recently remodeled building has won rave reviews for its lifelike ambience—and ability to engage even the most complacent adults.

The chamber is set in a small freshwater marsh that can be experienced via an easy, accessible trail complete with small bridges, benches, and viewing areas. The spawning run usually begins in late September and runs about five weeks. Around the first Saturday of October, the site is a focal point for the annual Kokanee Salmon Festival, a gala two-day event for the whole family that includes nature walks, educational exhibits, children and adult trail runs, and more.

The fun: What is it really like to be a fish in a stream, to look up and see the sun shimmering through the sheen of water? The recently remodeled stream profile chamber allows you to experience Taylor Creek from its inhabitants' perspective without getting your shoes wet. Begin your walk from the visitor center, where the 0.5-mile Rainbow Trail loops through a wetland. Jeffrey pine and aspen give way to the quiet, shaded trail, where frequent interpretive exhibits cue you to watch wildlife. You may see circling ospreys, hunting coyotes, or fresh evidence of chewed trees left behind by beavers.

About halfway through the walk you enter a building that takes you below ground level. The natural sounds of the creek and a gushing waterfall urge people to speak quietly as they walk into the softly lit subterranean chamber on a surface that feels similar to a creek bottom. The huge floor-to-ceiling glass windows reveal the creek washed in sunshine and filled with aquatic life. Fish swim by, oblivious to your presence. Crayfish scuttle along the gravel, a frog appears from nowhere, and insects flit back and forth on the surface. If you're there in October, you will see female kokanees using

During fall the stream profile chamber at Taylor Creek provides up-close, below-the-water views of spawning kokanee salmon and other stream life. ROBERT W. GARRISON

their tails to dig a redd, or a nest, for their eggs; the hooked-nosed males, stand by, ready to fertilize the waiting eggs.

If you feel like more walking, there are several additional trails. The Lake of the Sky Trail contours Taylor Marsh. You can stop at a viewing deck that looks toward the terminus of Taylor Creek at the lake and then follow the lake shoreline, ending near the boat ramp at the Valhalla pier. Summer visitors may see nesting Canada geese here or yellow-headed blackbirds perched on the cattails. Winter visitors may see wintering bald eagles, watching for the silvery glimmer of fish near the surface. Those with a taste for history should try the Tallac Historic Trail, which curves past former estates, a pond and arboretum, and other historic structures.

Special tips: Weather can be changeable and there can be huge differences between morning and daytime temperatures. Those who have not visited high-elevation areas before should take a day to acclimate before climbing and strenuous activity.

Food and lodging: Extensive food and lodging opportunities surround the lake, from motels and lodges to cabins and condominiums. There are numerous campgrounds. Fallen Leaf Lake is close to Taylor Creek and is operated by a private concessionaire. Overnight fee is $18; call (877) 444–6777. Check the USDA Forest Service Web site for other camping information at www.fs.fed.us/r5/ltbmu/.

Next best: Just too many to mention! The Tahoe Rim Trail is a 165-mile hiking, biking, and equestrian path with breathtaking views that contours the entire lake, passing through scenery at elevations between 6,300 feet and 10,300 feet. You can see the big picture, savor the big lake, take a hike, or have a meal at the top by riding the Heavenly gondola from Stateline (775–586–7000). The Squaw Valley Tram also offers superb views (530–593–6985). The *Tahoe Queen* (800–238–2463) and MS *Dixie II* (775–588–3508) offer lake cruises, some at sunset or midnight. You can enjoy stargazing through a 30-inch telescope at Squaw Valley's High Camp (530–583–6955). Contact South Lake Chamber of Commerce at (530) 541–5255 or www.tahoeinfo.com.

For more information:
Lake Tahoe Basin Management Unit
35 College Drive
South Lake Tahoe, CA 96150
(530) 543–2600
www.r5.fs.fed.us/ltbmu/

Wine, Wetlands, and Italian Charm

Imagine a day of wine touring and tasting at one of Sonoma County's most interesting wineries. Envision yourself ending your tasting with an Italian picnic, sipping wine at a villa reminiscent of Tuscany—all while overlooking legions of ducks and geese resting peacefully on a cattail-lined wetland.

Site: Viansa Winery & Italian Marketplace, about 4 miles north of California Highways 121 and 37 and San Pablo Bay.
Recommended time: Wetlands best October through March. Winery wonderful anytime!
Minimum time commitment: Three hours.

What to bring: Binoculars, your favorite bird guide, and an appetite.
Hours: Open daily 10:00 A.M. to 5:00 P.M.
Admission fee: None for Marketplace. If you put together a group and call in advance, you may enjoy a wetland tour for a fee.

Directions: From U.S. Highway 101, take CA 37 *east* to CA 121. From Interstate 80, take CA 37 *west* to CA 121. Located north on CA 121, about 4 miles past the Infineon Raceway (formerly called Sears Point).

The background: If you like waterfowl and wetlands, and wish you could combine them in a setting reminiscent of old Tuscany complete with fine wine and gourmet food, a visit to Viansa Winery, wetlands, and Italian Marketplace is a must.

Founded by Sam and Vicki Sebastiani, the 125-acre estate and vineyards are also home to 91 acres of wetlands. The name "Viansa" combines the founders' names (*Vi-an-sa*) and blends their love for Old World Italy with Sonoma County elegance. The winery is viewed by many as the gateway to wine country.

The area's unique Carneros soil provides the perfect setting to grow a wide variety of traditional but perhaps unfamiliar Italian grape varietals, from Sangiovese, Nebbiolo, and Vernaccia to Pinot Grigo. The grapes are transformed into wine in fermentation and cellaring rooms, some with 2-foot-thick stone walls that are decorated with fresco-style hand-painted murals. The wines are sold only at the winery.

The Italian Marketplace is an Old World villa complete with a gourmet deli, seasonal outdoor Tuscan grill, and unique packaged gourmet foods for sale. Many of the foods have been created by Vicki Sebastiani, with herbs and vegetables grown in estate gardens. The family even grows, bottles, and sells their own olive oil on-site.

A picnic area overlooks a lush ninety-one-acre wetland restored by Sam, with help from Ducks Unlimited. It is one of California's largest privately restored wetlands. The marsh attracts more than 150 species of birds numbering in excess of 13,000 during peak periods between October and March. The Sebastianis are very committed to this restoration project. "We think wetlands are a vital part of our ecosystem, so we dedicate a portion of the sales of two wines we produce—our Riserva Anatra Rosso and Riserva Anatra Bianco (Duck Preserve red and white wines)—to Ducks Unlimited to help protect them," says Joe Sebastiani.

The fun: As you enter into the winery estate, you'll drive past well-tended vineyards toward an impressive red-tile roofed Italian villa situated amid gently rolling hills. The moment you set foot on the patio, you will enter an atmosphere of warmth, comfort, and welcome.

If you've come for the wine, you may wish to start at the tasting room. You may sample many wines and rare varietals and hear a wealth of information about each. You'll want to browse in the Marketplace store for exquisite foods, from pestos and winery-grown olive oil to grilling sauces and glazes.

Come at mealtime and purchase a picnic lunch at the deli, or on select weekends from May through November order food grilled before your eyes on the Tuscan grill in the picnic area. Take your treats to seats located under a grape trellis or olive trees and savor the peaceful wetland scene, viewed against a backdrop of the Sonoma Valley. Enjoy live music through the summer months.

Whether you're an avid birder or a novice, bring out your binoculars and enjoy spotting many of the migratory species that rely on the winery wetlands. More than two dozen species of waterfowl visit, from flashy tundra swans to sleek mergansers. Shorebirds prowl the mudflats, and golden eagles and northern harriers can be seen teaching their youngsters to hunt. Chances are there will be other visitors who can help you identify some of the birds. Although you cannot walk to the wetland unless you prearrange a tour, you can enjoy the bird-watching right from the villa.

While sipping on famous Viansa wines, birders and wine lovers can enjoy views of the wetlands Vicki and Sam Sebastiani have restored. VIANSA WINERY

Viansa offers many events, from special wetland days to summer music festivals. To learn more about these events, or the wetland, call or visit the winery Web site.

Food and lodging: The area is known for its many fine restaurants and cafes. A wide range of lodging is available in Sonoma, Napa, and numerous surrounding communities, from traditional motels to health spas and bed-and-breakfasts. Contact the Napa Chamber of Commerce at (707) 226–7455 or www.napachamber.com or the Sonoma Valley Visitor's Bureau at (707) 996–1090 or www.sonomavalley.com.

Next best: For another unusual winery experience that takes in a view of nature, consider the aerial tram ride up steep forested slopes to Sterling Vineyard, near Calistoga. The Wine Train also transports you to wineries through beautiful Napa Valley scenery (800–427–4124) Nearby San Pablo Bay offers extensive wildlife viewing just a short drive from Viansa. The Sonoma Valley has more than 13,000 acres of parks and natural areas for exploration.

For more information:
Viansa Winery & Italian Marketplace
25200 Arnold Drive (CA 121)
Sonoma, CA 95476
(707) 935–4700
(800) 995–4740
www.viansa.com

Celebrating the Return of the King

Thousands of huge king salmon fight their way up the American River to return to the place of their birth to spawn and die, oblivious to the state's largest wildlife festival celebrating their return.

Site: Nimbus Hatchery in Rancho Cordova, located 20 miles (thirty minutes) east of Sacramento.

Recommended time: The American River Salmon Festival occurs on the second weekend in October. King or chinook salmon return to the river in early October, but the hatchery fish ladder and spawning operation aren't opened until the river water cools to about 50 degrees, usually in early November. Salmon spawning continues through December, when steelhead trout begin arriving at the hatchery. The hatchery and visitor center are open year-round, and young fish and rainbow trout are always seen in the raceways.

Minimum time commitment: Four hours.

What to bring: Sun hat and sunscreen, comfortable walking shoes, day pack to collect goodies, water, lots of nickels.

Hours: Festival 10:00 A.M. to 4:00 P.M. Saturday and Sunday. Hatchery open daily 8:00 A.M. to 5:00 P.M.

Admission fee: Festival parking $5.00 event free. No charge rest of year.

Directions: From Sacramento, travel east on U.S. Highway 50 for 20 miles to Rancho Cordova. Take the Hazel Avenue exit north over freeway and follow signs to off-site parking (free shuttle bus to hatchery). For limited disabled parking during the festival and for the rest of the year, continue north on Hazel Avenue to Gold Country Boulevard. Turn left and then take an immediate right on Nimbus Road to the hatchery parking lot.

The background: The great rivers of the Central Valley once supported huge runs of chinook salmon and steelhead trout before the rivers were dammed to water the rich farmlands and cities of the state. Before the dams, salmon and steelhead traveled high into the Sierra Nevada and Cascades to spawn in the gravel beds. On the American River alone, more than 100 miles of spawning beds were lost when Folsom Dam was built in 1955. To offset the loss of spawning habitat, Nimbus Hatchery was constructed at the foot of Lake Natoma. The hatchery raises four million chinook salmon and 430,000 steelhead trout each year. Below the hatchery, salmon crowd the few miles of remaining natural gravel beds. Of the twenty to fifty thousand salmon that return to the American River each year, more than 80 percent are fish that spawn in the river.

The remarkable life cycle of the salmon and steelhead begins as the eggs hatch in the cool, oxygen-rich waters of the American River. As the tiny fry grow they become imprinted to the smell and taste of this part of the river. The fry eventually head to the ocean, where they spend two to four years following and feeding on the rich schools of bait fish in the northern Pacific. At maturity, the salmon and steelhead return to the place of their birth, following an ancient signal passed on from generation to generation.

Steelhead spawn and return to sea, but salmon die after they spawn. One of the most awesome wildlife viewing experiences is watching a thirty pound salmon, scarred and battered, use its last reserves of energy to struggle up the fish ladder to complete the cycle of life. Visitors crowd the ladder, a series of stair-step waterfalls, cheering on the fish as they make one more step only to be swept back to the lower pools. Once in the upper holding ponds, the fish are sorted by readiness to spawn, and on most weekday mornings the hatchery staff artificially spawn the fish. The whole process can be seen from viewing windows in the visitor center or on a video presentation at other times.

The fun: Nimbus Hatchery has been a popular attraction since it opened in 1955. Many visitors first came to the hatchery with their parents or on a school field trip. Now they bring their children and grandchildren each year to watch the spawning adults and feed the young fish. Fish food dispensers still cost a nickel for a handful of food. The young fish boil to the surface when a few food pellets hit the water. In recent years the hatchery has added an excellent visitor center, complete with interactive exhibits, video presentations, and a viewing window into the spawning room. A new nature trail overlooks natural spawning beds in the river below the hatchery, and naturalists are on hand daily to answer questions. Additional hands-on exhibits are planned in the near future.

The American River Salmon Festival kicks off the spawning season with a bang. This family-oriented event offers about every conceivable salmon-related activity you can think of. Try the salmon maze, "Extreme Salmon Challenge," or salmon golf. Storytelling, puppetry, and art activities introduce the river and salmon in fun and imaginative ways. Take in a guided cruise, culinary demonstration, and the giant aquarium filled with local fish species before you break for some music and food. The menu you ask? Why salmon of course (as well as many other types of food).

The festival stretches out over Nimbus Hatchery and adjacent Lake Natoma State Park and the American River Parkway. There is plenty of room for the more than 20,000 participants who attend the two-day event. Shuttle buses transport guests between the two locations and to and from the remote parking lot. Arrive early in the day to beat the crowds.

Special tips: Mid-October can still be quite warm. Most of the festival is outside, so wear a sun hat and sunscreen and drink plenty of water during the day.

Food and lodging: Rancho Cordova and Folsom offer a variety of accommodations and restaurants. Contact the Sacramento Conference and Visitors Bureau at (800) 292–2334, or visit www.discovergold.org.

Next best: Take a bike ride down the American River Parkway (see Weekend 11), and stop frequently on the bluffs overlooking the river to watch salmon working their way upstream. The water is quite clear, and you should be able to see the fish on the gravel beds. Dead salmon litter the edge of the river during the spawning season, attracting a wide variety of wildlife that take advantage of the yearly feast. Bring your binoculars and watch for coyotes and vultures along the water's edge and common mergansers and other ducks feasting on salmon eggs. Effie Yeaw Nature Center offers exhibits on the natural history of the parkway. Head upstream to Lake Natoma and Folsom Lake to bike, hike, and camp.

For more information:
Nimbus Hatchery
California Department of Fish and Game
(916) 385–2820
www.salmonfestival.net

Emerald Springs, Silver Mountains, and Sapphire Skies

Hike on uncrowded trails, camp in an alpine meadow, and soak in hot mineral water from middle earth—all in Alpine County, the least-populated county in the state.

Site: Grover Hot Springs State Park, located 3.5 miles from Markleeville (southeast of Lake Tahoe).

Recommended time: The peak season for the hot springs is late April to mid-September.

Minimum time commitment: Four hours for a short soak and picnic; a full day to add in a hike.

What to bring: Bathing suit, pool shoes, towel, layered clothing, sun hat, sunscreen, toiletries, picnic, binoculars. The weather can be very changeable, so come prepared.

Hours: Pool complex days and hours of operation vary. Call for current hours prior to making your trip. The pool complex is closed for two weeks during September for maintenance and on Thanksgiving, Christmas, and New Year's Day.

Admission fee: $3.00 for adults, $1.00 for children age sixteen and under.

Directions: From California Highway 89 and Markleeville, travel west on Hot Springs Road 3.5 miles to the park. Markleeville is located southeast of Lake Tahoe and can be reached via U.S. Highway 50 southeast to Meyers. Travel southeast on CA 89 to Markleeville.

The background: Six thousand feet above sea level, a glacier-carved valley borders the Mokelumne Wilderness. Within this beautiful valley of pine forests, meadows, and streams lies Grover Hot Spring, a 700-acre park known for its relaxing campground and a soothing hot pool fed by natural hot springs.

The hot springs formed millions of years ago when the Sierra Range was in its infancy. Deep faults and fissures developed as the young mountains rose. Water constantly seeps into these openings, traveling thousands of feet below the earth's crust, where it is heated among the hot rocks. It returns to the surface, dissolving subterranean minerals before it emerges west of Markleeville.

Water from eight springs feed one of the park's two pools, where the water is actually cooled to a comfortable 102 to 104 degrees Fahrenheit from its original 148 degrees. The end result is a broth of minerals full of healing virtues, according to old-timers and modern-day healers. The hot pool water is naturally disinfected with bromine, which reacts with the minerals in the water, giving it a light green color. The remaining water flows into Hot Springs Creek, which bisects the park meadow. The creek is often stocked with catchable trout below the campground bridge, making this one of several great local fishing spots, along with Silver Creek and the Carson River.

John Fremont and Kit Carson explored this rough backcountry of the Sierra Nevada Range, and the area's silver mining history is captured in local names such as Silver Creek, Silver Mountain City, and Mt. Bullion. The nearby town of Markleeville is named for Jacob Marklee, who used his mining claim to establish a bridge and toll station. Local restaurants the J. Marklee Toll Station and Wolf Creek provide dining and a taste of the town's early history.

The silver boom ended a quarter of a century after it started and, with it, Markleeville's growing population. The tiny town has remained small and charming. Alpine County is the least-populated county in the state, a boon for visitors who can enjoy the area's colorful history, laid-back lifestyle, and a true respite from crowds.

The fun: During an era when backyard spas are almost as common as bathtubs, it is rare to experience what entrepreneurs have tried to imitate. There are a number of natural hot springs in California, but few can accommodate a crowd. What the soaking pools at Grover Hot Springs lack in aesthetic appeal, they possess in usability. The cement pools are located in a peak-bordered meadow with gorgeous views. They are also easy for the park to maintain and keep safe and clean. The fencing that surrounds the pools may not be visually appealing, but it helps maintain pool hours and security—and is quickly forgotten once the water begins to work its magic.

Many park visitors come only for the water and don't even make a pretense of exercising before they soak. They don a bathing suit in the changing rooms, take a shower, and then settle into the near-heaven of the soothing mineral water.

If you're in good condition and want to work your muscles before you soak, you don't have to travel far. Take the Burnside Lake Trail, which begins at the overflow parking lot. The trail climbs as it provides views of alpine scenery and a gushing waterfall while it switchbacks up a steep slope.

You can even get in some wildlife viewing as you walk the nature trail to the pools. The forest and meadow are home to long-eared chipmunks and Douglas squirrels. During spring and summer the canopy shelters many feathered travelers, including colorful mountain bluebirds and western tanagers. You may hear the sweet trilling of warblers or the tapping of woodpeckers. As you sit and soak, you may be able to see a variety of hawks cruising the skies above, from dainty American kestrels to big red-tailed hawks and turkey vultures.

You don't have to camp here to enjoy the hot springs. Hikers, cross-country skiers, and other travelers throughout the area often end their outing with a stop at the springs. The pools are normally open until dusk, and there is nothing more relaxing than the chance to soothe your muscles in the company of friends beneath a deep blue sky.

Whenever you visit, you must be prepared for what can turn into wild weather. Summer weather can sometimes reach the 90s during the day to the 60s at night. But thunderstorms are common in July and August, particularly in the afternoon. By fall the daytime temperatures are in the 70s, but overnight your camp water bucket will have ice on it. The same cold weather that turns the aspens into bright yellow and orange torches also heralds winter, where snowstorms can be severe, closing roads and felling trees. The steaming pools are open during snowstorms, even blizzards, but they close during thunderstorms.

Special tips: The park closes its pools if lightning is within 1 mile (five seconds) of the complex. They remain closed until a half hour after the storm passes. For your comfort, bring layers whenever you visit, and if you are a winter visitor, come prepared! Check with road conditions to find a route that is open. Call (800) 427–7623 or visit www.dot.ca.gov/hq/roadinfo.

Food and lodging: Markleeville and Woodfords offer limited food and lodging. The park has a seventy-six-space campground that is open from the end of April through the beginning of October. Winter overnight camping is available in the day-use area. Call (800) 444–7275 for reservations during summer. Camping is also available at Indian Creek Reservoir (north of Markleeville) and Turtle Rock Park (between Markleeville and Woodfords). Contact the Alpine County Visitors Center at (530) 694–2475 or www.alpinecounty.com/grover.html.

Next best: Bring your canoe or kayak and enjoy Indian Creek Reservoir. Topaz Lake is just 25 miles east, over scenic Monitor Pass. Lake Tahoe is about 35 miles north. If you come during summer, don't forget the wildflowers at Carson Pass (see Weekend 29) or Hope Valley. Plan a winter snowshoeing or cross-country skiing adventure, and stay at Sorensen's Resort on California Highway 88/89, a half mile east of Pickett's Junction, offering cozy cabins and great food in one place. Visit the Alpine County Museum in Markleeville to absorb some of the local area history.

For more information:
Grover Hot Springs State Park
(530) 694–2248
Pool information: (530) 694–2249
www.parks.ca.gov

Granite Spires and Golden Oaks

Take a bike ride beneath the granite monoliths of El Capitan and Half Dome while, along the valley floor, the golden foliage of the black oaks competes for your attention.

Site: Yosemite Valley, Yosemite National Park.
Recommended time: Spring for waterfalls, summer for crowds, fall for autumn colors and minimal crowds. Winters are cold but spectacular for those prepared.
Minimum time commitment: One day.

What to bring: Bicycle (or rent), helmet, camera, day pack, warm and cold-weather clothes, hiking boots, water bottle, binoculars.
Hours: Bike trails always open.
Admission fee: $20 for a seven-day pass, $40 for an annual pass.

Directions: From the south, California Highway 41 from Fresno or California Highway 140 from Merced. From the west and north, California Highway 120 from Manteca. From the east, CA 120 from Lee Vining (closed during winter).

The background: Yosemite Valley never fails to impress. About one million years ago, massive glaciers estimated to be more than 4,000 feet thick carved the U-shaped valley from the Sierra Nevada granite. The glaciers left behind the vertical cliffs and hanging creeks that form the spring waterfalls that cascade to the valley floor. In autumn, most of the falls are bone dry, but the dramatic cliffs and brilliant yellows of the black oaks, cottonwoods. and willows easily make up for the lack of water. Nevada and Vernal Falls tumble down the Merced River Canyon year-round, so waterfalls are available— they're just not the torrents seen in spring. The Merced River meanders through the flat valley floor, creating crystalline pools that reflect mirror images of the surrounding peaks and colorful foliage.

Black oaks and Ponderosa pines are the predominant trees of the valley floor. As the oaks prepare for winter, leaves turn a brilliant yellow and acorns fall to the ground, supporting a host of wildlife. Black-tailed mule deer graze in the oak-lined meadows; gray squirrels, Steller's jays, and acorn woodpeckers busily collect and store the acorns for winter use. Prior to the

Black oak leaves frame Half Dome at Yosemite National Park. ROBERT W. GARRISON

valley's discovery and invasion by the Mariposa Battalion in 1851, the Southern Miwok lived here, relying on the bountiful supply of acorns they collected in fall and stored in granaries for their yearly needs. Today the grand oaks still share their bounty with valley visitors, but now in the form of fall colors and summer shade.

Within a decade of the valley's discovery, visitors began arriving by horse and wagon and later by stagecoach to see the grand sights. Entrepreneurs soon built hotels and houses, and cattle roamed the valley floor. Concerns over the exploitation of the valley led to federal legislation signed by President Lincoln in 1864 that granted the federal land to the state of California as an "inalienable public trust" for public use and protection. This action led to the creation of the first national park at Yellowstone in 1872. Famed conservationist John Muir fought to protect the high-mountain meadows surrounding the valley in subsequent years, which led to the formal creation of Yosemite National Park in 1890. Today the park draws millions of visitors from around the world, and park managers continue to struggle with balancing resource protection with the needs of the public. The valley's free shuttle service and bike trails, established in the 1970s, allows visitors to park their cars for the duration of their visit and reduce their impact on the valley.

The fun: If you enjoy quiet and solitude, visit Yosemite in the fall. You can almost hear the valley sigh with relief as the roar of spring waterfalls and crush of summer crowds recede and the valley prepares for winter. Cold nights and frost-tinged mornings are quickly replaced by warm days, perfect conditions for a bike ride or hike. Bicycles provide the perfect mode of transportation to explore the valley. Flat terrain makes for easy peddling, and 12 miles of bicycle trails take you to all parts of the valley. Chances are you will have the trails almost to yourself. Take your own bikes or rent them at Curry Village or Yosemite Lodge for $5.50 per hour or $21.00 per day.

This is a great time of year to hike the Mist Trail to the top of Vernal and Nevada Falls. Granted, there is little mist at this time of year, but the views are spectacular and there is plenty of water plunging down the falls. This is a strenuous 7-mile round-trip hike, but the good news is the last 3.5 miles are all downhill! Allow five to six hours for the hike. Another option is to take the free hikers shuttle to Glacier Point and hike the 8.5-mile Panorama Trail past Illilouette Falls and down the Mist Trail back to the valley floor. It's all downhill, it takes about the same time as the first hike, and you see new terrain around every corner.

Unless you have cold-weather camping gear, stay in one of a variety of heated rooms ranging from heated tents with a shared bath to luxurious rooms at the grand Ahwahnee Hotel. Make your reservations ahead of time, because accommodations fill up even in fall. Some of the food and visitor services will be closed for the season, but there are a number of dining options, and you can prepare meals in the picnic areas if you prefer. By all means, take your camera—and keep it handy.

Special tips: Carry and drink plenty of water when you bike and hike. Children under age seventeen must wear bicycle helmets, but to be safe everyone should.

Food and lodging: Curry Village, Yosemite Lodge, and Ahwahnee Hotel offer accommodations and food services in the valley. The Wawona Hotel is located at the southern entrance to the park. All are managed by the park concessionaire, DNC Parks and Resorts. They can be reached at (559) 252–4848 or www.yosemitepark.com. For information about accommodations, restaurants, and activities outside of valley, visit www.yosemite.com.

Next best: The Wawona Hotel, near the south entrance to the park on CA 41, is a great lodging option for a second night in the park. The historic hotel retains the feel and ambience of times past. Visit the Mariposa Grove of Sierra redwoods and Glacier Point while you are in this section of the park. A nice nine-hole golf course adjoins the hotel, and it is usually a great place to watch black-tailed mule deer in the evening. Take a drive over the Tioga Pass Road to Tuolumne Meadows, and hike through the open meadows and granite domes of the high country.

For more information:
Yosemite National Park
(209) 372–0200
www.nps.gov/yose/home.htm

Prehistoric Songs and Ceremonial Dances

The sandhill crane's ancient lineage stretches back to the age of the dinosaurs, when their trilling calls and elaborate dances graced the prehistoric landscape. Their ancestors, thousands strong, return to the Central Valley in the fall, when a celebration marks their return.

Site: Sandhill Crane Festival and Isenberg (Woodbridge) Crane Reserve, Lodi.
Recommended time: Late September through early March to see the cranes. The first or second weekend in November for the festival.
Minimum time commitment: One day to take in a few field trips and workshops.
What to bring: Warm clothes, rain gear, binoculars, bird guide, water, and snacks.

Hours: Festival headquarters, Friday 2:30 P.M. to 8:30 P.M., Saturday and Sunday 6:30 A.M. to 5:00 P.M. The reserve is open sunrise to sunset.
Admission fee: None at Isenberg Crane Reserve. Festival, $10 general admission; field trips $10 to $20 each. Tours of reserve on nonfestival weekends, $8.00 donation.

Directions: Isenberg Crane Reserve: From Interstate 5 between Stockton and Sacramento, exit on Peltier Road. Go east to Thornton Road and then south 2 miles to Woodbridge Road. Turn and travel west for 2 miles to parking area on left.

Festival Headquarters: Hutchins Street Square at the corner of Hutchins Street and Pine Street in Lodi.

The background: The haunting trill of the sandhill crane's call echoes across the landscape long before they come into view. The silhouette of Mount Diablo and a golden sunset frame the evening sky as hundreds of sandhill cranes fly in formation back to their communal sleeping areas along Woodbridge Road. Flooded fields provide the perfect night roost, safe from predators. At first light the cranes return to harvested fields of corn and rice to graze on missed grain and the occasional snail and crayfish.

Two subspecies of sandhill cranes return to the Sacramento–San Joaquin Delta in the fall. The lesser sandhill cranes come from as far away as Siberia, Alaska, and northern Canada. The greater sandhill cranes, a few inches taller than their lesser cousins, arrive from northeastern California and eastern Oregon and Washington, where they nest in wet meadows. Only about 7,000 greater sandhill cranes survive today in California, and the majority of the threatened birds overwinter here. Standing 5 feet tall with a wingspan of 7 feet, the gray cranes sport a handsome red crown. The males and females look alike (to us). The birds pair for life, and you can watch them perform ceremonial dances designed to strengthen their life-long bond.

The elegant dances consist of synchronized dips, wing spreads, bows, and leaps. The displays generally are more frequent early in the morning and prior to their spring migration back to their nesting areas. The dances have inspired many artistic reflections in dance, poetry, and painting. The exuberance for life captured in their displays, calls, and flight continue to inspire people throughout the world.

The fun: The Sandhill Crane Festival celebrates the cranes and the region over three days of field trips, workshops, lectures, performing and visual arts, and exhibits. More than fifty-five tours explore the delta and foothills by boat, by bus, and on foot. While some tours focus on crane viewing, many emphasize other wildlife of the region, including bald eagles, waterfowl, and shorebirds. Register early to ensure that you get your first choices of field trips and activities. Enjoy Lodi wines and hors d'oeuvres at the opening of the crane fine art display on Friday evening.

If you can't make the festival, visit the crane reserve on your own or take a guided tour. The two-hour sunset tours occur on a part of the reserve not regularly open to the public. A large viewing blind blocks the wind and rain and hides you from view as hundreds of cranes fly overhead and into the flooded fields to roost for the night. The popular weekend tours are offered by reservation only when the cranes are in residence, call (916) 358–2353.

Self-guided tours occur at a viewing mound adjoining Woodbridge Road. This is an isolated and primitive reserve with no drinking water or restrooms. The small parking area leads to the viewing mound, which provides a vista over the flat landscape. If no cranes are in the adjoining fields, drive to the end of Woodbridge Road and watch for them. More than a thousand birds regularly use this area, but they move from field to field throughout the day.

Stop at Lodi Lake Park on your way to or from the crane reserve to use the restrooms and bird-watch along the Mokolumne River. Located on

Turner Road midway between I–5 and California Highway 99, the park at first glance appears overly developed, and the lake may be dry. Bear to the right as you enter the park, and proceed to the nature area parking lot. From here a trail adjoins the mature riparian forest, where birdlife abounds.

Special tips: Farm trucks zoom down Woodbridge Road. Do not stop your car in the middle of the road; use pullouts to stop and view.

Food and lodging: Lodi offers an assortment of food and lodgings. Contact the Lodi Chamber of Commerce at (209) 367–7840 or www.lodi chamber.com.

Next best: In the heart of the Central Valley Delta, Lodi and the crane reserve are surrounded by rich farmlands and vestiges of the wetlands that once dominated the valley. The Cosumnes River Preserve (see Weekend 23), Brannan Island State Park, and Stone Lakes National Wildlife Refuge protect some of the best remaining habitats. Pick a driving route along the winding delta levee roads to see the diverse crops that feed the nation and the world. Stop in the historic Chinese community of Locke to view the old storefronts, and drop in for a steak at Al the Wop's on Main Street.

For more information:
Isenberg (Woodbridge) Crane Reserve
California Department of Fish and Game
(916) 358–2353

Sandhill Crane Festival
Lodi Chamber of Commerce
(209) 367–7840
www.lodichamber.com

WEEKEND 46

November

Bald Eagles, Ospreys, and Endangered Salmon

Thousands of fall-run chinook salmon crowd Battle Creek to spawn in the shallow gravel beds and at the nearby hatchery. In the upper reaches of the watershed, other runs of salmon facing extinction are given a helping hand to reverse a century of abuse.

Site: Battle Creek Wildlife Area and Coleman National Fish Hatchery, about 12 miles east of Anderson.

Recommended time: October and November to view natural and hatchery spawning fall-run chinook salmon. January to March to view hatchery spawned late-fall run salmon and steelhead. Winter and spring to view bald eagles and osprey. Any time of year for birds and other wildlife.

Minimum time commitment: Four hours.

What to bring: Warm clothes, rain gear, extra shoes for muddy conditions, binoculars, bird guide, lunch, and water.

Hours: Wildlife area open from 6:00 A.M. to 10:00 P.M.; hatchery from 7:30 A.M. to 5:00 P.M.

Admission fee: None.

Directions: From Interstate 5 northbound, take the Jellys Ferry Road exit beyond Red Bluff. Continue about 15 miles to Coleman Fish Hatchery Road. Turn right to Battle Creek Wildlife Area and Coleman Hatchery. From I–5 southbound at Anderson, take the Deschutes Road exit; drive east for 2.3 miles to Balls Ferry Road, and turn right. Drive 3 miles to Ash Creek Road and turn left. Travel 1.2 miles and then turn right onto Gover Road. Drive 1.6 miles and turn left onto Coleman Hatchery Road.

The background: Great changes are under way on aptly named Battle Creek. A tributary to the Sacramento River, Battle Creek is fed by a series of volcanic springs on the slopes of Mount Lassen, providing a year-round source of cool, clear water for salmon and humans. Farmers first tapped the water to irrigate their crops and built check dams and canals to move the water to their land. In 1901 the first of eight dams were built to divert water to generate electricity. Fish ladders, designed to allow the fish to bypass barriers, were included in most of the dams, but many were ineffective. Other conditions, including low stream flows from water diversions and the trap-

Cold, clear water and deep gravel beds provide the perfect habitat for spawning fall-run chinook salmon. CALIFORNIA DEPT. OF FISH AND GAME

ping of young and adult fish in canals, all had devastating effects on Battle Creek winter- and spring-run chinook salmon. Coleman National Fish Hatchery was built on Battle Creek in the 1940s to compensate for the construction of Shasta Dam on the Sacramento River and produces more than thirteen million fall- and late-fall-run chinook salmon and 600,000 steelhead trout.

Over thousands of years, chinook salmon began to spawn at different times of the year, creating four distinct species, or runs, which are named for the time of year the adults first enter fresh water from the ocean. All four runs—fall, late-fall, winter, and spring—can be found in Battle Creek and the upper Sacramento River, the only remaining places where this occurs. The winter and spring runs are in serious trouble and have been listed as endangered and threatened, respectively. These fish must travel to the upper reaches of the watershed to spawn. Their young, born in late spring and summer, require cool, shady water to survive until winter rains wash them out to the Sacramento River and ultimately to the ocean. Only a few non-hatchery winter-run and about a hundred spring-run chinook were counted in Battle Creek in 1998.

Over the past five years, planning has begun to restore the Battle Creek watershed for salmon, steelhead, Pacific lamprey, and other wildlife. While hatcheries will continue to play an important role in maintaining fall- and late-fall-run salmon and steelhead populations, biologists believe the best long-term solution is to restore historic spawning habitats that support all types of fish. Hydroelectric dams will be removed or improved to allow fish to migrate upstream freely. Screens will be placed on diversion canals, water flows will be increased during summer and fall, and degraded habitats will be restored. Battle Creek Wildlife Area and other public lands have been purchased to protect critical streamside habitats, which in turn support a variety of wildlife, including nesting bald eagles and osprey. Come and see how Battle Creek is being transformed from a battleground over water use to a cooperative community effort that benefits humans and wildlife alike.

The fun: Head to Battle Creek Wildlife Area in October and November to see wild fall-run salmon breeding in the lower stretches of Battle Creek. There are very few places in California where you can see hundreds of salmon crowding shallow gravel beds to spawn. Close to the water, cotton-woods, sycamores, and alders shade the banks and provide roosts for bald eagles, ospreys, and kingfishers. Away from the water, giant valley oaks grow in the rich, deep soils. Acorn woodpeckers send scolding calls to other woodpeckers—and to you—from their granary trees, drilled with thou-sands of individual holes stuffed with acorns. A loop trail begins at the park-ing lot and proceeds along the creek and through the oak woodlands.

Thousands of salmon will continue upstream to Coleman National Fish Hatchery, adjoining the wildlife area. The hatchery has exhibits on the life cycle of the salmon, and you can observe spawning operations from a viewing platform (call ahead for estimated times and dates of spawning). The hatchery also offers a nature trail along the creek, where spawning salmon, bald eagles, and ospreys can generally be seen—a unique opportu-nity to contrast natural spawning with mechanized hatchery spawning.

Bring your binoculars and spend some time hiking the trails. Find a quiet spot along the creek, sit down for a half hour, and let the water and wildlife envelop you. The salmon run attracts wildlife from afar to feed on the protein-rich eggs and dead fish. Watch for normally shy coyotes and

Bald Eagles, Ospreys, and Endangered Salmon

Redding

5

273

44

Deschutes Rd.

44

N

0   Kilometers   5

0   Miles   5

Dersch Rd.

Dersch Rd.

Black Butte Rd.

Wildcat Rd.

Wildcat Rd.

Anderson

Balls Ferry Rd.

Ash Creek Rd.

Asín

Gover

Coleman Hatchery Rd.

Battle Creek Wildlife Area

Coleman National Fish Hatchery

Cottonwood

Manton Rd.

36

36

36

Hogsback Rd.

36

99

Red Bluff

36   99

5

99

foxes on the edge of the creek and ducks and wading birds in the water. Plan your visit near dawn or dusk to possibly observe raccoons, ring-tailed cats, and other nocturnal animals coming down to feed.

Special tips: The trails can be wet and muddy; bring a change of shoes.

Food and lodging: Anderson, Red Bluff, and Redding offer an assortment of restaurants and lodging. Contact or stop by the Anderson Welcome Center for more information. The staffed welcome center has excellent exhibits and brochures on other things to see and do in the region. Call (800) 474–2782, or visit www.shastacascade.org.

Next best: Travel up to Redding to the Turtle Bay Discovery Center (www.turtlebay.org), a new nature center complete with a stream profile chamber where you can see life below the water's surface, permanent exhibits on the area's cultural and natural history, and rotating art exhibits. Fishing along the Upper Sacramento River is always great. Book a guided float trip or fish from shore for trout and salmon. (Outfitters and fishing reports are listed on the Shasta Cascade Web site: www.shastacascade.org.) To view the upper Battle Creek watershed, drive up to Darrah Springs State Fish Hatchery. Ask for directions at Coleman Hatchery.

For more information:
Battle Creek Wildlife Area
(530) 225–2300
www.dfg.ca.gov/lands/newsites/wa/region1/battlecreek.html

Coleman National Fish Hatchery
(530) 365–8622
pacific.fws.gov/Fisheries/Coleman.htm

November

Featherlight Butterflies and Rock-rimmed Tidepools

With sun and surf, pocket beaches, and trees with fluttering butterflies, Natural Bridges State Beach offers incredible scenery, an education, and a welcome respite from Santa Cruz boardwalk crowds.

Site: Natural Bridges State Beach.
Recommended time: From mid-October through the end of February for monarch butterflies. Check tide table for low tides and best tidepool viewing.
Minimum time commitment: Three hours.

What to bring: Sun hat, sunscreen, day pack, layered clothing, extra shoes if you want to go tidepooling, camera, and a picnic if desired.
Hours: Daily, 8:00 A.M. to sunset.
Admission fee: None, but a $5.00 parking fee inside park. There is street parking outside, but it's a walk!

Directions: From California Highway 1 in Santa Cruz, take Swift Avenue west (left). Or follow West Cliff Drive north along the in-town bluffs until it ends.

The background: For years on end, wind and waves gnawed at the mudstone cliffs buttressing the Santa Cruz coast, undercutting here, pounding there. By the early 1900s these forces had created three natural rock arches that were gradually severed from shore. Locals called these landmarks the natural bridges. Since then, nature has continued its rough treatment. Only one of the three arches still stands, but the name Natural Bridges remains.

Its rugged coastal scenery, sheltered pocket beach, glistening tidepools, and upland trails would alone make Natural Bridges State Beach a draw for people and coastal wildlife alike. But it is a small, velvet-winged traveler that gives this state beach its special distinction. Every year, tens of thousands of monarch butterflies return to Natural Bridges to spend the winter. The park was established in 1933 specifically to preserve this important monarch butterfly wintering site, and is one of a few monarch preserves in the state.

As fall temperatures drop in the valleys west of the Rocky Mountains in the United States and Canada, these featherlight travelers leave the plentiful milkweed that has sustained them to migrate to warmer climates, some traveling 2,000 miles to their wintering sites. They travel to numerous central California coast locations, but one of the largest gatherings in the western United States occurs each year at Natural Bridges State Beach. They are drawn to the stately eucalyptus groves within the park, where they rest in clusters, sometimes covering great sections of the trees. When it is cold they intertwine their legs to gain better purchase on the tree limbs, helping one another withstand wind and rain. When their wings are closed, they are a dull tannish gray, hiding their rich markings. If the temperature rises above 60 degrees, the warmth can transform the tight, drab clusters into a fluttering orange-and-black tapestry. Sometimes a great mass of monarchs lightly flutter from the trees all at the same time to search for a sip of nectar.

The fun: If you have children, the butterflies may not be able to compete with Santa Cruz's famous half-mile-long boardwalk with its Giant Dipper (thought by some to be one of the best roller coasters in the nation) and other carnival rides, cotton candy, and people strolling to and from the beautiful adjacent beach. After your binge of rides and "comfort" food, a trip to Natural Bridges is a must—and it is just minutes from town.

An accessible boardwalk within the eucalyptus grove leads to a viewing deck that provides outstanding views of these dainty travelers from October through March. There is often a hush among the crowd as people marvel at a creature that weighs fractions of an ounce but is tough enough to fly miles through wind and storms. While at Natural Bridges, they feed on nectar; but milkweed is their preferred food for about half the year and is the only place they will lay their eggs. Time your visit for a weekend to take advantage of the excellent tours provided by park guides. They are offered from October to mid-February at 11:00 A.M. and 2:00 P.M. You should sign up in advance at the visitor center. The park celebrates the monarchs' arrival with a Welcome Back Monarchs Day the second weekend in October and their departure in February with the Migration Festival.

Include a visit to the demonstration milkweed patch next to the visitor center to watch the feeding monarchs and to see their bright green chrysalides hanging beneath the walkway railings in spring and fall. As the winter wears on, the monarchs move toward breeding, often flying inland to find patches of milkweed upon which to feed and lay their

MONARCH BUTTERFLIES—THE CYCLE OF SEASONS

Late in the fall, after the crush of summer tourists have left the coast, up to a hundred million new visitors arrive. Carried by velvet wings on a migration that can span several thousand miles, monarch butterflies arrive to winter at about a hundred sites between Mendocino County and northern Baja California in Mexico.

The mystery and miracle of the monarch butterfly lie in its migrations, for the parents mate and then die before leaving the wintering site. The young butterfly that emerges from its chrysalis begins the migration to a summering site it has never visited. These individuals will breed and die en route, and it will take several such matings and generations to make the entire trip to summer habitat scattered throughout the western United States. In fall a single generation of butterflies will make the entire one-way trip to the California coast, a destination they have never visited. They use the position of the sun and an instinctual compass to guide them with unwavering accuracy, returning in fairly predictable numbers to these coastal sites.

The monarch butterfly is the most widely distributed and recognized butterfly in the United States. Natural Bridges State Beach claims one of California's largest populations, but you can also see gatherings at George Washington Park in Pacific Grove, Point Lobos State Reserve, Morro Bay State Park, and Pismo Beach State Beach.

eggs. There are numerous trails through the butterfly preserve and adjacent Moore Creek estuary.

Spring brings low tides and a chance to explore the park's amazing tidepool life. Urchins, anemones, sea stars, and other marine life cling to the ocean-bathed rocks. Check the tide table in advance so that you can time your visit for low tide. Tidepool life is extraordinary, not only adapting to differing saline conditions but also to long periods when they are either completely submerged and battered by the tide or exposed to the dessicating wind and sun. Like many other California beaches, Natural Bridges is also a magnet for surfers, wave boarders, and others who enjoy water sports. Beachcombers enjoying this shelter beach might also see shorebirds, whales, seals, and sea otters.

Special tips: The boardwalk through the monarch grove has been designed to avoid close contact, but try to avoid disturbing these delicate creatures in areas outside the grove. The last remaining arch is very fragile; climbing is not allowed. Enjoy the tidepools—but no collecting.

Food and lodging: Santa Cruz and surrounding communities abound with great restaurants and lodging of all varieties. Contact the Santa Cruz Conference and Visitors Bureau at (831) 425–1234 or (800) 833–3494 or www.scccvc.org/index.html. Camping opportunities are also plentiful. For more information and to make reservations, visit www.reserveamerica.com or call (800) 444–7275.

Next best: Butterflies also winter at Lighthouse Field State Beach, where you can see sea lions on offshore rocks and rare black swifts. The lighthouse on West Cliff Drive also houses the state's first surfing museum and is the site of a Santa Cruz Christmas tradition, Caroling Under the Stars. There are numerous state parks and beaches within driving distance, from Henry Cowell in the redwoods to Año Nuevo (see Weekend 49) to the north. History buffs should plan a stop at the Santa Cruz Mission State Historic Park, while motorcyclists will want to visit the Harley Museum in Santa Cruz.

For more information:
Natural Bridges State Beach
(831) 423–4609
www.parks.ca.gov

Friends of Santa Cruz State Parks
(831) 429–1840
www.parks.ca.gov

November

A Birding Bonanza from Your Vehicle

Take this rare opportunity to enjoy one of the Central Valley's top birding locations from your vehicle. See grasslands literally flocked with white geese, crowds of ducks, and ribbons of shorebirds. Stretch your legs on one of many easy hikes for close-up viewing.

Site: Grasslands of western Merced County, located around the city of Los Banos.

Recommended time: Birds best October through February. Tule elk rut occurs August to October. Vernal pool wildflowers spectacular April to May.

Minimum time commitment: Four hours for a quick experience; a day if you want to make a few stops.

What to bring: Binoculars or spotting scope, hat for sun or rain, layered clothing and rain gear so that you can enjoy taking a hike, water and picnic or snack, your favorite bird guide.

Hours: The driving loops on public roads are open twenty-four hours a day. National Wildlife Refuges are open every day of the year during daylight hours. State wildlife areas have seasonally changing access hours; contact them before your visit.

Admission fee: None for San Luis or Merced National Wildlife Refuge or the county road driving tour; $2.50 per person day fee or valid hunting or fishing license at Los Banos Wildlife Area.

Directions: The driving tours begin in Los Banos; see map on page 210.

The background: Central Valley travelers on California Highway 99 or Interstate 5 often push the speed limit to pass through what appears to be a monotonous landscape of flat farm fields and orchards that extends for miles. Unseen by the motorist, much of the year several huge wildlife oases offer an exciting diversion and a respite from freeway travel. High above California's busy roads, each fall millions of waterfowl, shorebirds, birds of prey, and songbirds navigate highways in the sky to escape harsh northern weather and pass the winter in the temperate Central Valley.

Long before gold called people with dreams westward, California's Central Valley had lush native grasses that were so tall a traveler could get

WETLANDS—RE-CREATING WHAT HAS BEEN LOST

Over eons, generations of migratory birds have traveled long distances, sometimes battling storms and fierce winds, to leave their northern breeding grounds to winter at temperate California wetlands. A wetland is an aquatic habitat that forms in any depression that holds water.

At one time, wetlands were strung like pearls along the state's 1,100-mile coastline. Coastal wetlands were shaped by tides that waxed and waned twice each day, enriching offshore waters, tidepools, and mudflats with nutrients and marine life that sustained birds, fish, and other organisms. Wetlands also sprawled across the Central Valley's vast river floodplains. Here winter rains filled basins or pushed rivers and streams beyond their banks. The resulting seasonal ponds and pools awakened dormant seeds and organisms within the soil and a banquet of plants and other foods were available when the migratory birds arrived.

In the late 1780s in the lower forty-eight states, the cycle of chang-

lost in them. Oaks shaded grassy savannas studded with vernal pools. Rivers ran free, swelling with winter rain and spilling across the floodplain to form vast seasonal wetlands. Over eons, the "wind" birds arrived each fall, relying on this smorgasbord of habitats and food to sustain them through the winter.

Then settlers came, first grazing cattle on the virgin grasslands and later tilling the rich soil to provide food for the world's larders. Much of the native grassland disappeared. Rivers were harnessed with dams, providing water for farms and communities. The seasonal wetlands also vanished, until only about 5 percent remained. Though their numbers diminished, the wind birds still came.

One of the enduring magnets for migratory birds is the grassland of Merced County. Vast tracts of farmland now also provide vital foraging areas for sandhill cranes, ducks, and geese. These farmlands lie among a patchwork of state, federal, and privately owned wetlands, where scarce water must be conveyed through canals and ditches to re-create seasonal wetlands. A small army of workers moves the water to just the right spot, in the right amount, at the right time of year to be ready for the millions of migratory birds that visit. The area isn't known for its stunning scenery, but it is a five-star Hilton for migratory birds—and a birder's paradise. People come here

ing seasons produced about 221 million acres of wetlands. As America was settled, enterprising farmers found ways to dry out wetlands, tilling their rich soil for crops. As rural areas were colonized and urban areas expanded, communities learned how to harness the power of rivers with dams. The floodplains no longer filled with winter rain, and the seasonal wetlands gradually disappeared. In little more than 200 years, the nation's wetlands dwindled, and today barely 105.5 million acres remain. The losses have been the greatest in California, where about 95 percent of the wetlands have disappeared. These aquatic habitats are vital to wildlife. Eighty percent of the nation's commercial fisheries reproduce in wetlands, and almost half our endangered species rely upon them for survival.

Many national wildlife refuges and state and local areas have been protected to preserve natural wetlands. When you visit a wetland, remember that in many cases the natural-appearing habitat you are observing has been created with water purchased and pumped at a high cost, conveyed through human-made ditches and canals, and precisely timed for the winter stay of a legacy of migratory birds.

from around the world to see this huge gathering or to spot a yellow-billed magpie, tricolored blackbird, Ross' goose, curlew, or another bird missing from their life list.

The fun: Imagine the sight of thousands of snow geese foraging on a wetland, flocks of ducks darkening the sky as they move to feed, or shorebirds of various sizes and shapes fanned out on the mudflats—all from the comfort of your vehicle. On this 180,000 acres of public and private land, you can count on seeing the unexpected. You can travel all or some of three tour loops that cover 100 miles of paved roads and more than 30 miles of gravel road contouring the valley's largest block of wetlands and native grasslands. Stretch your legs en route at more than a dozen subunits of the two national wildlife refuges and two state wildlife areas.

For a quick drive, the south loop leads to Mallard Road, where you'll often be close to intensively managed wetlands; the scene buzzes with activity. Snow geese lift up, then settle, with a cacophony of calls. Ibis and other wading birds wade quietly in the shallows along with an assortment of feeding ducks. Use your binoculars or spotting scope to locate songbirds in the grasslands. Look skyward for a chance to see golden eagles and prairie falcons hunting for a meal.

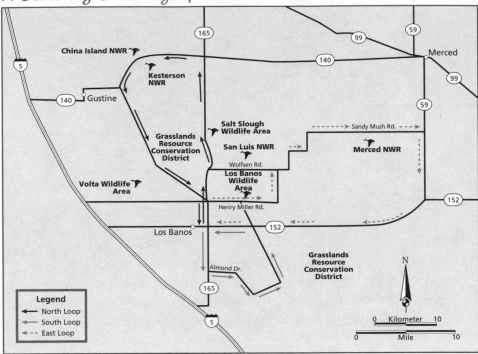

The popular north loop leaves Los Banos on California Highway 165, past fields with resting ducks, ibis, and shorebirds. Take a break at Los Banos Wildlife Area, the state's oldest wildlife area. Stop by the office for directions for an easy half-mile walk to Buttonwillow Lake. The trail is open on Wednesday, Saturday, and Sunday only, from mid-October to January. As you walk, look in the willows and cottonwoods for perching great horned owls or red-tailed hawks; skirt uplands dotted with alkali sacaton, a native grass; and then pause at the lake overlook. Even from a distance, huge flocks of snow geese, Ross' geese, gadwalls, and pintails may be visible.

Continue road viewing as you drive north 3 miles, turning right onto Wolfsen Road, through the Salt Slough Wildlife Area, to San Luis National Wildlife Refuge. Watch for perched raptors and circling white pelicans as you pass marshes packed with waterfowl. Plan a stop at the platform overlooking a 760-acre enclosure that is home to a thriving herd of tule elk, a species found only in California. The rut has usually ended by October, but through the winter you can see males with heavily branched antlers protecting their hard-won harems.

The route continues north along CA 165, going through 8,000 acres of native grassland adjacent to 8,000 acres of restored habitat in the Great Valley Grassland State Park and the Freitas and Bear Creek Units of San Luis NWR. The auto tour route at West Bear Creek has been a favorite resting area for swans in January and February, along with ducks, ibis, and shorebirds.

The north route continues to California Highway 140 and then west past China Island, Fremont Ford, and Kesterson before the turn onto Sante Fe Grade, a route that provides safe public access through the heart of 107,000 acres of private duck hunting clubs, if the road is not too wet. The route ends in Los Banos.

Don't forget the east loop. In addition to the roadside viewing, a 5-mile auto tour with two observation platforms and a 0.25-mile walking loop at Merced National Wildlife Refuge offer the chance to see thousands of ducks and shorebirds, 50,000 Ross' and snow geese, three species of owls, and up to 20,000 lesser sandhill cranes—the largest concentration in the Pacific Flyway.

Special tips: Morning fog is common October through February. Some views are distant; you will need at least binoculars to enjoy the detail.

Food and lodging: Los Banos offers many choices for food and lodging. Contact the Los Banos Chamber of Commerce at (209) 826–2495 or (800) 336–6354, or visit www.losbanos.com. Several state recreation areas offer camping for $11 to $14 per night. You can make reservations at www.reserveamerica.com.

Next best: You easily can spend a weekend visiting sites on the grasslands tour. If you have extra time, during winter and spring O'Neill Forebay and Reservoir offers outstanding opportunities to see a dozen species of diving ducks in a few hours. Sixty-pound striped bass have been taken here, and the steady breeze makes it a haven for sailboarding. Among the many state recreation areas, San Luis Reservoir offers viewing and water sports. Also check out two small riparian gems, McConnell and George Hatfield.

For more information:
Los Banos Wildlife Area
(209) 826–0463
www.dfg.ca.gov

San Luis National Wildlife Refuge
(209) 826–3508
http://sanluis.fws.gov

WEEKEND *49*

December

Elephant Seals on Parade

From a solitary pup born on the beach in 1975 to well over 2,000 births a year today, the beaches and dunes of Año Nuevo State Reserve support the second largest mainland colony of northern elephant seals in the world.

Site: Año Nuevo State Reserve, 20 miles north of Santa Cruz.
Recommended time: December 15 through March 31 for guided tours of breeding colonies, April through November for self-guided tours of yearlings and molting seals. Elephant seals and other marine mammals viewable year-round. The elephant seal viewing area is closed December 1–14.
Minimum time commitment: Five hours.

What to bring: Hiking boots, layered warm clothing, hooded rain gear, binoculars, camera, day pack, water.
Hours: Guided tours 9:00 A.M. to 2:30 P.M. daily December 15 through March 31. April through November, permits for self-guided tours in seal area available 8:30 A.M. to 3:00 P.M.; other areas of reserve 8:00 A.M. to sunset.
Admission fee: $4.00 parking fee. Tours $4.00 per person; children under age three free.

Directions: From Santa Cruz, travel 20 miles north on California Highway 1 to the reserve. From Half Moon Bay, travel 27 miles south on CA 1.

The background: By 1892 decades of commercial hunting reduced the vast colonies of northern elephant seals to just one colony of fewer than one hundred animals on Guadalupe Island off Baja California. The seals were officially protected by Mexico and the United States in the 1920s and slowly began to recolonize the islands along the Pacific coast. By 1955 solitary elephant seals arrived on Año Nuevo Island, and the first birth occurred there in 1961. As the island population grew, adults began moving to the mainland beaches, where the first pup was born in 1975. Today the mainland beaches and dunes of Año Nuevo State Reserve support the second largest mainland colony of northern elephant seals in the world. The largest mainland colony occurs at Piedras Blancas, north of San Simeon.

In December the two-and-a-half-ton bulls arrive on the beaches to establish breeding territories. Bloody battles ensue as males fight for the best real estate, the areas that will attract the most females. By late December, pregnant females arrive on the beaches to give birth. Crowded conditions lead to barely controlled chaos as the bulls vigorously defend their harems from a host of ready successors, often plowing through mothers and pups in the process. By the end of March, most of the adults have left the breeding colonies and returned to the ocean.

If the pups survive the dangers of the crowded breeding colonies, they grow from 75 pounds at birth to between 250 and 300 pounds in about a month. The pups normally nurse only on their mother's rich milk, but more gregarious pups may nurse from other females and grow to 600 pounds. About twenty-four days after giving birth, the females come into season and breed with the dominant male. They soon abandon their young and return to the ocean to feed for the first time since arriving on shore.

The weaned pups, called weaners, remain on land until mid-April; they molt and learn to swim in the shallow tidepools and freshwater ponds. Hunger drives the weaners to sea, where they hunt for rays, small sharks, and other types of fish along the Washington and British Columbia coast. Great white sharks patrol the waters around Año Nuevo for young and adult elephant seals, as well as for harbor seals, California sea lions, and Steller sea lions that inhabit the island off the point.

The fun: From CA 1, Point Año Nuevo gently slopes to the sea, passing through farm fields, meadows, and dunes to Año Nuevo Island with its abandoned lighthouse. The island and land adjoining the coastline are protected as a state reserve. Within the reserve, active sand dunes slowly blow across the end of the point and shelter elephant seals, brush rabbits, bobcats, foxes, and a host of bird species. A visitor center created in a historic dairy barn interprets the natural and cultural history of the reserve.

Docent-guided walks of the elephant seal colonies give you a close-up view of nature in the raw. Blood and death are balanced by birth and motherly nurturing. It is a spectacle not to be missed. The moderately strenuous 3-mile hike begins at a staging area about a mile from the visitor center. The windblown point lacks shelter, so prepare for wind, rain, and sun. The walking route constantly changes to accommodate the movements of the animals. Part of the fun and adventure of the hike is trying to outmaneuver the seals that may block your route, forcing a march up and over the dunes. Bring your binoculars to watch the animals along the shoreline or to get a really close view of the seals in the dunes.

State park rangers and docents do an excellent job of balancing the needs of the visitors and seals. The two-and-a-half-hour, twenty-person walks depart every fifteen minutes throughout the day. The guided walks are very popular, and the weekend tour slots quickly fill. Reserve your tour before you arrive; while there may be some no-show spots available, chances are you will not get on a tour without reservations. April through November you can pick up a permit at the visitor center and take a self-guided tour through the reserve. There are generally some elephant seals in the reserve throughout the year, but the real action occurs in winter.

Special tips: Tour guides will direct you away from the seals, but remain at least 25 feet from any animal. Do not get between a mother and pup or a bull and his harem. Poison oak is common in the uplands, and ticks occur throughout the reserve in spring and summer.

Food and lodging: There is a selection of small lodges and restaurants between Davenport and Pescadero. A greater assortment is available in Santa Cruz. Contact the Santa Cruz County Conference and Visitors Council at (800) 833–3494 or www.scccvc.org. Camping is available at nearby Butano State Park, and upscale tent cabins can be rented at Costanoa right next to the reserve (www.costanoa.com). Or try the youth hostel at Pigeon Point Lighthouse a few miles up the road.

Next best: Año Nuevo State Park, a separate unit from the reserve, was recently created and extends up into the redwood-clad canyons on the east side of the highway. A 2-mile trail climbs to the upper sections of the watershed with great views of the coastline. Pigeon Point Lighthouse is closed to tours, but the grounds are open for visits. Butano State Park preserves some beautiful old-growth redwood groves. Pocket beaches north along the coast are great for a picnic on a sunny afternoon.

For more information:
Año Nuevo State Reserve
(650) 879–0227 (recorded access information)
Guided walk reservations: (800) 444–4445
www.parks.ca.gov

Savor a Living Legacy for the Holidays

An avenue of ancient redwoods, the winding Eel River, and small towns with backcountry charm provide the perfect setting for an old-fashioned holiday outing.

Site: Avenue of the Giants, located 20 miles (thirty minutes) north of Garberville.
Recommended time: Any time of year, though the best weather occurs June through September.
Minimum time commitment: Three hours.
What to bring: Layered clothing, rain gear during winter, waterproof walking shoes, binoculars, camera, day pack, water and snacks.
Hours: Daily, sunrise to sunset in day-use area. Visitor center open Thursday through Sunday 10:00 A.M. to 4:00 P.M. (winter) and 9:00 A.M. to 5:00 P.M. (summer).
Admission fee: None for the drive. Park fee is $4.00 per adult.

Directions: Take U.S. Highway 101 north to Garberville, and then continue 20 miles. From Eureka travel south on US 101 for 45 miles.

The background: Driving by lot after lot of cut Christmas trees, have you ever longed to walk in a grove of living trees so old and so tall that it would take a Paul Bunyan to fell them? Fortunately for Californians and visitors to the state, the Save-the-Redwoods League made sure that the heart of California's coastal redwood legacy, some of the oldest trees in the world, was preserved. In 1921 the League purchased a pristine redwood grove north of Garberville, deeding it to the state and establishing the first holding of Humboldt Redwoods State Park.

Over the years, the League and the state continued to expand the park, which now protects 53,000 acres and is the largest redwood park in the state system. Humboldt Redwoods straddles old US 101, and its best known feature is undoubtedly the Avenue of the Giants, a 32-mile drive through towering redwood groves that hug the Eel River. The Founder's Grove is named for the early preservationists who had the audacity to set aside a redwood preserve in the midst of logging country. One of the grove's lofty redwoods, the 346-foot Founders Tree, is considered among the tallest in the park. For many years it stood just in the shadow of the park's biggest tree, the Dyerville Giant, but that behemoth—measuring 372 feet—toppled in a 1991 storm. Even reclined on its bed of needles and rich humus, the Dyerville Giant is longer than a football field—a riveting reminder of the north coast's former grandeur.

The park's superlatives seem unending. Its 10,000-acre Rockefeller Forest protects the largest continuous old-growth redwood forest in the world. It was named for the renowned family that donated the land so that this international legacy could be preserved. Clearly, old-growth redwoods that are a rarity elsewhere are the norm here. Many in the park are thousands of years old. The experience of walking within this living cathedral of venerable trees on duff-lined trails where silence and majesty reign is both humbling and fills the soul. It touches something spiritual and common within all of us.

Of course, juxtaposed with the sublime are the expected tourist attractions and anomalies. Small gift shops sell everything from fine art to redwood trinkets. You can also take a picture next to the Shrine Drive-Thru Tree in Myers Flat, with its sign boasting that the widest car can drive through it.

The fun: Forty years ago, US 101 washed out and a new route was created. Old US 101 was repaired and remains—a two-lane backcountry road threading through the filtered light of the Avenue of the Giants. During the summer season, the 32-mile drive may include a stretch or two that become clogged with vehicles slowing to savor the view, but the inconvenience is relative—the park remains one of the least crowded in the state. During winter it can be foggy and rainy, so the area retains its "off the beaten track" feeling.

View the avenue in your vehicle or by bicycle, if you visit when it is dry. There are numerous places to stop and admire the view or to walk into the redwood forest. The park boasts 100 miles of hiking trails, something for every ability and time commitment. Located just a few minutes from the highway, one of the most popular is the easy 0.5-mile Founder's Grove Nature Trail. Park your car and look for the box at the trailhead with brochures describing the walk. It's hard to know which is more compelling, the sight of the Dyerville Giant in repose or the canopy of living giants that shade your walk. If you want a long hike away from roads but still want big trees, try the Bull Creek Flats Trail. After contouring the stream for 4 miles, you'll arrive at the Big Tree Area, where you will feel dwarfed by trees that are 10 feet in diameter. If river scenery and fishing are your preferences, stop at the Allen's Trail trailhead. But instead of taking this arduous walk, head north to High Rock and try your luck at this popular winter spot for shoreline steelhead fishing. Salmon and steelhead fishing abound on the Eel River.

If you're looking for a great Christmas getaway, or just gracious holiday ambience, put the Benbow Inn in Garberville on your list. This Tudor-style hotel, which opened in 1926, was designed by Albert Farr, who designed the Wolf House in Glen Ellen for author Jack London. It was built by the local Benbow family and has hosted many celebrities and public figures. The inn has been restored by its current owners, whose efforts also have placed it on the list of National Historic Places. Its monthlong Christmas celebration and holiday decorations are world renowned; it is a fine place to stop for a warm drink or stay during your redwoods adventure.

Special tips: Bicyclists using roads with vehicle traffic should wear bright clothing. Some roads have no shoulders and can be busy during the summer months. It can be cold and very rainy in December. Dress accordingly so that you can enjoy some outdoor time in the redwoods. Some businesses close during winter. If you want to spend the night, make reservations in advance.

Food and lodging: There are numerous motels, hotels, lodges, and cabins in Garberville and surrounding communities. Contact Garberville/ Redway Chamber of Commerce at (707) 923–2313, (800) 923–2313, or www.garberville.org. Camping is available at Humboldt Redwoods and at several nearby state parks. Make reservations at (800) 444–7275 or www .reserveamerica.com. Fees vary seasonally, from $7.00 to $17.00. Horse camps are available.

Next best: If you haven't had your fill of big trees, nearby redwood parks include Richardson Grove and Standish Hickey State Park, each with miles of hiking trails. The ocean is just 24 miles away at Shelter Cove, within the huge, secluded King Range National Conservation Area. The black sand beaches north of Shelter Cove are considered quite rare. Humboldt Bay is just 45 miles to the north.

For more information:
Humboldt Redwoods State Park
(707) 946–2409
www.parks.ca.gov
e-mail: hrsp@humboldtredwoods.org

Beautiful Lake and a Holiday Break

An active volcano sleeps on its western shore, mineral springs bubble up from its depths, and migratory birds from other nations seek sanctuary at Clear Lake, where tranquility and a slow pace reign throughout the winter.

Site. Clear Lake, located 18 miles (thirty-five minutes) east of Hopland and 65 miles (seventy five minutes) west of Williams.
Recommended time: Any time of year. Birding best fall through spring; sometimes up to a half million wintering birds. Water sports best in summer. Hot springs open year-round.
Minimum time commitment: Half day.

What to bring: Binoculars, layered clothing and rain gear, sun hat, day pack, water and picnic, your favorite birding guide.
Hours: Numerous public and private access points. Clear Lake State Park open 8:00 A.M. to 10:00 P.M. Anderson Marsh State Preserve open from April through September 8:00 A.M. to 8:00 P.M.; October through March open 8:00 A.M. to 5:00 P.M.
Admission fee: $4.00 per day at state parks.

Directions: From the Bay Area, take California Highway 29 north to Lower Lake. To reach Anderson Marsh State Historic Park, continue north 0.5 mile on California Highway 53. To reach Clear Lake State Park, from Lower Lake take CA 29 north to the Kelseyville exit. In town, turn north onto Gaddy Lane. At Soda Bay Road, turn right and follow signs. Park is 3.5 miles from Kelseyville. From Williams, take California Highway 20 west. Turn south onto CA 53. Anderson Marsh is 0.5 mile before the town of Lower Lake. Follow directions above to reach Clear Lake State Park.

The background: The holidays are almost here and you can probably use a break from shopping, crowds, and life indoors. While natural areas near urban settings are probably jammed, a quiet slice of nature may be just a few hours' drive for many northern Californians. Most think of Clear Lake as a summer lake, with its strong reputation for water sports and fishing. But the state's largest natural lake set in an oak savanna also has an incredible Pomo Indian presence, boasts outstanding winter birding, and can offer a beautiful, uncrowded respite during the busy holidays.

A doe rests in a meadow bordering Clear Lake. JEANNE L. CLARK

The lake is thought by some to be one of the oldest lakes in North America, more than a million years old. Clear Lake was formed when a landslide blocked a valley near the Russian River. Water backed up until it found an outlet through Cache Creek, eventually forming the lake. Some of the lake's water comes from runoff; the rest bubbles up from giant underground springs at Soda Bay, located at the foot of Mt. Konocti.

Rugged Mt. Konocti, the product of lava flows and the violent folding of the earth's crust, dominates the western shore. The 4,200-foot mountain is a spiritual place for the area's Pomo Indians, whose ancestors lived along the lake's shore 6,000 years ago. The Pomo are thought to be among the oldest Indian tribes in the state. Anderson Marsh State Historic Park on the lake's southern shore is an archaeologist's paradise, with mortars, petroglyphs, and other evidence of American Indian presence dating back perhaps 10,000 years.

The early Pomo lived off of the lake's incredible resources. The historical presence of huge wintering bird populations endures today and is quantified during Audubon Society Christmas Bird Counts, an annual event that occurs across the nation. According to the local Redbud Audubon Chapter, during the fourth Great Backyard Bird Count, Lake County ranked first in the state and eighth in the nation for the highest number of species counted.

The Pomo were also the first to discover some of the area's many mineral hots springs. Lake County is known for its geothermal resources, and at one time the mineral springs at numerous resorts drew crowds. You can still enjoy soaking, for a price, at the area's resorts and health spas. Be aware that clothing is optional at some locations, and many guests exercise this option.

The fun: Clear Lake is more than 19 miles long and 9 miles wide, providing huge stretches of unbroken shoreline views. While the southern end of the lake has a slightly more commercial feel to it, the rest of the lake feels more pristine.

Perched on the western and southern shores are two outstanding state parks, Clear Lake and Anderson Marsh. If you visit in winter, you may see killdeer feeding along the creek's muddy banks just west of the Clear Lake State Park Visitor Center. As you cross the bridge, look in the water to the east for several types of wading herons. Continue to the beach, but keep a sharp eye out for many land birds in the brush and trees, from California quail to acorn woodpeckers. During winter the lake's open water usually

WHAT'S SO SPECIAL ABOUT A CATTAIL?

A single marsh plant can sustain and link many species. If you've been to a marsh, you've undoubtedly seen tall, green, flat-bladed plants topped with thick brown spikes growing in clumps along the shore. They are cattails, the emblem of the freshwater marsh.

Cattails are amazing plants. Emerging cattails bind the soft mud with a web of stems and roots that shelter frogs and insects. Muskrats eat the roots and shred the sturdy stems for their lodges. Wrens and blackbirds use the standing dead stalks to hold their spring nests. Wood ducks, rails, and other secretive species find cover among the maze of blades and grasses. The wandlike leaves and stalks sway in the water, softening the effects of the wind and waves. When the brown seed head splits open, the featherlight seeds are carried by the wind and catch on birds' and animals' feathers and fur, perhaps lodging somewhere to form a new plant.

American Indians found numerous uses for cattails, from weaving the slender leaves into baskets and containers to using the absorbent seed heads to line their cradle boards. Even when dead, the cattails are still working; their hollow tubes transport air to the fleshy rhizomes below the surface, nurturing a new plant for the coming spring.

draws the state's largest population of western and Clark's grebes, both conspicuous with their sleek black-and-white bodies riding low in the water. You should also see white pelicans. While you're at the park, be sure to take in the Indian Nature Trail near the entrance, where you can learn how the region's Indians used plants for food and medicine. The quarter-mile walk passes through the site of a former Pomo village.

If this combination of cultural history and nature is appealing, make the 18-mile drive from the park to Anderson Marsh State Historic Park. Anderson Marsh packs a lot into its 900 acres. Begin at the historic ranch house that serves as the site's discovery museum. The entire park is considered an archaeological site. One hill has produced rich yields of relics, from obsidian arrows and stone tools. If you visit on the first Saturday of the month, at 9:00 A.M. you can join a guided Audubon tour of the marsh. The willows lining the shores provide perches for bald eagles and hummingbirds alike, while the lush tules shelter pond turtles, ducks, and small mammals. During the summer, the marsh sustains a great blue heron rookery.

If you bring or rent a boat, you can explore the shoreline and travel from town to town. As you putt or row slowly along the shore, savor this tranquil setting that is a world unto itself—and a world apart from the commercial aspects of the holidays.

Special tips: Birding is best before 10:00 A.M. Binoculars will improve your sightings. Winter weather can be changeable, so come prepared. If you want to spend the Christmas or New Year holiday, make reservations well ahead of time.

Food and lodging: There are numerous motels, inns, and cabins in the communities surrounding the lake. The south end is most developed. Contact Clear Lake Chamber of Commerce at (707) 994–3600 or www.clearlake.ca.us/chamber. Camping available at Clear Lake State Park; rates vary with season from $12 to $19 per night. You must have reservations March 1 through September 30; camping is first-come, first-served the rest of the year. Call (800) 444–7275 or visit www.reserveamerica.com. Camping also available at nearby public lands.

Next best: The lake holds several major bass fishing tournaments. Summer visitors may get a kick out of the lake's annual Worm Races on July 5. Stop at a local store and take a look at the area's famous Moon Tears. These diamondlike stones of volcanic origin are found nowhere else on earth. Make a side trip to see the hissing fumeroles and springs of the geysers at Cobb Mountain, or take a soak at Harbin Hot Springs. If you're driving to or from the lake on CA 20, watch for tule elk near Cache Creek Basin Recreation area.

For more information:
Clear Lake State Park
(707) 279–4293
www.parks.ca.gov

Anderson Marsh State Historical Park
(707) 994–0688
www.parks.ca.gov

December

Climb a Mountain at Year's End

Reflect on the natural gifts that enrich our lives in so many ways and contemplate the future year from the summit of Mount Diablo.

Site: Mount Diablo State Park.
Recommended time: Winter hiking between storms for crisp mornings, green hillsides, and crystal-clear skies. Spring for wildflowers and nesting birds. Summers are hot and dry, but sunsets are spectacular. Fall for colorful leaves and cooler days.
Minimum time commitment: A full day to hike from bottom to top and back; four hours to hike the perimeter trail around the summit.
What to bring: Good quality hiking boots, day pack, water, lunch, hat, sunscreen, binoculars, warm clothes, a notebook for your New Year's resolutions and reflections.
Hours: 8:00 A.M. to sunset.
Admission fee: $6.00 per vehicle.

Directions: There are two entrances to the park. These directions are to the south entrance. From Interstate 680 in Walnut Creek, travel south to the Diablo Road exit. Turn east (left) onto Mount Diablo Scenic Boulevard. Turn left to park.

The background: At 3,849 feet, Mount Diablo may not be the tallest peak, but what it lacks in height is more than made up for by its setting. Sitting on the western edge of Central Valley and surrounded by much lower Bay Area foothills, Mount Diablo rises from the plains and dominates the skyline. From the top, views extend in all directions—west over San Francisco Bay and the Farallon Islands, north to Mount Lassen, east over the delta and Central Valley to the Sierra Nevada, and south to Mount Hamilton and the Santa Cruz Range. No other mountain in California offers views over a larger portion of the state.

A young mountain by geologic standards, Mount Diablo grew as ancient rocks buckled deep within the earth and pushed up through 6 miles of sedimentary layers over the past one to two million years. The oldest rock, and the core of the mountain, is the 160-million-year-old Franciscan formation, comprising a mixture of sedimentary and volcanic rock. This ancient red rock is found at the summit. Younger rock layers, deposited in shallow seas in what is now the Central Valley, unfold as you progress down the mountain. Fossil-rich sandstone, mudstone, and limestone display many of the sea creatures that once lived in these shallow waters. Remains of more recent saber-toothed cats, mastodons, and three-toed horses have also been discovered on the lower slopes of the mountain.

The plant and animal life of Mount Diablo represents a microcosm of the habitats found throughout California. Grasslands and oak woodlands intermingle on the lower slopes. Riparian forests of alder, maple, bay, and sycamore line the creek bottoms. Higher up the mountain, fire-dependent chaparral plants including manzanita, foothill pines, and knob-cone pines cling to the rocky soils. Finally, black oaks mirror those found in the Sierra Nevada.

The fun: The hiking options are about as diverse as the park's habitats and geology. For this end-of-the-year trip, two options are proposed; both are strenuous. One starts at the base and climbs more than 3,000 feet to the summit; the other circles the top of the mountain. If these hikes are too strenuous, drive to the summit, stop in and enjoy the summit visitor center, and ask for advice on choosing one of the many other hiking options. The 0.7-mile Fire Interpretive Trail at the summit is partially paved for wheelchair accessibility.

The 6.2-mile Summit Trail trailhead is located just inside the park boundary on South Gate Road. Unless you're a glutton for punishment, take two cars and park one at the summit so that you don't have to backtrack. From the small parking lot, hike through Dan Cook Canyon past Live Oak Campground and on to the summit. The trail crosses the main park road a few times on the way up. This route offers views to the west and south. This is definitely the trail to take if you want to "bag a peak" or explore many of the habitats found in the park.

The 6.8-mile Grand Loop Trail also includes a lot of elevation change, but it tends to follow the contours of the mountain. This is the best hike for views of the surrounding countryside, and on foggy days the summit will often be in full sun while the base is shrouded in clouds. Park at the summit and backtrack down the road to the Juniper Trail. Head northeast and hike in a counterclockwise direction to avoid tough uphill sections between Deer Flat and Prospectors Gap.

No matter which trail you choose, take your time and plan plenty of stops to soak in the surrounding beauty. In our rushed and frantic world, nature often takes a backseat. Take along your family or a friend, and get reacquainted with them and the earth. Write a poem, sketch a tree, or find an unusual fossil and share it with the others. Breathe deeply, smile often, and give thanks.

Special tips: Check the weather conditions before you go, and postpone your trip if heavy rain or snow is forecast. The weather patterns can change dramatically from the bottom of the mountain to the top or from the leeward side to the windward, so carry a jacket even if it is warm at your starting point. Carry plenty of water, and drink it.

Food and lodging: San Ramon, Danville, Concord, and Walnut Creek offer a variety of accommodations and restaurants. Camping is available in the park. Contact the Contra Costa Conference and Visitors Bureau at (925) 685–1184 or www.cccvb.com for Danville, Concord, and Walnut Creek listings. Contact the Tri-Valley Convention and Visitors Bureau at (925) 846–8910 or www.trivalleycvb.com for San Ramon listings.

Next best: The Blackhawk Museum in Danville displays a fantastic collection of vintage cars in an opulent setting. The museum also displays many of the different fossils found on the slopes of Mount Diablo. Tour Eugene O'Neill's Tao House in Danville, now a National Historic Site that offers guided tours of the Nobel Prize–winning playwright's home and archives. Call (925) 838–0249 for tour times and reservations. In nearby Martinez, visit John Muir's home and National Historic Site.

For more information:
Mount Diablo State Park
Information: (925) 837–2525
Weather conditions: (925) 838–9225
www.parks.ca.gov

Best Bets

Best Trips for Families

Best Trips for Hikers

Best Trips for Birders

Best Trips for Photographers

29. Glacial Lakes and Colorful Bouquets at Carson Pass—Carson Pass

30. Biking and Kayaking into the Past—Angel Island State Park

31. From Skyline Redwoods to the Pacific Ocean—Big Basin Redwoods State Park

33. North Coast Getaway with Lots of Options—Redwood Parks

34. From Boiling Mudpots to Icy Lakes—Lassen Volcanic National Park

35. Serenity and Solitude in California's Alps—Trinity Alps Wilderness

36. Wildlife and Wild Seas at the Point of the Sea Wolves—Point Lobos State Reserve

39. Bay Vistas and Hawks That Ride the Wind—Hawk Hill/GGNRA

44. Granite Spires and Golden Oaks—Yosemite Valley

47. Featherlight Butterflies and Rock-rimmed Tidepools—Natural Bridges State Beach

48. A Birding Bonanza from Your Vehicle—Grasslands, Merced County

49. Elephant Seals on Parade—Año Nuevo State Reserve

50. Savor a Living Legacy for the Holidays—Avenue of the Giants

52. Climb a Mountain at Year's End—Mount Diablo State Park

Best Trips for Bicycling

10. Waterfalls and Spring Flower Displays—Feather Falls

11. Down by the Riverside—American River Parkway

13. Whales, Wildflowers, and Elk—Point Reyes National Seashore

24. Everything's Possible on the Bizz Johnson Trail—Bizz Johnson Trail

28. Rain Shadows, Rare Cranes, and Steam Trains—Shasta Valley

30. Biking and Kayaking into the Past—Angel Island State Park

31. From Skyline Redwoods to the Pacific Ocean—Big Basin Redwoods State Park

33. North Coast Getaway with Lots of Options—Redwood Parks

34. From Boiling Mudpots to Icy Lakes—Lassen Volcanic National Park

44. Granite Spires and Golden Oaks—Yosemite Valley

50. Savor a Living Legacy for the Holidays—Avenue of the Giants

Best Trips for a Rainy Day

2. Winter Sports with an Environmental Twist—Claire Tappaan Lodge

4. Festival at Former Navy Shipyard Celebrates Wildlife—Mare Island

5. Salt Marsh Heaven in a Sea of Humanity—Palo Alto Baylands

8. Elegant Plumes and Fuzzy Youngsters—Bolinas Lagoon Preserve

Best Trips for Wildlife (Other Than Birds)

Best Trips for Wildflowers

Best Trips for Scenery

Best Trips on the Water

Best Trips for Something Different!

Easiest Trips

Driving Tours

Best Trips for Mobility Impaired

Index

eucalyptus trees, 24, 204

Eureka, 80, 81, 82, 83, 143, 146, 216

F

Fairfield, 33, 36

Fairy Falls, 78

fairy shrimp, 68, 69

falcon, 140

Fall River, 49

Feather Falls, 47–50

Feather River National Scenic Byway, 122–24

Felton, 138

fens, 105, 122

field guides, 56–57

fish hatcheries, 53, 184–86, 198–202

fish ladder, 53, 198

fishing, 31, 75, 91, 92, 111, 188, 202, 218, 223

Fitzgerald Marine Reserve, 99–101

Folsom, 51, 186

Folsom Dam, 184

Folsom Lake, 54, 118, 120, 186

forest birds, 104, 105

Fort Baker, 134

Fort Bragg, 102, 104

Fort Jones, 127

Fremont, 71

G

Galt, 70, 84, 88

Garberville, 216, 218

geese, 10, 11, 17, 55–59, 208, 209

George Washington Park, 205

geothermal mudpots, 147, 149

glacial lakes, 128–31

Globally Important Bird Area, 140

Godwit Days Festival, 80–83

Goethe Park, 53, 121

Golden Gate Bridge, 65

Golden Gate National Recreation Area, 20, 134, 171–75

Golden Gate Park, 134

Golden Gate Raptor Observatory, 174

Graeagle, 124

grapes, 180

grasses, 68, 102–3

grasslands, 73, 78, 85, 103, 207–11, 225

Gray Lodge Wildlife Area, 12, 79

great blue herons, 37, 40, 222

great horned owls, 19

Great Valley Grassland State Park, 211

great white sharks, 214

grebes, 116, 222

Green Trinities, 154

Gridley, 12

Grizzly Island Wildlife Area, 33–36

Grover Hot Springs, 128, 131, 187–90

gulls, 116

H

Half Moon Bay, 99, 101, 213

Harbin Hot Springs, 223

harbor seals, 38, 100, 101, 103, 141

Harley Museum, 206

harvest mouse, 23, 26, 35

Hat Creek, 149

hatcheries, 53, 184–186, 198–202

Hawk Hill, 20, 171–75

About the Authors

Jeanne L. Clark has worked in the field of natural resource communications for nearly twenty-five years and has written numerous books, magazine articles, video scripts, brochures, and reports. She is the author of the coffee table book *America's Wildlife Refuges: Lands of Promise,* a commemorative book showcasing the National Wildlife Refuge System centennial anniversary. She also has written the *California Wildlife*

Viewing Guide and the *Nevada Wildlife Viewing Guide.* Jeanne has worked with numerous government agencies and private organizations. For the past seven years, she has served as editor of *Out & About,* an award-winning quarterly newsletter published by the U.S. Fish and Wildlife Service/Pacific Region and has written many other Fish and Wildlife Service publications. Jeanne lives with her husband, Bill, a retired Fish and Game wildlife biologist, in the foothills near Auburn, California, where the beauty of nature and march of the seasons help shape and enrich her writing.

Robert W. Garrison is the owner of Nature Tourism Planning, a private consulting firm founded in 2000 and focused on the development of sustainable wildlife recreation and tourism programs and facilities throughout North America. He has more than twenty years of experience as an interpretive planner and naturalist and has worked on many natural and cultural history projects throughout California. He served for ten years as the state coordinator of interpretive services and aquatic education for the California Department of Fish and Game and ten years as an interpretive planner for the California Department of Parks and Recreation. He has written many wildlife articles published in *Outdoor California* magazine. Bob lives with his wife, Lisa, and son, Sean, in Sacramento.